CAMINO DE SANTIAGO

IN 20 DAYS

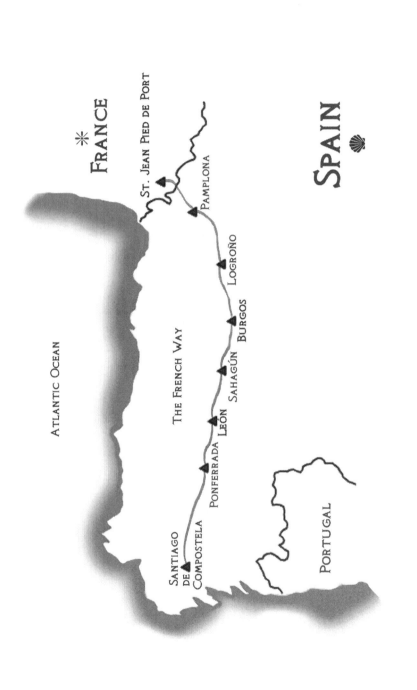

CAMINO DE SANTIAGO IN 20 DAYS

MY WAY ON THE WAY OF ST. JAMES
ST. JEAN PIED DE PORT TO SANTIAGO DE COMPOSTELA

RANDALL ST. GERMAIN

WOLF SHIELD
PUBLISHING

Camino de Santiago in 20 Days: My Way on The Way of St. James
Originally Published in 2011 by Wolf Shield Publishing
Surrey, B.C., Canada
For more information, please contact: info@caminomyway.com

Library and Archives Canada Cataloguing in Publication
St. Germain, Randall
Camino de Santiago in 20 days : my way on the Way of St. James : St. Jean
Pied de Port to Santiago de Compostela / Randall St. Germain.

Includes bibliographical references.
ISBN 978-0-9877090-0-4

1. St. Germain, Randall–Travel–Camino de Santiago de Compostela.
2. Camino de Santiago de Compostela.
3. Pilgrims and pilgrimages–Camino de Santiago de Compostela.
4. Hiking–Camino de Santiago de Compostela.
I. Title.

DP285.S25 2011   914.6'1104   C2011-906838-9

Editing by Mirabella Mitchell
Cover Design by Sebastian Weber
Interior Design and Map by Anna Karin Tidlund
Front Cover photo of Cirauqui, Navarra by Randall St. Germain
Back Cover photo by the author's camera using the self timer

For more information, including photos, the author's blog, and
links to social media, please visit
www.caminomyway.com

FOR MY MOTHER

I THINK OF YOU EVERY DAY

DISCLAIMER

This book recounts the author's experience while preparing for and while walking the Camino de Santiago and is not intended to be a guidebook or provide any advice. As to be expected with an 800 kilometer walk, there are risks and dangers. The author and publisher have made every effort to ensure the information is correct and assume no liability for injuries, death, or damages sustained by readers of this book. Before you leave, please consult your doctor, physiotherapist, trainer, family, and friends. Make sure you have the appropriate gear and are prepared mentally and physically. Please be honest with yourself. There are already plenty of pilgrim memorials along the Camino de Santiago.

The opinions expressed by the author are soley his and are based upon his observations. Except for the author's, the names of people in this book have been changed to protect their privacy. Names of accommodations where the author stayed have not been revealed, as conditions can change rapidly along the Camino. Please ensure you carry a current guidebook.

CONTENTS

IX   PROLOGUE

1   SOMEWHERE OFF THE WEST COAST OF SPAIN....

7   MY CAMINO - THE BEGINNING
13   TRAVEL ARRANGEMENTS AND PLANNING
14   CHECKING OUT MY MIND AND BODY
15   GEAR REFLECTION AND SHOPPING
19   TO THE END OF THE WORLD

26   DAY 1: HAVING FLESH TORN FROM MY BODY BY A PACK OF WILD DOGS

38   DAY 2: THE BED SHOOK LIKE AN EARTHQUAKE ROLLING THROUGH THE HILLS OF NAVARRA

49   DAY 3: CANADIAN BOY

59   DAY 4: SOMETIMES, IT ONLY TAKES ONE OR TWO PRICKS TO DO THE JOB

66   DAY 5: DID I JUST ASK FOR VIAGRA?

74   DAY 6: *FRÍO, FRÍO*

82   DAY 7: HEY BUDDY, YOU'RE NOT AT HOME!

90   DAY 8: I NEED TO LEARN HOW TO ROLL THE R'S

100   DAY 9: I FELT NO STIRRING FROM MY PENIS WHATSOEVER

108   DAY 10: TWENTY IS A NICE ROUND NUMBER

115   DAY 11: FUCKING WIND

122   DAY 12: I HATE TO LET YOU GO

132   DAY 13: I MISSED ALL THE SNORING AND FARTING

140   DAY 14: WHO ELSE WOULD I DREAM ABOUT?

150   DAY 15: WILD SPANISH LAVENDER

159   DAY 16: A GRUELING DAY

168   DAY 17: LUSH

176   DAY 18: WITH A HUGE GRIN, HE BEGAN TWIRLING HIS STICK LIKE A BATON

185   DAY 19: I CAN WRITE GOOD ENGLISH, CAN'T I?

191   DAY 20: *LA CATEDRAL*

197   LOOKING BACK

PROLOGUE

While some people plan their Camino de Santiago for years, I had less than two months. Seriously, I didn't know that much about the Camino until I booked my flight and started planning. I certainly didn't think about writing a book until the latter days of my journey. Even then, I wasn't sure. Initially, I felt too shy writing anything about myself, especially regarding personal matters. Since I'm basically a nobody, I thought readers wouldn't care what I had to say. Most of the time, I don't really care what I have to say myself. I started writing this as part reflection of my Camino, and part guidebook with historical notes. As I progressed, it was becoming evident that I was writing a book so large that nobody would be able to lift it, let alone pay a price that would make it economical. It was a mishmash without a clear focus.

After about three months of writing, I decided to take the guidebook portion out, keep the historical notes brief, and concentrate on my personal journey and observations. One day, however, I plan to release a guidebook on a twenty day French Way, but not yet.

I wanted to maintain the integrity of my Camino from St. Jean Pied de Port to Santiago de Compostela. My writing had to be honest and based on events which actually happened. I know some of it may be dry, but I wanted to keep my journey intact and not make up anything, including dialogue. Believe me, if I made shit up, this book would be far more entertaining.

I also wanted to tell my journey as someone who walked the entire French Way with a full backpack. I know if I was badly out of shape, packed poorly, or had too heavy of a backpack, I could get myself into situations that would be somewhat entertaining. However, I thought I was ready and reasonably in shape.

So with that said, please join me, and remember this book is rated.....

PDA
Pilgrim Discretion
is Advised

MY
CAMINO DE SANTIAGO

STARTS

Now

SOMEWHERE OFF THE WEST COAST OF SPAIN....

I woke up suddenly, my head screaming in pain. My eyes burned, my vision was blurry. I saw something – no, someone – looming over me – a large figure. A man. I lay flat on a soft surface, a bed, I thought, my arms stretched behind my head with my hands tied and feet bound with legs apart. I panicked and yelled as I tried to pull my hands free. The sharp wire dug into my wrists, and the pain shot through my arms and straight to my brain. I felt a deep thud from a forearm across my chest followed by large hands that pinned down each shoulder. A disgusting stench from the man overcame me. Rotting fish – no, rotting garlic – no, rotting fish topped by rotting garlic – it doesn't matter right now.

"You're gonna die, Focker," the man said in a deep, coarse voice followed by a laugh that resembled a hyena's.

This perplexed me, and for some crazy reason I thought I had been transposed into one of the *Meet the Focker* movies, somewhere just before the happy ending. The realism of this notion didn't immediately come into my mind. I wasn't an actor, nor had I ever been in a movie, T.V. show, porno, on Broadway, off Broadway, or in any theatre, come to think of it. Maybe the grade one school play, but that was many years ago and hardly enough of a résumé to allow me into one of the most successful movie franchises of all time. So without any consideration for logic whatsoever, I thought of only one word.

"Cool!"

I felt the pressure on my shoulders intensify. I thought, "If this is a movie, why am I in so much agony? Aren't there special-effects or something called acting?"

"You're gonna die, Fucker. You're gonna die." I heard that voice again, followed by a rush of foul breath. But this time I didn't hear "Focker" and was pretty sure it was "Fucker." As the large hands grasped around my neck, I began to choke. Droplets of sweat fell on my face, and at that very moment, my eyes began to clear. I looked at the man who towered over me and was overcome with disappointment. Hey, that's not Robert De Niro. Or Ben Stiller. I was fucked!

I had made a mistake and was embarrassed by it. An obvious gag, Focker, Fucker, yes, everyone had heard it, had seen it, and had their own laugh. But now I was in grave danger. Boris – I'll call him Boris because he looked like a Boris; for all I know, his name could have been Romeo – had a wrinkled face, a giant head with long gray hair, and a bushy Fu Manchu mustache. His eyes were mean and black, his nose pointy, his teeth chipped, almost fang-like. He wore a black T-shirt with the words "Welcome To My Nightmare" written in bright red, like a billboard across his wide frame. Now I got it. I was having my own nightmare within his nightmare. Just like in the movie, *Inception*. Okay, enough with the movie references.

Boris let go of my neck and walked across the room. A room that looked very odd. It wasn't my bedroom or any other I recognized. There were large packages and crates with addresses and waybills. And there was that sound, sort of like the engines of an airplane. Wait, I was in a plane, a cargo plane. I looked at my legs spread-eagled with my feet tied to the corners of the bed. My hands and arms were behind me; I couldn't see them. Boris went to the hatch, at first struggling with the lock, but it soon released, and he slid the door until it fully opened. The plane shook as air gusted into the hold, causing papers to blow all over. I saw someone's package fly out the window followed by another and another. Boris walked toward me but this time he went behind. I felt the bed nudge and then move slowly as he pushed me toward the opened hatch. I yelled and screamed "Who are you? What is happening? Can I have my iPhone back? I need to call 911."

A large envelope hovered momentarily in front of my face. It was addressed to a Delores Vickers in Muncie, Indiana, and that was all I saw before it flew out the door. Sorry, Ms. Vickers, it wasn't my fault you never got your letter. Boris appeared above me, behind the bed.

Even upside down, he looked evil. Just upside-down evil. He gave me another crazed, lunatic look, one that resembled Jack Nicholson's when he gave his "Here's Johnny" line in *The Shining*. Stop it, Randall! Get focused! Boris's saliva dripped onto my forehead, and I felt the sting. "Goodbye!" he screamed – I supposed he wasn't returning my phone. I felt another nudge from behind, and the hatch got closer. The front wheels went off the ledge and the bed dangled at a forty-five degree angle with my head above. Time slowed for a brief moment as I looked outside. What a breathtaking view. There was blue sky, not a cloud around. A large body of bright blue water was below and I could see land far in the distance. A peaceful land with ancient stone churches, lush green pastures, and large dogs that roamed free.

Dangling out the door, I felt another push from behind, but something was wrong. Boris gave an evil gurgling noise followed by an "Arghhhhhh!" Another push, but now I was no longer at forty-five degrees; I was almost vertical. Something had caught up underneath the bed. But then, I heard a loud bang from under me and the bed released. Because of the angle, I went feet first out the door, and then the bed, with me attached, twirled and flipped uncontrollably as it descended at lightning speed. Instantly, I felt sick and puked. My head rushed with pain, my eardrums exploded, and I pissed my pants. As the water came closer, before I lost all consciousness, I thought, "This is going to hurt."

And then I awoke.

It was that snoring. That damn snoring. I checked the time on my phone, the glare of the light blinded me for a moment. It was four-thirty, yes, in the morning. I could have slept for another two hours. Someone from across the room got up, and I closed my eyes, pretending to sleep. I sensed them walk past and slowly open the door. The hinges creaked followed by a small thud as the door closed. I heard footsteps, progressively quieter, followed by another creaking sound and a soft thud from the bathroom door closing.

There was silence for some minutes, maybe ten or fifteen. Then the toilet flushed, followed by running water from the faucet, the bathroom door creaked, and then a thud. The footsteps gradually grew louder, the hinges of the door in the room creaked, I closed my eyes and sensed someone walk by, followed by the shuffling of the bed and blankets. Then there was only a light snoring from the man below me. Moments later, I heard footsteps, but this time they were from above. The floor squeaked with every step and I heard a bump, possibly someone banged into the wall. The footsteps gradually grew louder, and I was sure they were on the stairs. For a moment, the steps were faint until the bathroom door creaked, followed by a soft thud, more minutes of silence, toilet flushed, water flowed from the faucet, hinges creaked, soft thud, and the sounds of the footsteps as they retreated upstairs.

Where was I? A five-star hotel? No, it wasn't even a one-star hotel. I was in a narrow room with two bunks holding four beds, all of them occupied. At least twenty other people slept in other rooms of the centuries-old building. I was in a hostel, a pilgrim hostel, otherwise known as an *albergue* in Spanish and French – with different pronunciations. I was in the town of St. Jean Pied de Port, France, and had traveled halfway across the world to be here. I had shuffled my life, put work and relationships on hold – or at least to the extent where they wouldn't demand my utmost attention. I made travel arrangements, shopped, researched, and trained. I was ready; at least, I hoped I was. I really, really hoped I was ready. In a few hours, I would begin a journey, one that would take me about 795 kilometers, or 494 miles, to Santiago de Compostela, Spain. Was I driving? Taking a bus, a train, a donkey? No, I was walking the entire way, with a backpack that weighed over thirteen kilograms or twenty-nine pounds and would contain almost everything I would need.

I would walk on roads built by the Romans, cross rivers on medieval stone bridges, walk through ancient cities, towns, and hamlets. I would see tiny churches, grand cathedrals, and everything in between. I would see vineyards, farmland, mountains, forests, and prairie. I would walk on grounds that Napoleon, Charlemagne, and hundreds of other monarchs, groups, and peoples once traveled through and battled on. I would sleep in places I never thought I ever would – such as, the one I was at now. I would meet many people, although often not for very long, and I would have a lot of time to think. Lots and lots of time. For a short period of my life, I would become a pilgrim, walking arguably the world's most famous pilgrimage during the 2010 Holy Year – something I never would have imagined months earlier. I was about to walk the French Way on the Camino de Santiago, The Way of St. James.

My Camino was not only a walk. It was a personal challenge.

While some people were happy just to finish and others gave themselves a month or longer, my goal was to be standing on the plaza outside the Santiago de Compostela Cathedral in twenty-one days. The schedule would be grueling and require walking about thirty-eight kilometers, or twenty-four miles, every day without a day off. It would require planning, discipline, and careful decisions. Then there was the thought of injury, which I had had my share of during the previous two years. All it would take was one bad step – a muscle strain or snap, a knee twist, a rolling of an ankle – and my Camino would be over.

Most importantly, I had dedicated my walk to the memory of my mom who had passed away only three months earlier. It was a trying time, an experience I had never been through before and hope to never again. I watched Mom, apparently healthy a year earlier, become stricken with a disease and with further complications that made an operation impossible. Mom spent seven and a half months fighting, but every time she made one step forward in her progress, it would be followed by two or three steps back. She fought right to the end but lost her battle on the night of February 5, 2010. I was by her side as I held her hand. She opened her eyes wide, stared into mine, grasped my hand tightly, and took her last breaths. Mom and I spent so much time together and became closer during her illness. In this time, I gained a greater respect for Mom. For her strength, her courage, her determination, and her fight.

My Camino de Santiago was for her.

MY CAMINO
THE BEGINNING

My first exposure to walking in Spain was from the movie, *Belle Époque*, which I watched on television sometime during the mid-1990's, a few years after it won the Academy Award for Best Foreign Language Film. The opening sequence shows a young man walking along a path through the scenic Spanish countryside. He was a deserter during the Spanish Civil War and befriended an older man who invited him to stay in his large farmhouse. The older man had four daughters, including one played by a young Penelope Cruz. Over the course of the movie, the deserter made love to each of the daughters before he chose one to marry. I thought this plot was very intriguing and wondered why nothing like that ever happened to me. I haven't seen the movie since, but I always remember the farmhouse, villages, and countryside with fondness. I would be disappointed, however, if I found out the movie was filmed somewhere around Hollywood.

I never thought much more about walking in Spain until the last Saturday in August, 2009. I had awoken early and turned on the radio to a local news talk station. A man was being interviewed by the host; I had tuned in late and missed his name. Although I was groggy, what I heard was interesting and inspiring. They talked about this walk through the north of Spain, a pilgrimage called the Camino de Santiago. There were mountains, countryside, and ancient churches and bridges. It was a long walk, I missed exactly how far, and would take about four to six weeks. One day possibly, but not now or anytime soon.

Most of my concentration and energy was spent on looking after my mom who, at that point, had been very ill for over two months. I couldn't think of going anywhere for more than part of a day. That summer and fall, Mom had three stays in the hospital and almost died twice. She became progressively weaker, and by January, she had trouble walking, and I spent many hours with her every day. Often, I stayed overnight when she needed me or when I was worried about her condition. It was so stressful and sad to watch her deteriorate. Mom didn't want to leave her home, so we managed the best we could.

After dinner, we would usually watch the television shows *Two and a Half Men*, *The Daily Show with Jon Stewart*, and *The Colbert Report*. These times we spent together started years before, and they were very special to both of us. We looked forward to having a laugh together; however, I must admit, when there was graphic humor, or bleeped-out four letter words, I was embarrassed and couldn't look her way. Mom often laughed, sometimes hysterically, although as she got sicker, her laughs became more and more subdued.

One evening, Mom started talking about places she had always wanted to visit but now would never get to see. At the top of her list was Cuba, and she talked with regret and sadness about her dream destination. I tried to be positive and told her not to give up. She asked where I wanted to travel, and I admitted that I hadn't thought of anywhere for a long time. The first destination that came to my mind was the Camino de Santiago, although I still didn't know much about it. She smiled and told me she wanted me to make plans to go and she would pay for my trip. It was a considerate thought − a moment I remember clearly − but I told her I wouldn't be going anywhere until she got better. A few days later, it was Mom's 78th birthday, but she was too ill for other company, so only she and I were together. A few days later, we had a small gathering that included my girlfriend, Sarah, and her son, Adam.

One week after Mom's birthday, I had spent the afternoon with her and went home around six o'clock. About two hours later, she called and said she felt very ill. When I had left for home, she seemed fine, but when I returned, she couldn't walk or stand. I called the ambulance; they arrived about fifteen minutes later and took her to the hospital. It was a horribly busy night, and we waited in the hallway until after 1:00 A.M., when a bed in the emergency room became available. Although she was stable when I returned later that morning, we knew something was wrong. Two days later, Mom's doctors informed us the tests revealed she had a terminal condition, and there was little else they could do. Mom was sent to a hospice where the treatment changed from fighting to keep her alive to keeping her comfortable and pain-free.

On Monday morning, I arrived at the hospice very early. It was so tough to see Mom in such a grave state. When she awoke, I told her that I had trouble coping with her being in palliative care. Over the past seven months, I had done my best not to show my emotions in front of her. I left that for when I was alone. Mom held my hand and in a low voice told me she loved me and needed me to be strong. She thanked me for all the care I gave her and told me she would have died long before if it wasn't for me. Then she looked me in the eyes and told me to go on my journey. It was a sad and touching moment. I could no longer control my emotions, and I broke down in front of her. It was the last time I could talk with Mom. She deteriorated rapidly over the next few days, and I began a vigil. Staying overnight with her in a room where perhaps thousands of people had died was unnerving and haunting. Mom fought right to the end. She would appear to struggle but then would open her eyes as if to say, "I'm not ready to go, yet." On Friday, Mom had visitors during the day, and then I was alone until Sarah and Adam arrived. Mom seemed stable, but at ten-thirty, her breathing became deeper and her breaths were spaced farther apart. Half an hour later, with Sarah by my side, Mom passed away.

Over the next few weeks, I didn't have much time to think at all. I was immersed with dealing with my mom's cremation and her estate. My personal investment work had been delegated to an afterthought for most of the past several months, but now I had to get focused. My relationship with Sarah demanded more time, and when the 2010 Winter Games in Vancouver took place, we attended the festivities. On the last Saturday of February, Sarah and I had an argument over something silly, which led her to ignore me for a few days. During this time, I really started thinking about Mom's words and the radio interview I had heard the previous August about the Camino de Santiago. I emailed the talk show host and was informed the man's name was John Brierley, author of *A Pilgrim's Guide To The Camino de Santiago*.

I googled "Camino de Santiago" and read the Wikipedia page – hey, I had to start somewhere. From there, I checked other websites, saw photos, read blogs, and then thought about travel arrangements.

How would I get to St. Jean Pied de Port anyway? I started checking out flights to Europe and found I could get a good deal to London, a city I had wanted to visit for many years. I hadn't been anywhere recently, and with all the stress and responsibilities, I needed a break. A week after our initial argument, Sarah and I finally talked, but our fight only intensified, and in the heat of the moment, we ended our relationship. After I hung up, I checked my calendar. I knew if I filed some papers for the estate, I would have about a six-week window until they were accepted and returned. I went to an airline website, chose a flight departing near the end of April, and booked my flight to London. My Camino de Santiago had officially begun.

I didn't know much about the Camino but wanted to learn more. Camino is a Spanish word meaning "way." It also refers to a road or journey. Santiago is Spanish for St. James, one of Jesus' apostles, who traveled to Spain after the crucifixion. According to legend, Santiago's bones rest in the Santiago de Compostela Cathedral.

The Camino de Santiago, or The Way of St. James, is not only one route but a network of different routes that lead to and from Santiago de Compostela in the northwest of Spain. Different routes originate from all over Europe, including Britain and Scandinavia to the north, Russia to the east, and Italy – and by some accounts, North Africa – to the south. By far, the most popular route is the French Way, or *Camino Francés*, which originates in St. Jean Pied de Port in the southwest of France near the Pyrenees Mountains. It travels about 795 kilometers west to Santiago de Compostela. Most other Caminos will join the French Way at some point, although a few are separate and originate or terminate in Santiago de Compostela. One is the Camino Finisterre, which travels eighty-seven kilometers from Santiago to Finisterre on the Atlantic coast. During medieval times, many people thought that Finisterre was situated at the end of the world – *Finis terrae* means "lands end." Finisterre captivated me from the start, and I immediately included it in my plans. To the end of the world!

Much of the Camino de Santiago was originally a Roman trade route, and it wasn't until the ninth century that it became popular as a pilgrimage. During that time, the Moors had overtaken much of Spain, and it is thought by many that the remains of Santiago himself at the cathedral are a legend, and was promoted to expand Christianity in Spain to a feverish level. Christianity began to flourish, and the different regions and kingdoms began to win back territory from the Moors. Later, the *Codex Calixtinus*, considered to be the first modern era travel guide, was published in the early 1100s for pilgrims walking the Camino. In 1189, Santiago de Compostela was declared a Holy City, and ever since, Holy Years have been the most popular for pilgrimages. A Holy Year at the Santiago de Compostela Cathedral occurs when St. James Day, July 25, falls on a Sunday.

In the early years, some of the towns and villages vied to be included as part of the Camino. Often, most or all of the businesses in the Camino towns were situated along one main road. Churches and monasteries were built for the pilgrim traffic and were important for prayer and worship. Other buildings and infrastructure such as roads, bridges, hospices, and hospitals were built to make the pilgrimage more hospitable and as convenient as possible. The pilgrimage flourished during the Middle Ages, but the number of pilgrims diminished during times of war, plague, or political unrest.

For many years preceding the 1980s, the popularity of the Camino had fallen drastically; pilgrims often numbered less than one hundred per year. *Albergues* and business diminished, and some villages and hamlets became near ghost towns. During the 1980s, the pilgrimage regained popularity. In 1982, the Pope visited Santiago, and in 1987, The Way of St. James was declared the first European Cultural Route and a UNESCO World Heritage Site. According to the Delegation of Peregrination website (peregrinossantiago.es), a whopping 272,703 pilgrims were received at the Pilgrim Office in Santiago de Compostela in the Holy Year of 2010. The majority would have been those who walked all or part of the French Way, myself included. The total doesn't include pilgrims who started the Camino at various points but quit because of injury, tiredness, or lack of time. Since the early days, the symbol of the Camino has been a scallop shell, which pilgrims attached to their backpack or attire. It shows they are in the process of walking the Camino or have completed it. In early times, pilgrims received the shell upon completion, however now they are handed out at the Pilgrim Office in St. Jean Pied de Port before commencing.

Everyone has their own reasons for walking the Camino. They may include religion, spirituality, fitness, or cultural and historical interest. For most people, it's a combination of any or all of those. I was – and still am – very interested in the historical and cultural aspect of the Camino. The fitness aspect was also very intriguing. Whether or not the remains of Santiago rest in the Santiago de Compostela Cathedral, there's no doubt that religion is the major factor behind the pilgrimage, and most of the historical features and landmarks are there because of it.

Many people said how difficult the walk is. How difficult could it be? Well over 100,000 people complete the French Way every year. It's not climbing Everest, hiking the entire Appalachian Trail, or running across the Sahara. However, it's still an eight hundred kilometer walk over varying trails and terrain. One of the main questions everyone has is how long it will take to complete. I desired more of a challenge with the Camino de Santiago somehow. Maybe it lay in the number of days it took to complete the journey.

After I got off the phone with Sarah and booked my flight to London, I read and thought about my upcoming journey. There were so many aspects of my preparation that needed to be considered, among them travel arrangements, shopping, and attention to my fitness, not to mention dealing with my personal responsibilities. I had a busy time ahead and had to be organized.

I woke up early the next morning and went to a spinning class at the gym, my first day of getting back in shape. After the class, I received a phone call from Sarah. She wanted to see me and came over to my place later that afternoon. We talked reasonably and made up, although I had never expected it. I told her I had booked my flight to London and I'd be walking across Spain on the Camino de Santiago.

"That's crazy, That's really crazy!" she said.

Sarah didn't believe me, so I showed her the map, "You're really, really crazy!" After her initial shock, which took many minutes to recover from, I told Sarah that I wanted to do it and needed her full support. Seriously, if I hadn't thought we were apart, I'm not sure if I would have made travel plans at all. Often, I had been in relationships and procrastinated or delayed trips, only to regret it later. It was too late now; the airline didn't allow changes, cancellations, or refunds.

We made up, and then Sarah and I made beautiful love that lasted all afternoon, evening, and well into the night. Okay, it wasn't quite like that. If you've picked up this book hoping for erotica or sex scenes, you're going to be very disappointed. I suggest you put this down right now and grab a copy of *Lady Chatterley's Lover*, which, although I've never read it, is, I presume more erotic than this one. Before I go on, I must admit the upcoming section is kind of dull. Honestly, it almost put me to sleep writing it. I would recommend reading it before bedtime to ensure a good night's sleep, as it may make you drowsy. Please do not read it before driving or operating heavy machinery. Lame joking aside, shopping and planning were very important to my Camino. I chose to include my list and discuss my preparation here but have tried to be as brief as possible. I shall continue.

TRAVEL ARRANGEMENTS AND PLANNING
Hmmmm... What Have I Gotten Myself Into?
or
What, Exactly is a Biarritz, Anyway?

Since I had planned to visit London before the Camino, I booked a Ryanair flight from there to Biarritz in the southwest of France. From nearby Bayonne, I would take the bus to St. Jean Pied de Port. I booked a hotel room in Bayonne and an *albergue* in St. Jean. Booking dates along the Camino was too constraining, and I left everything open, depending on how I was feeling and how far I walked each day. Furthermore, not knowing where I was staying on the Camino seemed so exciting.

For my planning, I used two guide books – John Brierly's *A Pilgrim's Guide To The Camino de Santiago* and Bethan Davies and Ben Cole's, *Walking the Camino de Santiago*, updated by Daphne Hnatiuk. I also bought, *The Pilgrimage Road To Santiago* by David M.Gitlitz and Linda Kay Davidson, which I didn't read much before my departure but found an important historical reference when I returned. If it wasn't so big and heavy, it would have been great to carry on the Camino.

The internet has websites with good information, although some are better than others. There were two forums I used – www.caminodesantiago.me.uk and www.caminodesantiago.me. In the end, I used all the resources to influence my decisions but never relied on one person or source. Nobody knew what my Camino was, and at that point, I was still trying to figure it out for myself.

CHECKING OUT MY MIND AND BODY
Don't Worry, There's No Nudity

I am driven most of the time and like to accept challenges, even those I make myself. In this case, I wondered how long it would take to complete the French Way. Most of the guidebooks and online resources said about a month to five weeks. Very few people talked about completing it in less than a month, and those who did were often criticized by people who say it's not how fast you go but how much you enjoy the journey. Or whatever. In my opinion, three weeks is a long enough walk. However, early on, I was in the same camp; I figured it would take a month or even longer if I got hurt. Then, I thought about it more. I had hiked for years on rough trails in the mountains near Vancouver, up to forty kilometers, or twenty-five miles, a day, and up to 1,800 meters, or 5,900 feet, of elevation gain. However, that was only hiking one day, and I always had a long time to rest afterward. The Camino was probably an easier trail most of the way, but I knew there would be cumulative effects from walking long distances every day. Although it seemed crazy even to me, I thought three weeks would be an achievable goal – an average of almost thirty-eight kilometers per day. Early on, I was part of one of the forums and contemplated walking with someone else. When I decided to challenge myself, I chose to go alone. Seriously, walking eight hundred kilometers in three weeks is not many people's idea of a fun, relaxing holiday.

At my best in recent years, I was in good shape for an average person but certainly never in my life close to being an athlete. In the previous ten months, I had hiked very little and visited the gym infrequently. My cardio was well below my level of previous years and not ready for strenuous activity. Added to that, I was 44 years old and had experienced three injuries over the previous two years, which forced me to take time off to recover. I had torn my groin two years prior, and in the previous year, I tore a calf muscle and then strained my knee two months later. Those injuries were always in the back of my mind during my training and on the Camino. One of the first appointments I made was with my doctor, and I followed that with two visits to my physiotherapist. They both said I was fine and ready to go.

During those seven weeks, I put myself on a better diet and got back to the gym, although not as much as I would have liked. At the gym,

I concentrated on cardio workouts – the bike, elliptical, and stepper. I didn't run or participate in any activities with impact or where I felt I could get hurt. My goal was to get as fit as I could without tiring or wearing myself down before I started. As I walked the Camino, I would further increase my fitness. I didn't see the point of carrying a heavy backpack for twenty or thirty kilometers before I left. I knew I would carry my backpack in Europe for two or three days before starting the Camino, although I hoped to have one day off.

Everywhere I went, I tried to walk fast. I started on sidewalks in the city and then moved up to trails I thought would be representative of the Camino. I used my GPS to monitor my time and distance; my goal was to reach and sustain a pace of five kilometers per hour. If I could sustain that pace for many hours, there was a possibility of walking forty kilometers a day. Of course, that was easier said than done. I also had a heavy backpack to consider. There would be times when I felt great and could keep a good pace, but I knew there could also be parts of days or entire days when I felt like shit and would be slower. I knew beforehand that I would push my mind and body well past their comfort level. Motivation and determination would be a major factor during my Camino. I had to be focused.

After seven weeks, it turned out that I had had little time and didn't exercise nearly as much as I hoped. However, it ensured I wasn't worn down physically. Mentally, I was already burnt out. All my responsibilities had left me with little free time and sleep. Furthermore, my aunt had recently fallen and needed some of my attention, too. I was thinking too much about my upcoming trip. I was already stressed out and hadn't gone anywhere. Maybe going away was what I needed.

Gear reflection and shopping
Can Someone Lend Me $1,000?

Much of the little free time I had was concentrated on shopping. I could always get in shape on the Camino, but couldn't buy the gear I needed. I had no idea what the shopping would be like in France and Spain and didn't expect much in the small towns and villages. Before I started shopping, I had to assess the gear I had. In the past, I shied away from expensive, lightweight gear and clothing, so I didn't have much I could use.

One item I already had was a Tatonka forty-five liter backpack I had bought the previous year. It had smart pockets, was adjustable and durable, and it only weighed 2.2 kilograms. There were good backpacks available just under two kilograms, but it wasn't worth the extra expense from my perspective. In addition, I was very happy with the fit.

I wanted boots that were light so I could walk at a fast pace and not feel them on my feet. They had to be waterproof, with a sole I could trust, one that was good on pavement and trails. After contemplating between a few, I chose a pair of Merrell boots with a Vibram sole. My rule with boots was important – break them in, but don't wear them out. Walking well over eight hundred kilometers before, during, and after the Camino would be enough wear. I started wearing my boots about three weeks before I left and gradually broke them in. I wore them on trails and around the city. For the trip, I also bought lightweight trail runners that could be used if my boots got wet and cheap flip-flops for around the *albergue* or outside in warm weather.

The sleeping bag was another concern. It had to be small and light but warm enough for the cooler spring nights. I chose a Chinook mummy bag rated at 2°C, or 36°F. It weighed 600 grams and measured approximately 29 cm x 11 cm when stuffed in its sack. If the temperature was cold, I had my silk liner and could always wear extra clothing to bed. The silk liner would work alone on nights that were too warm for a sleeping bag. In addition, and I'm not sure if it's true, I understood from a store clerk and many online resources that bed bugs don't like silk. Although I had my doubts, I took a tent. My main concern with walking long days was finding a bed. At 560 grams, or 19.75 ounces, the tent was light enough, but it still took up a good portion of the main compartment in my backpack.

Good quality, lightweight clothing was expensive. For the first time, I bought a proper wind jacket, a lightweight Arc'teryx, which I planned to wear often while traveling and walking the Camino, and around the towns and accommodations. I took a fleece sweater, a long-sleeve cotton shirt to wear around the *albergue* and to bed if it was cold, three T-shirts, two that were made of a quick drying material and a light cotton one, two pairs of well-cushioned hiking socks with a moisture repelling fabric, one pair of light socks to wear with my trail runners, and another pair for bed.

Rain gear was important, and I chose an extremely lightweight Montane rain jacket. I had never bought a Montane item in the past and wasn't sure what to expect. The hood had a small brim with adjustable drawstrings to cover much of my face. I bought a light pair of breathable rain pants and a lightweight poncho that was on sale after the 2010 Vancouver Winter Games. The poncho was good quality but was not made to go over a backpack. However, I didn't want the giant, heavy ones that draped down to the knees. I found those too restraining for walking fast. I also carried a rain cover for my backpack and half gaiters to wear on muddy trails and when it was raining.

I took two pairs of quick drying shorts. One was the main pair for walking and the other used for backup, in bed, and around the *albergue*. Lightweight travel pants were for wearing in towns and track pants were for days when it was cool but not raining. Base layer pants would be worn around the *albergue* and to bed. I hoped three pairs of cotton underwear and one pair of quick drying ones were enough. I brought a beige-colored sun hat, wool fingerless gloves, and a new pair of Eddie Bauer Windcutter gloves, which I initially thought might be too warm for the Spanish springtime.

Before I left, I put my clothes into compression bags to cut down on space. I also brought one carry bag to hold my personal items and a thick, plastic bag to hold clothes while I showered. I had a bath sponge for my shower and a quick drying towel for wiping. Another smaller towel was for me to carry on warm days when I sweated.

I intended to take many photos with my new Nikon fourteen megapixel point-and-shoot camera with a ten times zoom. It was tempting to take a DSLR, but they are also heavy. Of course, with the camera come a charging cord, extra battery, extra memory cards, USB drive, and SDHC card adapter, which I would need with an older computer. An electrical outlet adapter was also needed, the same one for France and Spain. My iPhone would serve me well when or if I had Wi-Fi, and I topped up my Skype account so I could make phone calls. However, I didn't inquire enough about finding a SIM card that would work in Europe.

Also important were sunglasses, because I would be walking toward the west, often in the evenings, and a headlamp, in case I walked in the dark, although it wasn't my intention. Both were put in separate cases that wouldn't break. A lightweight plastic cup was for the wine fountain near Estella. I didn't take a water bottle and would buy water and refill the bottle in sinks and fountains. I also took power gels and bars to last the first two days. The only guidebook I brought was John Brierley's aforementioned one, which I considered taking apart before I left because I didn't need many of the pages. However, I couldn't bring myself to do it and still have the book today. I also downloaded current *albergue* ratings off the internet onto my iPhone notes. Of course, whenever I had Wi-Fi or internet, I was able to do further research. I took one small notepad with a pen but planned to initially record my journal onto my iPhone and transcribe it later.

Wakey, wakey! Are you still with me? I know, it's tough. Just a little more.

With toiletries, it was important not to take packaging that wasn't needed. I kept everything small and used my postal scale to compare items. Travel bottles were lightweight; each one contained hair gel, sunscreen, shampoo, or body wash, which would double as a laundry detergent. With disposable razors, I cut the handles so there was just enough room to grasp between my fingers and thumb. I took a small container of shaving oil, which I hadn't used before, but was much lighter than a travel size can of shaving cream. I cut the handle of my toothbrush so it barely fit in my hand and the holder so it just fit the toothbrush. The tube of toothpaste was travel-sized, and with dental floss, I cut my normal-size lengths and put them into a small re-sealable bag.

The cotton swabs were cut so that the stem just fit between my index finger and my thumb, and then all the swabs were put into a re-sealable bag. I took a fistful of tissues and stuffed them into a luncheon bag and a half-roll of toilet paper and put it into another. My vitamins for the trip were smaller tablets than I normally took, and I counted out just enough for the days of my trip and placed them into a re-sealable bag. Ibuprofen and allergy pills were also taken out of packages and put into a re-sealable bag. The weight of travel-sized deodorants varied greatly, and I chose the lightest one. I bought a plastic hairbrush from a dollar store and cut off the handle and part of the back so it would just fit into my hand. Other items I brought included lip balm, nail clippers, earplugs, plastic clothes pegs, and a file for my toenails.

My first-aid kit consisted of a sewing kit with needles, scissors, adhesive strips or Band-Aids of various sizes, two fist-size piles of gauze, two rolls of tape, alcohol wipes, and a small tube of antiseptic ointment. I expected many blisters.

There were also personal items such as money, passport, credit card, and travel documents. Did I forget anything here? I hope not. Throughout my packing, I used the digital luggage and postal scales to weigh every item and get an idea of the total. I wanted my backpack to weigh no more than thirteen kilograms, because I knew with food and water, it could go over fourteen. A heavier backpack over a long distance would surely increase the risk of injury and jeopardize my Camino.

In the days before I left, I separated everything into two piles. One pile was comprised of items I needed, and the other was comprised of items I considered. A few days before my departure, I started placing items in my backpack. I stuffed the insides of my trail runners with extra gauze, and a few other small items. I contemplated each pocket and what would go inside. I really wavered on my decision to take the tent up until the last minute. I didn't want to take anything I wasn't going to use, especially something that large. But I didn't know. Walking the Camino was going to be a learning experience. I had an idea but honestly wasn't sure what was out there. I know some people say to leave certain things such as phones or cameras at home, but everyone has their items or gear that make them feel comfortable when they travel. My list was comprised of items I believed were needed to complete the Camino in three weeks. If my Camino was different, the list would have changed appropriately. I'm not saying my list is for anyone else. Everyone is different.

TO THE END OF THE WORLD

On April 25, Sarah and Adam took me to the airport in Vancouver. I enjoyed the time we all spent together and knew I would really miss them both. Sarah and I hugged and told each other to be good. I knew I'd be good and hoped she would be too. I thought of a time about two weeks prior, when I was sleeping at Sarah's and she woke me up in the middle of the night. She asked me if I minded if she went out for coffee with other men while I was gone. "Coffee?" I thought, "What does that mean?" I was only going away for five or six weeks, not a year. I lifted my head and said that was fine, but I added that I would go for "coffee" with women in Europe, too. I went back to sleep, and half an hour later, she woke me up again. She told me to forget about it; she would wait until I returned. "Yes dear, I'll wait for you too," I said and went back to sleep.

I flew to London Gatwick and took a bus to King's Cross station. For the next eight hours, I walked around London before I took the train from Liverpool station north to the town of Bishop's Stortford where I stayed the night. Although I took breaks during the day, I was exhausted, and my shoulders, neck, and back were sore from carrying the backpack. I had an hour of sleep at most on the plane and barely slept the night before I left. Although the bed-and-breakfast was comfortable and quiet, I left the next morning with no more than three hours of sleep.

From London Stansted, I flew to Biarritz on Ryanair. Outside the Biarritz airport, I met my first fellow pilgrims who gathered around waiting for the bus. One man asked me to join him in a taxi to St. Jean Pied de Port because he wanted to start the Camino right away. Since I had a hotel room booked in Bayonne and wanted to see the seaside resort town of Biarritz, I declined. I took a bus to the picturesque but very touristy downtown area and had my first taste of delicious Basque chocolates. I walked along the seawall and then by the beach, where I saw my first topless women sunbathers in Europe. They were the last boobs I would see for a long time.

Although I didn't rush, I was exhausted by the time I arrived at the lighthouse, north of the beach area. My backpack felt heavier and heavier in the warm afternoon. For about three hours, I had walked around Biarritz and now needed to get to Bayonne. I took the first bus I saw, which happened to be the wrong one, but I was just happy to get off my feet. After a forty-five minute bus ride and two circles around Biarritz, I transferred to the one that took me to Bayonne. My hotel, an ancient building near the station, didn't necessarily look run-down, only as if it hadn't been renovated or decorated for about fifty years. The clerk gave me my room key, which was attached to a one-kilogram fishing weight. She said I could leave the key at the front desk when I went out, as if I was going to carry it around with me. The hallway and room were dark, drab, and a little creepy. Not wanting to spend much time there, I dropped off my backpack, washed up, and went outside to the medieval city of Bayonne.

I walked through the narrow streets, looked in shops, and crossed over stone bridges. Later, I had a pleasant romantic French dinner by myself while sitting at a window table overlooking the Adour River. Dinner included a half-liter of red wine, which I hoped would ensure a good sleep. On my way back to the hotel, I stopped inside the train station to check the bus schedule for the next day. Normally, the train would be running, but the track was undergoing maintenance.

Although I should have slept easily, I couldn't. In my mind, I had a bed bug phobia developing, and I even used my silk liner in the bed. I envisioned a giant bed bug breaking into my room and having its way with me. I didn't dare answer the door. I read and then listened to a French podcast. It wasn't until two o'clock that I fell asleep but woke up at six, not fully rested. However, I didn't want to stay in the room, so I got ready and walked through the streets of Bayonne some more. Visiting the Bayonne Cathedral was an awe-inspiring experience that sent tingles up my spine when I first walked in. I was amazed by the architecture, sculptures, and art – the peacefulness. Afterward, I visited a shop that specialized in local jams and honeys. The clerk spoke English well and spent so much time explaining their products, I felt compelled to buy something. I chose two small jars of jam, which was ironic, since I had spent so much time and effort cutting down the weight of my backpack.

I bought my bus ticket for the eleven o'clock departure to St. Jean, went to the hotel room, and packed up. I was glad to leave that place behind, especially the weight that came with the key. As I waited outside the station, I met three other Canadians, including one from Northern Ontario who had an enormous four season sleeping bag, rated to minus 15°C. His sleeping bag alone was about the same volume as the large compartment inside my backpack. I asked him if he was walking the Camino de Santiago or the Arctic Circle. He said he didn't have much time to shop before leaving and took items he already had. His boots were well worn, and his backpack was old and tattered.

On the bus, seven out of the fourteen passengers were Canadians. It seemed odd, and I guessed it was a coincidence. Few of the people I knew back home had even heard of the Camino de Santiago until I mentioned it. It was a fine day for a bus ride as we traveled through valleys and small towns. In St. Jean, three other Canadians and I walked to the Pilgrim Office. Don was about my age, and the other two, Mike and Dave, were in their late 50's or early 60's. Mike had completed the Camino fifteen years prior and kept telling me how difficult it would be going over the Pyrenees. I told him that I had intended to get well past Roncesvalles, Spain on the first day, and he laughed and told me I'd never do it. Apparently, I'd get to Roncesvalles and collapse onto a bed in anguish, unable to move. Honestly, Mike was beginning to give me doubts; I started to wonder what I was in for. Maybe I had underestimated the difficulty of the Camino. Maybe I had overestimated my abilities.

St. Jean Pied de Port is a centuries-old town with narrow streets above the river and a more modern area on the lower side. As we walked up the small hill and joined the old, narrow street, I noticed Don was already breathing heavily. Upon entering the Pilgrim Office, we were greeted by the friendly staff. I paid a few euro, I forget exactly how much, and the smiling woman handed me a pilgrim passport, or *Credencial*, a scallop shell, and a supposedly up-to-date copy of *albergues* along the Way. She explained that I had to get a stamp on my pilgrim passport from each accommodation. My pilgrim passport would be proof that I completed the Camino and would allow me to get my *Compostela*, the certificate issued at the Pilgrim Office in Santiago. I said goodbye to Mike and Dave, who had a hotel room, while Don scrambled around to find a place to stay.

My *albergue* was across the street, and when I entered, Jacques immediately greeted me. He was a *hospitalero (hospitalera* is the feminine form), someone on staff who oversees or assists with the operations of an *albergue*. Sometimes they were volunteers, but in this case, I believe Jacques was the owner. While signing me in, he told me something I will never forget, "You have such a beautiful French name. It's such a shame you can't speak the language." Thanks, Jacques. He was right, and I was embarrassed by it. Despite being over half French, I knew little of the language. I could get by traveling but had trouble conversing with someone. I tried to learn French and Spanish before I left but concentrated on Spanish because I would spend more time in Spain. I bought books, and downloaded podcasts and apps, but my time and mind were often occupied, and it wasn't easy to learn. I think the only way I'll ever learn another language is if I'm dropped off on an isolated mountain village somewhere where nobody else speaks English.

The *albergue* was a former house with a large kitchen and dining area. It was clean, well-maintained, and spacious. Jacques led me to a narrow dormitory room on the downstairs level, with two double bunk beds against the wall. I put my backpack down and went outside to the pleasant patio. I met two of my roommates, Brian and his daughter,

Jenny, from England. Brian had just walked 740 kilometers on the Camino from Le Puy, France to St. Jean and had a badly swollen knee to show for it. Jenny had only met up with her father the previous day and would stay with him for a few more before heading home. After a brief visit, I washed some clothes and hung them out in the sun.

Dinner wasn't until later, so I had a few hours for sightseeing. I walked the narrow streets, visited the small cathedral, and then took a walk to the citadel, a stone and brick fortress, on top of the hill. By now, it was hot, and although I didn't have my backpack, my energy waned. I had also forgotten to bring water, which didn't help. From the citadel, there were views of St. Jean below, the Pyrenees Mountains, and the surrounding valleys of forests and farmland.

I joined Don, Mike, and Dave in the old town and looked in shops. Mike continued with his advice and gave me some tips that made me wonder. He explained, in a very spiritual manner, to leave my clothes on during a shower so the body and the clothes are all cleansed at the same time. Honestly, I had never even thought of that, but it sounded disgusting. Again, he continued to reiterate how difficult the Camino would be. This time, I thought I would test him and said boldly that I intended to complete the French Way in three weeks. Rather rudely, he laughed in my face and told me it was impossible. I must say, the Grand-daddy tagline for this book was written with Mike and a few others of all ages in mind. No offense is intended, just having a little fun.

In a Basque chocolate shop, I had an interesting conversation with the clerk, whose English was about as good as my French. We tried our best and talked chocolate; then she gave me samples. I left with a bag of delicious Basque chocolate-covered pralines, which, although heavy, would last a couple of days. At the *albergue,* I picked up my guidebook and jam, bought a fresh baguette, and went down the hill to a park by the old town's walls. I forced myself to relax, but after half an hour, I was bored with my own company and went to the nearby Camino option to make sure I understood the directions for the next morning.

An outside patio of a pub looked enticing, and I chose a table with a pleasant view of the old town across the river. After I ordered a beer, I called Sarah and checked the internet with my iPhone using the Wi-Fi. For a while, I just sat and thought. Was I ready for the Camino? I was tired and already felt drained. It had been five days since I had a good sleep, and I suffered from jet lag. My intentions were to have a full day of rest before I began my Camino, and I wasn't keeping up with my plan.

On the way back to the *albergue*, I met Don, who confided that he was nervous about walking alone and asked to join me the next morning. I had my concerns. Don hadn't exercised much before he left home and badly suffered from jet lag. He told me to expect him to be slow; he would need frequent breaks. Don wanted to meet me in front of my *albergue* at 8:00 A.M. I said if I saw him, we could at least walk out together. I never intended walking with anyone, especially if I didn't think they were ready or would slow me down.

It was a nice evening, and the communal dinner was served on the outside patio. Everyone who stayed at the *albergue* had promised to join the dinner upon their reservation being accepted. I met my other roommate, Chuck from St. Louis in the United States. He was in his 50's, a little overweight, and was having serious doubts. He really wanted to complete the Camino but was concerned with the 795 kilometers that got in the way between St. Jean and Santiago.

Before dinner, everyone introduced themselves in their own language, and Jacques, who apparently knew many, translated into English. The nationalities varied, but most pilgrims were from Europe. I was the only Canadian, and Chuck was the only American. The ages varied from mid-20's to early 60's, and men and women were about evenly split. We had a short prayer, and then it was time for dinner – the highlight was a Basque quiche. A carafe of red wine was brought to every table, and the staff made sure the guests were well taken care of. After dinner, a man who had already finished the Camino and on his way home showed off a few bed bug bites on his stomach he received in another *albergue*. They weren't bad, but he talked about one woman who woke up with one side of her face and neck covered with bites. Shit, that wasn't something I wanted to hear just before bed.

It was a good evening, bed bug talk excepted, and by ten o'clock, everyone started going back to their respective dorms. The clothes I had washed earlier were completely dry. Before I left home, I had concerns about washing clothes, but with weather like this, it should have been easy. I stopped at the washroom to drain my bladder, because I didn't want to disturb anyone in the middle of the night. I felt nervous in the dorm. Here I was, 44 years old, and I had never stayed in a hostel before. I was a hostel virgin.

I said goodnight to my roommates and shuffled into the sleeping bag liner. The room was warm, and I didn't need to zip the sleeping bag. The silk liner covered me like a mummy, with a hood that fit over my eyes to my nose. I brought ear plugs to drown out the expected snoring, but they were large and uncomfortable. I couldn't sleep with the plugs, and honestly, I had never tried them until that moment.

So after all the thinking, planning, preparing, shopping, spending, contemplating, procrastinating, worrying, training, and finally, urinating, I had one more sleep until I began my Camino. My mind wandered, and I couldn't help thinking about my days ahead. Then, I heard the first snores from the men in the room; I was sure it wasn't Jenny. I heard some noises upstairs and then footsteps – just someone using the washroom. More snoring, it was getting louder. Oh, please! Let me sleep. Sometime after midnight, I finally fell asleep but was restless. And even then, I was woken up after a crazy dream.

HAVING FLESH TORN FROM MY BODY BY A PACK OF WILD DOGS

Day 1
St. Jean Pied de Port to Zubiri
47 Km

When I climbed off the top bunk at six-thirty in the morning, I had already been up for almost two hours. My roommates were in various stages of awakening. Brian was getting dressed, while Jenny lay in bed, still inside her sleeping bag. She smiled but looked so tired, like she could sleep for another hour. Chuck looked dazed and sat on the edge of his bed, elbows on his knees and hands holding his chin. I heard footsteps, talking, and banging from upstairs. Everyone in the *albergue* was getting ready for their first day on the Camino de Santiago. I was nervous but couldn't quite tell what it was from – anticipation, excitement, wonderment – fear of injury, bed bugs, bandits, having flesh torn from my body by a pack of wild dogs? Probably a combination of everything. Nevertheless, I was excited and ready.

I had been warned many times about bed bugs in accommodations along the Camino. Just the thought of them made my skin crawl, and I wondered how I would feel if I really got any bites. I went to the washroom, pulled my shirt up and my pants down, and was happy there were none. I thought about my appearance. Should I wash my hair? Should I use hair gel? Should I wear my orange hiking shirt, or maybe my black one? Thankfully, these concerns would diminish over the next few days. I already hated the shaving oil. It felt and smelled oily, which I probably should have expected. It worked poorly, and I had to shave three times. How I missed shaving cream and my Fusion razor. I wet my hair but decided only to brush it and not worry about the gel. Would I even need hair gel? I wasn't going on any dates.

I hoped to take what a nurse friend of mine once referred to as a "bowel movement," but nature wasn't calling at the moment – for those who don't understand, I'm talking about taking a crap. No matter how hard I thought and tried to persuade myself to get regular, it wasn't happening. Maybe I should have bought prune juice instead of the jam. I waited for a few moments, but nothing; my body was still on Pacific

Coast time. I envisioned myself having to go later on some barren hillside in the Pyrenees, with not a tree, shrub, or boulder in sight. Just a few dozen pilgrims walking by.

I poked my head out the door, and, although slightly cool, it looked to be a fine day. In the dorm, everyone was dressed and almost ready. Brian's knee was so swollen, I suggested he take a couple of days off. He told me not to worry, he'd be fine. Chuck looked very nervous. He wondered if he was ready, if he was in shape, if he could make it to Santiago de Compostela. Jenny had no real concerns and seemed happy to accompany her father for a few days. I decided to wear shorts and the orange shirt with the quick drying fabric that I later found out from photos was not very flattering for showing off my upper body. Jacques asked me to sit down for the communal breakfast, but I had already been up for too long and was eager to start walking. I had a big day ahead. We all did. I still needed to pay for my stay, but Jacques was busy serving breakfast, so I waited. The lack of sleep made me a little cranky and impatient. I had already watched a few others leave and felt very late. After a few more minutes, I asked Jacques again, and he brought out his receipt book and took my money.

I bid farewell to Brian, Jenny, and Chuck and wished them the best. If I kept to my planned schedule, I likely wouldn't see any of them again. Jacques and the *hospitaleras* were friendly and made my first stay in an *albergue* comfortable. I hadn't perfected *Buen Camino* yet and didn't dare say it to anyone. I was fine with the *Camino* but not with the *Buen*. The Spanish phrase literally means "Good Way" or "Good Road" and would be the most popular greeting among pilgrims. It was so much more than just a greeting, though. It signified a common bond between pilgrims, no matter where they came from or their motivation for walking the Camino. It was an understanding that we all were putting our lives on hold and attempting a long and difficult journey. It was a wish of success for others to achieve what they hoped for and a wish for a safe Camino, free of injury and harm from others. At least that was my interpretation, but I didn't understand it on the first day. I was still working on my *Buen Camino*. For now, something like "Have a safe trip" would have to do.

It was seven-thirty, and much later than I had hoped to leave. I walked outside and looked down the cobbled street, lined on either side by centuries-old buildings, which framed the Pyrenees far in the distance. A young man took my photo toward the direction I was headed, and then I obliged for one of him. I stretched my body and made sure I covered every muscle and joint. I was so tight and hadn't even started yet. As I walked down the main street of St. Jean, I thought about Don, the fellow Canadian, who wanted to join me. He wouldn't enjoy my pace, so I didn't wait. Part way down the hill, two young and very cute Korean women, dressed in pink and baby blue outfits with matching backpacks, were walking back up. They had forgotten something and seemed to be in a slight state of panic. They stayed at the same *albergue* as I did but kept to themselves. I wished them well and they smiled back. I figured they wouldn't last long on the Camino but hoped I was wrong.

At the bottom of the hill, the Camino could be a little confusing with an option of two routes, both leading to Roncesvalles. One was the Route de Napoléon, the more strenuous route through the Pyrenees. The other stayed along the valley and had less of a climb. I had decided long before on the Route de Napoléon and knew the directions from checking out the spot the previous day. When I arrived at the option, four confused pilgrims huddled together, studying their map. I pointed out the direction to the supposed leader, a panicky English man who was engrossed in a map that was in such a small scale, it covered all of Spain and part of France. St. Jean Pied de Port was merely a tiny black dot. He wouldn't listen, even when I pointed out the other pilgrims on the road. I gave up and was glad I wasn't with him.

St. Jean Pied de Port literally means "St. John at the Foot of the Mountain Pass," and I began the gentle ascent through the Pyrenees along the side of the paved road. A small, unassuming metal sign showed the "Route de Napoléon," and I was thrilled to walk where Napoleon had long ago. There were many more pilgrims than I had expected – young, old, skinny, fat, and everywhere in between. Some carried giant backpacks resembling ones I would normally see on a multi-day wilderness backpacking trip. Others carried ones so small, I wondered where all their gear was. My forty-five liter backpack was about average size, and it was full. So full that, with embarrassment, I had to carry a shopping bag containing food.

I felt great and passed many others as I followed the hand-painted French flags that marked the French Way. By now, a thin layer of clouds covered the sky, but when the sun emerged, it would highlight a vast array of colors – greens from the pastures and trees, and browns and reds from the hillside shrubs. It was springtime, and the Pyrenees were coming to life. Sheep, horses, and cattle grazed in the fields, and I enjoyed the sounds of the animals and cowbells that echoed through the valley. I found out that wearing a cowbell wasn't restricted to cows but could be just as easily worn by a horse or a sheep. The first time I saw a horse with a cowbell, I had to look twice. I'm such a city boy and was lucky to even be able to tell the difference between a cow and a horse.

As I veered onto the first rough gravel path, I saw a tall man ahead who carried a huge backpack with a large sleeping bag strapped on the outside. He struggled and breathed heavily. His face was covered in sweat, and he already looked beat. I asked him how he was doing and he mumbled he was fine. He sure didn't look fine to me. Often, I saw items on the side of the road that people had already discarded – clothing, shoes, flashlights, bottles, cans, and a vibrator. Okay, I didn't see a vibrator – I think it was a sausage – but the piles were so messy and such a waste. The path was steep, and, although I wasn't tired, I stopped for my first break. I would take days to get in shape and didn't want to wear myself out on the first one. I took off my backpack, sat down on the grass, and ate a power gel and some Basque chocolate-covered pralines. I greeted the pilgrims as they walked by, many who I had already passed. I'm sure some thought I had problems from my early pace. Many people looked happy, while others grimaced with the steep climb. After my break, I felt energized and passed many of the same pilgrims again.

The gravel path led to the paved road, and soon I saw the *albergue* at the outpost of Orisson. It was a modern, natural-looking building, with the bottom three quarters finished in stone and the top quarter and shutters in oak. Since Orisson was only eight kilometers from St. Jean, it attracted pilgrims who started late in the day, preferred an easy first day, or had early difficulties and had to stop. Across the road, a patio hung on the hillside overlooking the hazy Pyrenees and St. Jean. I tried to talk to a man, tall and lean, about twenty-five years old with curly brown hair. He had an Eastern European accent and didn't say much. I couldn't tell if he had trouble with English or wanted to be left alone. I sat at an adjacent table and stared at the alluring green mountains and valley. I could have stayed there for hours.

Well, my break wasn't for hours, but merely ten or fifteen minutes. I continued the gentle ascent to the Pic D'Orisson, where the statue of the Virgin Mary sits on a rocky outcrop overlooking the valley. As I climbed, there were fewer trees and more open grassland. I watched horses as they scampered on the hillside above the road. They looked magnificent with their brown bodies and long manes against the green field and white clouds. I had expected pilgrim memorials for those who had passed away on the Camino, but the first ones made me think. One was a small, wooden cross with two blue hearts and a plaque attached. The other was a heart-shaped stone with an inscription on a brass plate. They reminded me that, no matter how much I thought I was ready, I was always vulnerable, and life could be gone in an instant. Nobody came to the Camino expecting to die.

Speaking of almost dying, I was surprised how many drivers didn't slow down. More than once, I jumped off the shoulder when it was obvious the car wasn't going to move.

I passed more people, although one, the Eastern European man, was faster than I was. If I saw someone far ahead, I would focus and try to catch them. It kept my mind occupied during uneventful stretches and maintained a good pace. The next landmark was a *cruceiro*, a large, cement cross, and, although not old, it looked impressive against the barren bright green hills. However, a photo of the cross alone was impossible due to an ugly, rusted, metal bar around the perimeter. At the base of the cross, "Paris-Le Puy" was etched along with "Camino," but the rest was in French and I couldn't determine what it represented.

My shoulders were already sore, and I took off my backpack and sat down on the soft grass facing the Pyrenees to the north. The site was a popular resting area, with at least a dozen people sitting on the hill. I only nodded or said *bonjour* and gave everyone space to enjoy the beauty. It was cool at the higher elevation, and I put on my fleece sweater. I pulled out my baguette from a bakery in St. Jean and my black cherry jam from a boutique in Bayonne. Here I was, so particular with reducing weight to the point where I cut most of the handle off my disposable razor, and yet I was carrying a jar of jam up the mountain. After my humble lunch, which also included a power bar and gel, I laid and closed my eyes for a moment. I opened my eyes and was happy that I wasn't dreaming, but truly in the Pyrenees. Sadly, I couldn't stay there all day and had to move on. I shuffled the contents of my backpack and finally managed to fit everything inside. Although I wasn't the only one who carried a shopping bag, I wondered how stupid I looked. As the Camino progressed, those concerns wouldn't bother me.

The Pic de Leizar Atheka, a rocky peak, was the high elevation point for the time being. I followed a path through a grass field, which led to a short, steep trail between the peak and a rocky knoll. At the top, there was a flat field with a mountain shelter on the edge, nestled in the rock and blending naturally with the landscape. I recognized a friendly man from New York City who was on the bus to St. Jean. We both wondered aloud why half the people on the bus were from Canada, but we couldn't figure it out. We talked briefly, and he took my photo with the mountain shelter in the background. I had no idea how old it was; I thought about Napoleon and wondered if he stayed there.

I said goodbye to the American and followed a well-worn path marked with hand-painted French flags and yellow arrows. A large group of pilgrims were gathered at a fountain, the Fontaine de Roland. It was named for Knight Roland, who most notably led the rearguard of King Charlemagne's army that was defeated in the area by the Basques, the Moors, or some unknown faction in the 778 Battle of Roncevaux Pass. The fountain was a popular spot, and the first water source since Orisson. I was always careful of the fountains and made sure my water bottle was filled in the towns. Years before, I had endured a bout with a waterborne illness that lasted months and have been paranoid about water sources ever since. If I wasn't confident in the source, then I wouldn't drink the water.

Just ahead stood the concrete border marker between France and Spain, and I was excited to enter a new country. Although I had never expected a border guard or someone to stamp my passport, it felt odd to simply walk into Spain. If I ever tried walking from Canada into the United States in a rural or mountainous area wearing a backpack, I would have helicopters, the National Guard, and a pack of foxhounds hunting me down. There was not a "Welcome to Spain" sign, but the marker simply stated the region – "Navarra" and "Nafarroa" in Basque.

Facing France, there were only symbols depicting mountains, a snow-flake, and something that resembled a paw print. The hillsides near the border consisted of barren grassland, with low shrubs and small stands of trees on the lower levels. This led to a peaceful beech forest with small patches of snow along the road. The early afternoon sun was warm, and it was a good time for a break. I picked a soft spot on the grass beneath a tree and took off my shoes and socks to air out my feet. Many pilgrims walked by, and I said *hola* to everyone, including a few I recognized. I saw the guy with the Eastern European accent who I had met in Orisson and a beautiful young woman with long blonde hair who I had passed only minutes earlier.

I ate more pralines and chased them with a power gel before I resumed walking through the forest. Soon, the landscape opened up as I climbed the steep road through a vast, scrubby hillside. Ahead, I saw the young woman and pushed hard up the hill until I caught up. Alja was from Denmark and was walking the Camino alone. She had concerns about safety, bed bugs, and whether she could even make it to Santiago. We talked about hiking and the outdoors. Alja loved mountains and wildlife and was particularly interested in the Canadian Rockies. She struggled on the steep hill and encouraged me to go on. Maybe she just wanted to get rid of me; I couldn't tell. Soon, Alja caught up at the Col de Lepoeder, where I was taking in the view of the mountains and valleys with Roncesvalles directly below. The col was the highest point of the day, and I was glad the climb of 1,400 meters, or 4,600 feet, from St. Jean was over. There was a choice between two routes to Roncesvalles, and I told Alja that I intended to stay on the French Way, which was more direct. Alja wasn't sure what to do, and as she thought, I said I would go ahead. The dirt trail descended steeply through the forest and I went slowly to take care of my knee. I stopped a moment for a rest as Alja smiled and passed. I never saw her again.

At the bottom of the hill, another Camino from the east joined the French Way. One day, I hope to explore some of these lesser-known routes. I crossed the bridge into Roncesvalles, an important historic site, not only for the Camino, but for the many battles that took place in the area, including the aforementioned Battle of Roncevaux Pass. King Charlemagne's army damaged some of the buildings in Roncesvalles, which leads me to believe it was the Basques that destroyed the rearguard. Of course, I have no real idea; I certainly am not an authority on the subject and most likely will never be one. Honestly, I don't anticipate a historical scholar calling me up one day and asking for my view or opinion. Who knows? I never thought I'd be writing a book either.

The church and monastery, Real Colegiata, an imposing brick and stone building, towered above me, although it wasn't extravagant from the exterior. Inside, the *albergue* was very busy as pilgrims waited in line for a bed. Roncesvalles is a popular spot for pilgrims to begin their Camino. It can be difficult to get from Spain to St. Jean by bus, and some people prefer to skip the climb through the Pyrenees. I even talked with someone who took the bus from Pamplona to Roncesvalles, walked to St. Jean one day, and then walked back to Roncesvalles the next. Now that's crazy!

It was only two-thirty and far too early for me to find a place to stay. I needed a break and went into the bar, but there were no tables available. It was a loud, busy place, with many pilgrims happy their first day of walking was over. I bought a Coke Light – same as a Diet Coke – and sat on the outside patio, which was far more pleasant on a sunny afternoon. I looked at my map and had to consider the rest of my day. There were no *albergues* from Roncesvalles to the village of Zubiri, about twenty-two kilometers away. The villages in between had private hostals or casas, but I preferred not to spend extra money on the first night. Not to be confused with a hostel, a hostal or *hostales*, is a private room found throughout Spain and Latin America. It's often smaller than a hotel room but also more inexpensive. My shoulders were a little sore, but otherwise, I felt great. I sure didn't want to stop yet. By the time my break was finished, it was three o'clock, and I had to get moving. Time would be tight to get to Zubiri before dark.

On the edge of Roncesvalles, a highway sign showed 790 kilometers to Santiago de Compostela. I think that sign was intentionally placed there by an official or someone as a joke to scare the crap out of the poor pilgrim. Supposedly, the distance to Santiago was about 790 kilometers from St. Jean, so I wasn't sure what had happened to the twenty-five kilometers I had just walked. The Camino veered off the highway and followed a flat, dirt path, on which I made excellent time. I thought I was the only pilgrim walking until I saw an older couple resting in the trees and contemplating whether to go back. The three kilometer walk to Burguete was very pleasant, traveling through grasslands and pine forests. When I arrived, the village was quiet, with few people on the streets. It was almost spooky and nothing like the busyness of St. Jean, or even Roncesvalles. I would learn that the period of siesta during the afternoon influenced many of my days on the Camino and often determined if I was able to buy food or supplies.

Many of the houses were two or three stories, white-washed, and finished with red or brown shutters and red tiled roofs. Larger houses had elaborate coats of arms above the main entrance. I stopped in front of the Hotel Burguete, one of author Ernest Hemingway's favorite places to stay in Spain. Hemingway loved Navarra and often wrote about the people, landscape, villages, and of course, Pamplona. Part of his 1926 book, *The Sun Also Rises*, involves the characters spending time fishing and relaxing around Burguete. There was one bar open, and all I wanted was an ice cream. No beer or wine, just an ice cream. My first attempt to order in Spanish didn't go well and I had to resort to pointing. Three people sat at an outside table, but otherwise, nobody else was in the streets. I stopped for a moment outside the church, a gray and beige, brick and stone building with a new clock in the center. It was a more rustic, with a less elaborate style of architecture than the ones I saw in France.

After Burguete, the Camino veered onto a gravel road and then joined a dusty dirt and gravel trail. I passed a shabby house with a very mean-looking dog on a long leash that lunged, barked, and snarled as I walked by. There were a few other homes and farms, but much of the landscape was scrubby and gently rolling. The walk was easy, and I made good time. Soon, I was back on the paved road, and ahead of me was the village of Espinal.

I needed a quick break and stopped at the bar for a drink. Only three other people were there, but they were all smoking, and the air was thick and stale. An overweight woman with a cigarette dangling from her mouth stared at me while I tried to order a Coke Light. I was sure the bartender understood but gave me a hard time. Sometimes it was faster only to say, "Coke Light" instead of making a sentence and confusing the hell out of someone. I sat far away from the others, but the smoke bothered me so much, I quickly finished my drink and left. The glass Coke bottles were so small but still cost about €3 in the bars. If I had two or three a day, it would add up to one of my largest expenses.

Espinal was another quiet village, and I didn't see anyone else until I stopped for photos in front of the modern church. The young man with the Eastern European accent walked up the street. We had passed each other a few times during the day, but I hadn't seen him since I took my break near the French-Spanish border. I introduced myself and was pleased he could speak English. His name was Jerry from Czechoslovakia, and, although he was much younger than I was, we immediately knew we had something in common – we were the only pilgrims walking in the late afternoon. We talked about our first day on the Camino and how it was both our intentions to walk long days. Jerry was concerned about getting to Zubiri, but I told him there wasn't much choice unless he wanted to splurge on a hotel room in Espinal.

Jerry didn't like my map and studied his for far longer than I thought was needed, so I said goodbye and took off. I walked at a fast pace through the village, but at one point, I realized there were no more Camino markers. I couldn't believe I had missed the turnoff and now had to backtrack two hundred meters. By the time I was on the proper path, Jerry was far ahead. I felt a little guilty for leaving him but didn't know what he was looking for on his map. I didn't think he was going to wait for me now, and he probably wondered what I was doing off the Camino.

It was warm, and I struggled on the gentle incline out of Espinal. My shoulders were sore, and my backpack felt very heavy. After the field, I entered a forest and was grateful to have some cover. I had more trouble climbing the one hundred meters of elevation gain to the Alto de Mezquiriz than I did the 1,400 meter gain from St. Jean through the Pyrenees earlier. Exhausted, I descended through a forest to the village of Gerendiain. It was a pleasant walk, and I don't think I could have climbed another hill right away. Sections of the path were recently laid with stone slabs; I supposed there was once a problem with mud. It was obvious that the government officials of Navarra took pride in the maintenance of the Camino. At least, it appeared so at this point.

Dark clouds were in the direction I was headed, and the air felt humid. Not wanting to be caught in a storm, I tried to pick up my speed, but my legs wouldn't respond. Gerendiain was also fast asleep, and the only person I saw initially was an old woman looking out her window. The village was clean and had garbage bins on every block. Jerry was near the church, inspecting his map. We talked briefly and decided to walk together. It was six o'clock, and with eight kilometers left to Zubiri, there wasn't any time to waste. We seemed happy with each other's company. Jerry had been going through relationship and work issues and was walking the Camino to clear his mind. I recently had a stressful year caring for my mom and watching her pass away. I needed to clear my mind, too.

After Gerendiain, there was a slight climb to another alto. I struggled and told Jerry to go ahead. I was concerned, trying to keep up with someone who was perhaps twenty years younger. My own pace was important, not only for my endurance during the day, but for the entire Camino. I couldn't push myself when I needed a break or my energy wouldn't last. I also didn't want to make myself vulnerable to injury.

Near the alto, I felt the first raindrops, and soon, we found ourselves bombarded by a heavy spring shower. I fumbled with my backpack cover and realized I had never put it on my backpack before. I'm such a fair weather hiker and normally won't go out with even the threat of rain. My poncho didn't fit properly with my backpack, and the hood kept shifting over and covering my face. I did the best I could with the rain gear, and we quickly descended the hill. At eight o'clock, we crossed the medieval stone bridge over the Río Arga and walked into Zubiri. The bridge had large cracks and looked to be in need of some maintenance. The unsightly blue barrels at the bottom of the bank sure took away from the experience of walking over an old bridge. We had made it, and now we had to find a bed. Oh, how I hoped there was a bed. I couldn't walk anymore.

We stopped at the first *albergue* and had success. The pretty *hospitalera* asked where we came from, and when we mentioned St. Jean Pied de Port, she looked at us with disbelief. She said it was far, and I told her I agreed. Jerry and I had walked forty-seven kilometers on the first day of the Camino. The last two hours were particularly difficult and exhausting.

We checked in and entered the dorm room with seven double bunks. Jerry immediately went to a lower bed near the window, which left me with no choice but to take a top one near the door. The wet clothes rack was full, but I made room for my soaked poncho. Before my shower, I realized there were toiletries all over my backpack. I had only been gone a few days, and my backpack was already unorganized. We had no trouble getting shower stalls, and there was plenty of hot water because the other pilgrims had arrived long before.

The *hospitalera* recommended the bar for dinner, not that there was anywhere else in the village that served food at that hour. The busy bar was smoky, which I didn't like, but Jerry smoked, so it didn't bother him. We both ordered an Estrella beer, which came to our table quickly. Jerry wasn't hungry, but I was. There was no menu, and our waitress didn't know English, nor could she understand my Spanish. She called to the back, and another woman came out to help. I ordered a sandwich with ham, *jamón,* but otherwise wasn't sure what I was getting. Jerry and I talked and got to know each other a little. He was also a hockey fan and gave a European perspective on the sport. We reflected on our first day, and, although tired, we were excited and proud. We decided to continue walking together and talked about the days ahead. I didn't know how long it would last, but I was willing to try.

My sandwich arrived, and besides layers of ham, it had peppers and was smothered with cheese. I was so hungry, and it easily took care of my fat intake for an entire week. After my dinner, we finished our drinks and went back to the *albergue.* Most of our roommates were already in bed, and I tried to be quiet as I looked for my bed clothes. I got settled and covered my head and eyes with the silk hood, just in time for the first snores of the night. I was tired but couldn't sleep. It was too dark to read, so I listened to a Spanish podcast. If the day behind me was any indication, I needed to learn a lot more Spanish soon. I fell asleep listening to beautiful Spanish words and phrases and wondering why it was so difficult to learn another language.

THE BED SHOOK LIKE AN EARTHQUAKE ROLLING THROUGH THE HILLS OF NAVARRA

Day 2
Zubiri to Uterga
39 Km

I found something out during the night – the more men there were in a dorm, the more snoring men there were in a dorm. Nothing very insightful, but I was too damn tired to think of anything else. If I did contribute to the snoring, it wasn't very much, because I only had a few hours of sleep at most. Sometime in the middle of the night, one guy across from me let out a series of loud, stinky farts that permeated the air in the room. To make matters worse, some idiot listened to his iPod at 1:00 A.M., and the bright light shone like a beacon every time he touched the screen. Sorry, I must admit that idiot was me.

When I realized I was up for good, I climbed off the bunk, grabbed my gear, and without making noise, or at least, too much noise, went to the communal room. It was only four o'clock, and I wondered how I would pass the three hours or so until Jerry got up. The computer was still on, and the internet was free, so I checked the news and emailed Sarah to tell her I had survived my first day. I was very concerned with the weather forecast for Spain. Apparently, spring would soon be replaced by a late bout of winter, which would last for at least ten days. I hated the cold and rain and normally wouldn't even think about going out in such weather. I didn't have a choice now. During my short time in England, France, and Spain, I had already taken about five hundred photos. I wanted to back them up, but when I plugged in my SDHC adapter into the old computer, it vapor-locked and took a few presses on the restart button to come back to life. I should have known better than to try it.

My backpack needed to be organized, so I unpacked the contents and spread everything over two tables. Moments after, two older women came into the room to get ready. They didn't speak English, and one gave me a funny look as she studied all my belongings. I felt uncomfortable and quickly stuffed everything into my backpack in a manner that was more unorganized than before. I looked at pamphlets, books, photos, and my guidebook for the third or fourth time. I was fascinated by a small, wicker basket, which contained about a dozen electrical outlet adapters that people forgot. These poor pilgrims likely used their adapter for two nights and then had to scramble to find another. I reminded myself to always double check that I had mine. I was dressed and ready by seven o'clock, but Jerry was still in bed. I became impatient and fidgeted some more. When he finally got up, I told him that I would walk slowly and he could catch up. I checked around my bunk to see if I had forgotten anything, and sure enough, my adapter was still in the electric outlet.

Although it was cool and cloudy, I was happy it wasn't raining. From Zubiri, a dirt path with patches of mud led through forest and overgrown pastures. I wore shorts and half gaiters, which I'm sure looked stupid, but they kept mud off my legs and socks. Immersed in solitude, I updated my audio journal, although at that point, I wasn't sure what I would do with it. The track was fast, with a few small ups and downs. Another section was recently laid with slabs of stone, and I had to be careful not to slip.

A pilgrim who resembled Jesus walked toward me. He was dressed in traditional pilgrim's wear – a long, shabby, brown robe. He had a fraying tan backpack, and held a walking stick, an old branch, with a white scallop shell attached. A panting Shih Tzu ran about his feet. The little dog was white with black patches, although I couldn't tell how much of that was fur, and how much was mud. I told him he was the first pilgrim I had seen walking toward St. Jean and asked where he was headed – I expected him to say St. Jean. "Roma," he said and smiled. His name was Fredrick from Germany and yes, he was walking from Santiago de Compostela, Spain to Rome, Italy, a distance of about 2,300 kilometers, or 1,400 miles. He didn't know how long it would take – four months, six months, it didn't seem to matter. I told him that was more than most people will walk in their lifetime, and he laughed. I said goodbye to both Frederick and his little dog and wished them a safe journey. And I thought *my* Camino was long.

There was no sign of Jerry as I continued through the peaceful green valley. Hamlets such as Osteritz were small, often with only a few houses and possibly an old brick and stone church.

After climbing to the top of a hill, I thought I saw Jerry far behind and waited, but it wasn't him. On the descent, I felt a few sharp pains in my knee, the same spot I had injured the previous year. I took a break and massaged the area. I knew if I strained my knee again, my Camino would be over. Jerry caught up near the hamlet of Illarratz and seemed fine. He seemed so fine that he walked at an incredibly fast pace. The little hill I had just climbed tired me, and now I had to keep up with him.

Just before entering Larrasoaña, we crossed again over the Río Arga on a medieval bridge whose thick green vines cascaded over the gray stone walls. Larrasoaña has been a pilgrim's stop for centuries, but the original hospices have long since disappeared. The church had a simple, square façade, with two giant bells in the overhead tower. Coats of arms with great detail sat prominently over the doorways of many of the larger houses. Few people were in the streets, and pilgrims who had stayed here had left hours before. We couldn't find anywhere to eat on the main street until we had almost reached the end of the village and saw a small café.

When it was my turn to order, I fumbled with my Spanish and mixed in some English. The waiter wasn't impressed and gave a slightly dirty look. After two tries, I was able to get my pastry and Coke Light and joined Jerry outside on the quiet patio. This morning was a much easier walk, but I didn't have the same adrenaline as I did the previous day. My shoulders hurt, at times, the sharp pains shot right up my neck. Jerry smiled and said he'd had an excellent sleep. He was accustomed to a hostel or dormitory environment and said he could sleep through almost everything. I was jealous. I had not had a good sleep since I was home and barely slept the night before I left. The warm sun made me tired, and when I began to yawn, it was time to leave.

Jerry and I left Larrasoaña on a dirt and gravel path through pastures and overgrown fields. We walked along the Arga Valley through Akerreta and crossed the river again just before Zuriáin. A short stretch along the narrow shoulder of the highway followed, and my eyes fixated on a tiny white cross that sat on top of a jagged, rocky outcrop. Jerry took few photos but would wait while I took mine. Sometimes we walked together and other times apart. Sometimes we talked and other times were silent. One thing we both did was walk fast and pass almost everyone.

We crossed over the Arga again and followed a dirt path for a short climb to an alto, where we looked across the valley with farmland and scrubby hills. This scene was spoiled, however, by a huge pillar of smoke that rose from a chimney of an old mill. Many pilgrims rested in front of the centuries-old church in the hamlet of Irotz. I heard my first *Buen Camino* of the day and turned around to see an Asian man nervously smiling at me. I gave a simple *hola* but I don't think he was impressed. I didn't mean any disrespect, but I was still having some trouble with my *Buen* which to me, sounded closer to "boing." It just wasn't ready. As I left him, I quietly worked on my *Buen Camino* and repeated it over and over.

Jerry and I sat on a wooden bench in front of the church, its walls sloppy with patches of peeling cement and mortar over the bricks. Some of the pilgrims we had passed earlier caught up, and I especially admired a French couple in their 60's. They seemed so happy walking together, and I hoped it would last for the entire Camino. The man smiled and shook my hand again as they went by. I dug out what was left of my black cherry jam and two-day-old baguette. The baguette was hard, and I only used enough to finish the jam. I was concerned with my sluggishness and the pain in my shoulders. Jerry said his shoulders were sore but didn't seem too bothered by it. Zabaldica was another pleasant hamlet and had an old church, with its overgrown yard and cracked walls that had seen better days. I wondered how many parishioners attended the churches in these hamlets. Better yet, how many people were left in these hamlets? Nearby, a beautiful stone house had attached to its walls a lovely lilac shrub with purple flowers in full bloom. I could smell the scent from across the road but walked right up to a flower for a closer whiff. I closed my eyes as my mind and body ingested the sweet smell.

I don't know if it was the scent of the lilac or the sugar from my black cherry jam, but I felt energized as we climbed steeply. Jerry and I took turns with the lead on the narrow trail, which led to an alto from which we could see Pamplona and its suburbs in the distance. We descended to a rest stop in a park-like setting that had one of the few public washrooms along the Camino. I tried to convince myself that now was a good time, but nothing happened.

The trail joined a road, and soon we faced an impressive medieval stone bridge with a curved span over six arches. Downstream, short, man-made waterfalls crossed the Río Ulzama, with huge tufts of brown and green grasses protruding from the water. The river banks had three- and four-story apartment buildings painted in yellows, beiges, and oranges. We walked over the bridge onto the cobblestone street of the quiet suburb of Arre. The streets were clean, and, although where I come from, hanging clothes from a line out the front window often looks terrible, here it brought character. The first neighborhood gave way to one that looked shabbier. There were unkempt houses and peeling murals, and here, clothes hanging from a front window didn't look good.

In the suburb of Burlada, Jerry and I took a break on one of the many benches along the busy road. For the past hour, I had felt a stone or something on the bottom of my right foot, so I took off my boot, but there was nothing inside. Then I removed my sock to find the beginning of my first blister. A group of pilgrims walked by, and one woman explained to me that, if I wanted to prevent blisters, I had to take it easy and not walk so much every day. I said I didn't consider that an option but politely thanked her. Another woman told me to use Vaseline on my feet, which I had never considered before. A friendly woman from Ottawa, Canada who saw my Canadian flag also took an interest in my stinky foot. She claimed to be a nurse and informed me, with a giggle, that I had a blister. I gave a slight laugh and thanked her for her examination. She was walking with two Irish women, and they all giggled as they left. I was sure they had already been drinking.

The walk through the housing and sprawl took longer than I had expected, but finally we arrived at the fourteenth century Magdalena Bridge over the Arga. Arches, cut out like windows, were inside the two main abutments, or supports. At the entrance to the bridge stood a very detailed *cruceiro* depicting St. James. We entered Arga River Park, with its old deciduous trees and pleasant paths. Ahead, towering over us, were the imposing ancient city walls of Pamplona. We stopped for photos at the Portal de Francia, the French Gate, with its huge coat of arms overhead, and then walked through to Calle Carmen and into the old city of Pamplona.

Pamplona, the capital city of Navarra, is probably best known to foreigners for the Running of the Bulls during the San Fermin Festival every July. The city was founded by the Romans in the first century BC, written about passionately by Hemingway, and in possession of a rich Spanish and Basque history. It had been the site of many battles and wars – fought or held by Romans, Basques, Moors, Franks, and various monarchs. As with other cities, Charlemagne also destroyed the city walls, pissing off the Basques even further. Jerry and I walked the cobbled streets with buildings five stories high, painted in oranges, beiges, yellows, and pinks. Each had different features and colors, with rarely a pattern. Shops and cafés were on the ground level, with homes above. The streets were clean, and police officers watched the pilgrims, tourists, and locals. We walked the same streets that were home to the Running of the Bulls, but on this day, there were no bulls to be seen, only crowds of people.

I know the Running of the Bulls is on some people's bucket lists, but I wonder if it could ever be on mine. Really, do I need to go to a foreign country and spend a whole bunch of money, just to get my ass pronged by a ferocious beast? I'm sure – if I was so inclined – I could get a similar sensation somewhere near my hometown. Seriously, I might watch the Running of the Bulls and attend the festivities, but I wouldn't go to a bullfight. It's far too gory for me.

In the Plaza Consistorial, I looked in awe at the Pamplona Town Hall. It had exquisite architecture highlighted at the top with gold and silver lions with crowns flanking a statue of a boy playing the bugle. On the corners were statues of men that appeared to be swinging baseball bats, I couldn't tell.

Jerry and I took our time as we looked at shops and stopped for a drink. We arrived at the end of the old city and crossed the street, while a few rough-looking men watched us closely. At the entrance of the Parque de la Taconera, we walked through the Portal de San Nicolás, which, if I read the sign correctly, was originally built in 1666 but reconstructed in 1929. Jerry and I sat on a park bench in the shade while three more possibly unscrupulous characters watched us from across the path. Although I felt uncomfortable, I wanted to see the park and took a quick loop around. The gardens were not as rich and the flowers not as plentiful as the ones I had seen in London. However, it was still picturesque, with statues and fountains among the tulips and trees. Nobody else was around, and I felt nervous so I went back to the bench. I looked at the map and was concerned we had missed much of Pamplona. Jerry had been here a week earlier and didn't seem like he wanted to walk back. I convinced him, and we backtracked many blocks to the Plaza del Castillo. I was surprised by the vastness of the plaza. It was surrounded by many grand buildings with bars and cafés on their ground levels. In the middle was a huge grandstand where children played and people posed for photos. The Plaza del Castillo is known as a meeting place for tourists and residents of Pamplona. It has hosted festivals, and long ago, was a venue for bullfights.

Afterward, we saw statues, churches, and more shops before we joined the Camino again. I was disappointed that so many of the statues and art had graffiti. It didn't seem to matter if the piece was modern or centuries-old. After the long detour, we were back at the Parque de la Taconera. I knew from the outset that I wouldn't have time to see everything in the bigger cities. I would likely have a few hours and would have to do my best. I had missed the cathedral, which was near the entrance to the city, and it would have to wait for another time. Jerry didn't take photos in Pamplona, but I took many. Sometimes he would walk ahead, look back, and wait. Although he seemed patient and didn't complain, I felt a little rushed and didn't want to hold him up. Certainly, he didn't have much choice if he wanted someone to walk with all day. It was a relationship, a walking relationship, with a little give-and-take.

Another park, Parque Vuelta del Castillo, was more open, with lawns and scattered trees. Next, we followed a sidewalk beside a busy road onto the University of Navarra grounds. Here, in the middle of the afternoon, there were mostly students and no other pilgrims. Jerry was very observant and noticed the many attractive, young Spanish women. Since I had a girlfriend back home, I was only looking at the flowers and trees. Jerry smacked his lips and proclaimed his devoted admiration for Spanish women. Until Pamplona, we didn't have too much exposure to attractive Spanish women, but he was right, there were many around. Although he didn't divulge all the details about his recent breakup, I could tell Jerry was a little heartbroken. I tried to explain some of the positives of spending some time alone. One obvious example was walking the Camino. Relationship stress can be like no other. Sometimes, it's good to have a break and a chance to renew. Once we exited the university grounds, relationship- and woman-talk was over. It was time to walk.

We crossed on the small, stone bridge over the creek-like Río Sadar. Ahead was the small suburb of Cizur Menor, on top of a hill about two kilometers away. It was at least 20°C, and I didn't know if it was the sun or the long walk, but I was drained and let Jerry lead. After the freeway, we began a gentle climb on a sidewalk into Cizur Menor. We passed the Iglesia de San Miguel, which looked more like a castle than a church, and stopped at a park next to a school. On the lawn, four men were having their siesta. They slept, rose for a while, and then lay down again. I didn't know if they had jobs or homes, but they were dressed fine and didn't look homeless. Jerry was also tired, and I was glad it wasn't just me. I took off my shoes and socks to discover one blister had already popped, and another was forming. Earlier, I had placed an adhesive strip on the first one, but it came off. I scrambled around my backpack for my first aid bag and covered the blisters with adhesive strips and tape. They would require better attention later.

I felt refreshed as we walked out of town onto a gravel path through a bright green hayfield. Or was it a wheat field? I couldn't tell. Please remember, I'm a city boy. Jerry went ahead as I updated my audio journal. I thought we walked at a good pace but a man and woman, out for an evening walk, passed us easily. They seemed happy, probably because they weren't carrying backpacks. In the distance was the ridge we had to cross, and along it was something new to me, a wind farm. At times, shrubs with white flowers lined the path. Other times, it was only farmland. The ruins of a castle stood on a hill; the light brown stone rose from the bright green field.

I stopped at a memorial for a pilgrim, and even though I had already seen a few, this one was unique. The cross was handmade out of iron, with a yellow Camino scallop shell on the top. Under the man's name, in the center, was a photo of him with a backpack. At the base, sat a recently-placed bouquet of artificial roses, which looked real. The man looked so happy, and I felt sure he had passed away doing something he enjoyed.

Soon after, there was a graveyard enclosed by stone walls. A tall tree with broken branches stood in the middle; it, too, had died. I looked back at Pamplona, and it seemed so far away. Only hours earlier, we had been on the hills on the other side when I had had the same thought.

Two pilgrim cyclists went by as we climbed slightly along the gravel path towards Zariquiegui. The hamlet had an *albergue*, but we believed we could get to Uterga on the other side of the ridge. Now we had to drop and then climb to the ridge that was still over two kilometers away. The landscape on the upper parts of the hill was scrubby, with sections of hay and recently plowed fields. Yellow mustard flowers often lined the path, and the contrasting colors were striking. As we climbed, the trail got rougher and rockier. We met the couple who had passed us earlier as they descended the ridge. They weren't friendly for some reason. I didn't think I smelled that bad.

One last push, and we made it to the top, the Alto del Perdón, with the wind turbines towering over us. I looked up and listened to the humming sound. It was amazing. On the ridge sat a memorial for pilgrims that featured life-sized shapes of adults, children, donkeys, a horse, and a dog – all cut out from wrought iron.

The only others at the alto were three young people who had driven to the top and one lonely pilgrim. She was a woman in her 60's who somehow got separated from her husband and had no idea where he was. She obviously had trouble with route-finding and had earlier spent many hours walking the wrong route. The Camino was well marked on the alto, but for some reason, she started to follow the road to the south. We called and pointed her in the right direction toward Uterga. I asked if she wanted us to wait, but she smiled and told us to go ahead.

A scary-looking storm with dark, purple clouds was approaching. Uterga was still over three kilometers away, and I wanted to get there before the rain did. The trail from the ridge was rocky, rough, and steep. Jerry flew down the mountain, but I slowed to take it easy on my knee. We descended to a wide gravel path and then walked fast, with the dark clouds overhead. When we arrived in Uterga, Jerry and I headed straight for the *albergue* and just beat the rain by minutes.

We were relieved there were beds available. The pretty *hospitalera* wanted to check our country passports, which was the first time someone asked for mine. I felt uncomfortable showing it, but Jerry told me it was mandatory at most places. The cost to stay was €10, and Jerry was surprised it was so much. He had limited funds and had based much of his budget on paying a few euro each night. I was just happy to find a bed.

The *hospitalera* showed us the dorm, and although it was only seven o'clock, people were already sleeping. Jerry took the last lower bunk on one side of the long narrow room, leaving me with a choice of either of the tops of two bunks across from each other. On the lower bed of one bunk was a rather large man, while on the other was a rather large woman. I said *hola*, but neither one of them said anything and only gave cold looks. I knew they were trying to rest, but it was still early. The couple looked beat, as if they had already walked for a month. Instead, it was more likely a few days. I looked at each bed and they both gave me a look as if to say, "Don't you dare take that bed above me." The woman muttered something in French to the man and he muttered something back. They were obviously a couple, hell, they almost looked the same. I thought about it for a moment. Who would snore the least? Surely the woman, I hoped. I chose the bed above her, and she wasn't happy.

I looked for my shower items and clean clothes, but since I had thrown my gear in the backpack that morning, I had less of an idea where everything was. As I rummaged, the woman glared into my eyes and made me very nervous. Honestly, I really wasn't that noisy. To ease the hardship that I had brought to the poor French couple, I grabbed my backpack and went into the hallway.

After my shower, I washed clothes and hung them outside on a small clothes rack beneath an overhang. They wouldn't dry, but at least they would drip overnight. The thunderstorm was intense, and I thought about the woman on the alto and hoped she was fine. I was out of food and thought I'd try the pilgrim dinner. Jerry joined me, but he had already eaten something from his backpack. We reflected on the day; we had walked thirty-nine kilometers, plus all the backtracking in Pamplona. We were pleased, though we knew we couldn't walk forty-seven kilometers every day. Jerry went back to the dorm, and the pretty *hospitalera*, who was now my pretty waitress, explained in her best English the set menu. I told her to bring everything, and she soon returned with a tasty lentil soup which alone filled me up. Then came a quarter of a chicken with fries, followed by a cheesecake. The dinner made me feel bloated, and I realized that if I wanted to finish the Camino in three weeks, I couldn't eat like this often.

When I first got to the bar, there were only a few people, and maybe two smoked. Since it was Friday and this was most likely one of the few places of entertainment in the village, the bar gradually filled up during my dinner and created a cloud of thick smoke. In Canada, smoking had been banned in restaurants for many years, and I was accustomed to smoke-free meals. I felt uncomfortable, and it was difficult to enjoy even a simple meal in this environment.

I said goodnight to the waitress and thanked her for being patient with my Spanish. I checked the internet but was too tired to look at the screen. It was only nine o'clock when I got back to the dorm. The French couple were fast asleep and I walked softly, hoping not to disturb them. When I unzipped a pouch on my backpack, the woman's eyes opened wide, and she looked pissed. I took off my shoes and began to climb the ladder to the top bunk. With each step, there was a loud squeak. I crawled into the bunk – more squeaking – and shuffled myself into the liner and sleeping bag – yet more squeaking. Although I was tired, I couldn't fall asleep. My earbuds were in my backpack, but I didn't dare go back down and get them. I just laid there and listened to the rain and the odd snore.

Soon, from below, I heard these gurgling sounds and some of the loudest snoring I had ever heard. Then from across the room, I heard more gurgling sounds and more of the loudest snoring I had ever heard. I couldn't believe it. It was snoring in stereo, but in this case, I was above the loudest speaker. When I chose the bunk, I hoped if the woman snored, it would be like a kitty cat purring. Instead, she snored like a mountain lion. Every time the woman turned, the bed shook like an earthquake rolling through the hills of Navarra. I'm not religious, but that night, I prayed she wouldn't tip over the bunk. And more than a few hours of sleep would have been nice, too.

CANADIAN BOY
Day 3
Uterga to Villamayor de Monjardín
38 Km

It was only 4:00 A.M. when I decided I couldn't take it any longer. Enough with the French snoring symphony. Enough with the snoring from everyone. The dorm had at least thirty people, and it seemed like every fifteen minutes, someone got up to use the washroom. I don't know how much I slept, but it wasn't much. I grabbed my gear and went to the communal room. Unlike the previous morning, the computer was off and all the books were in Spanish. I sat on the couch in a dazed blur for at least an hour before I heard the first rumblings from the early risers. I began a morning ritual of assessing blisters and then taping them up. There were two bad ones on the bottom of each foot and I had to drain the one on my right. And I hadn't even started day three yet.

I was ready by six-thirty, but Jerry was still sleeping. As I waited, my patience started to wane. He woke up around seven o'clock and was surprised to see me ready. I told him about the French couple who had left an hour earlier. He laughed and told me he had an excellent sleep. When he turned his back I mimicked, "I had an excellent sleep. I had an excellent sleep." Since it was cold and had rained during the night, my clothes had barely dried. I hated the thought of carrying wet clothes all day. Stretching my tired and stiff body proved to be a challenge. We left the *albergue* in a light rain at seven-thirty. I had already been up for over three hours.

With a good sleep, Jerry had so much energy. I, on the other hand, was a slug. I was fortunate the terrain only rolled slightly, because I don't think I could have handled a steep climb. The dirt path had muddy spots and many puddles, which we had to skirt around and jump over. The rain showers came and went, annoying me. We passed a crude paper sign that stated, "Santiago 747 km, *Buen Camino.*" I was cranky and really didn't need to be reminded how far I still had. I knew it was fucking far, thank you. I let Jerry go ahead while I recorded my audio journal. I didn't feel like saying much, anyway.

In Muruzábal, we stopped briefly to admire the church. It was rather simple in design but had colorful stained glass windows, with one featuring a large flower in the center. I felt better after the village, even with the minor climb to Obanos. We passed the first vineyard on the Camino – the trunks were thick with deep grooves, and the leaves had recently sprouted on the vines. In Obanos, Jerry needed something to eat and went inside a bakery while I bought my first Pepsi Light in Spain from an outside machine. I drank, ate a chocolate bar, and admired the buildings around the plaza. The church, with its elaborate stained-glass, was much more impressive than I would have expected in a small village. A woman and a man – I believe they were mother and son – unrolled a canvas of an oil painting and took photos of it displayed in front of the church door. Obviously, the painting was special to them. They laughed and were in a better mood than I was. At least they didn't carry a garden gnome across Spain. Jerry spent at least ten minutes in the store, and I had no idea what he was doing. Meanwhile, I was getting very cold. When Jerry came out, he sat and started eating. I couldn't get warm watching him as he savored the banana and the crumbling pastry. After a minute, Jerry mentioned how cold he was, gobbled up the rest of his food, and we left.

The Camino descended gradually past vineyards and farmland. I saw the first red poppy, and soon, there were splashes of red along the path. We arrived at Puente la Reina and were greeted by a large metal statue depicting St. James. Puente la Reina has catered to pilgrims for centuries and is best known for its magnificent Romanesque bridge. The town, whose name means "Bridge of the Queen," refers to the queen in the eleventh century who commissioned the bridge to span the Río Arga. The Iglesia del Crucifijo, near the entrance of the town, had an octagon-capped bell tower separated from the main building by a portal. Storks, as if on guard, stood on top of the tower. The grounds around the church were clean and peaceful but deserted in the cold weather. For centuries, the Camino has followed a narrow street with four- and five-story brick and stone buildings. Bars, cafés, and small shops were on the lower levels, with houses above. Because of the angle from the narrow street, the Iglesia de Santiago proved difficult for good photos. Jerry and I backtracked and then went two blocks off the Camino for a better view of the octagon bell tower.

Jerry went into a bakery while I looked in a liquor store. The price of the wine surprised me. One bottle was €1.65, and many were in the two to four euro range. It was too bad I couldn't carry any. We walked to the edge of the old town and looked at the most impressive bridge I had seen. It was the beautiful Puente la Reina, which had six main arches, along with five abutments. Similar to the Magdalena bridge just before Pamplona – although grander – each abutment had an arch cut-away similar to a window. I couldn't believe I was walking on an eleventh century bridge. I took my time as Jerry went ahead. The river was wide, and I could understand the problems it created for travel before the bridge was built.

I was bewildered by two pilgrims' attempt to make their Camino more comfortable. They pulled a contraption that resembled two long ski poles connected to a wheel, with a backpack placed on top of the poles. Although it took weight off the shoulders, I'm sure pulling and pushing this thing all day would still tire out muscles in the shoulders along with the back, arms, and hands. I felt sprinkles as we crossed the bridge, and soon it was pouring rain. Jerry needed another break, and we escaped the rain under the cover of a freeway overpass. I sat for a moment but really didn't need a break. Jerry looked like he'd be a while, so I put my rain gear back on and told him I'd walk ahead. I looked forward to the upcoming section of the Camino with the Roman road.

A lovely South African woman in her 60's saw my Canadian flag and wanted to talk. She had family in various parts of the world who were concerned that she walked alone. I told her about my recently departed mom, and I could feel her sincere sympathies. Her company was enjoyable, and her words were very soothing. We talked about each other's Camino and what we hoped to achieve. First, we hoped to get a good sleep one day. We both had trouble with all the snoring in the *albergues* and already had our share of stories – my low point was sleeping so close to the cranky French couple. As we walked, the rain stopped and soon, patches of blue sky were overhead. The dirt path glistened, with many sections covered in thick mud.

The landscape began to change after Puente la Reina, where the reddish-brown soil was so prominent. The terrain rolled as we gently climbed a dirt path lined with red poppies and mustard in full bloom. It was Saturday, and many Spaniards were on day hikes. Most were friendly, but some younger people went by with barely an *hola*. I had already taken so many photos, my camera battery had died. I told the

South African woman to go ahead because I knew it would take a while to find my spare battery. I looked through my pack, and after ten minutes, I finally found it in the top compartment. Of course, it was the last place I looked. Jerry caught up, and with much of the contents of my backpack spread under a tree, I told him to go ahead; it would be my turn to catch up.

Mañeru was a small village, and I particularly paid attention to the doors. One arched double door was made of oak and had dark metal fittings, including a door knocker in the shape of a hand. Another door was much older, covered with deep cracks; its ancient fittings were rusted and weathered. Jerry wasn't in Mañeru, so I continued past the French couple from the *albergue*. Although it wasn't raining, they wore their giant ponchos that covered their backpacks to well below their knees. They looked so grumpy, and I didn't say a word to them. Thankfully, I never saw them again.

The emerging sun brightened a landscape of many colors, one of which was the red of the mud, which built up, despite my best efforts to knock it off, on my boots. In the distance, I saw the village of Cirauqui in a setting that was typical in this part of Spain. Most often, the village would be on top of a hill, with the dome or steeple of the church being the highest point. I was tired but continued at a fast pace, hoping to catch up with Jerry, wherever he was. My feet were sore from the blisters, and I knew there were now more than two on each foot. Back home, I was accustomed to day-hiking, and if I got blisters, they would have many days to heal. On the Camino, I was walking every day, and there was little or no time for my feet to recover.

A thick plume of smoke rose from the near side of Cirauqui. I had no idea what it was and hoped there wasn't a building on fire. Soon I smelled something I never had before – the odor of a Spanish barbecue. I walked the last muddy section to the village and the origin of the wonderful odor. A group of about fifteen men were drinking beer and barbecuing chicken and huge sausages. There was not a woman around. It was a private party, but I hoped they could sell me a delicious-looking sausage and bun. The two men who guarded the barbecue didn't understand my Spanish. I tried pointing to the sausages but they just nodded their heads and smiled. I was disappointed that I failed in my quest for a barbecue sausage and walked through the well-preserved village. The locals were friendly and greeted me as I passed by.

Finally, I found Jerry eating something in the small plaza. I was exhausted and didn't say much as I went into the store for a Coke Light and a Magnum ice cream. Magnums are vanilla ice cream coated in milk chocolate, sometimes with almonds or caramel. I really enjoyed them and felt myself getting hooked. It was also one of my best sources for energy. As I ate, Jerry became impatient, but I really needed a damn break. After I finished my ice cream, Jerry got up, and I followed him through the portal, where a bonfire burned right on the street. It was attended by a family that spanned three generations. They talked and laughed as the rain began to pour. I wished I could have stayed with them. Or the guys with the barbecue.

From Cirauqui to Lorca was the most important stretch of Roman road left on the French Way. The path started gently rolling through vineyards and farmland. A group of pilgrims rested at an old stone bridge, which I thought would be a good place for us also. However, Jerry was one hundred meters ahead and not looking back. I began to get frustrated, and it was obvious that we were on individual Caminos. I walked the Roman road and took many photos. The original road was not always clear, but when I saw the laid-out stones, I slowed and watched every step. I couldn't worry about Jerry and took my time. Millions of pilgrims had walked on this very road, and I felt special and honored to be able to join them. My mom would have been excited to know where I was, and I wished I could have called her. I climbed the short hill, past the abandoned village of Urbe and down to the Río Salado. Here, there was a wonderful medieval bridge with a curved span over two large arches. It looked well maintained and had been rebuilt many times over the years. The sun was shining, and it would have been nice to join the dozen or so other pilgrims who rested. However, I didn't see Jerry anywhere. I took my photos of the bridge and started the gentle climb toward Lorca. I was exhausted; it was well past my break time. I was not having fun.

Lorca is a village built on a hill, with more modern buildings than I would have expected. I had no idea where Jerry was. He could have been in a shop or somewhere far ahead. I continued my climb and finally found him waiting on a bench. I had made up my mind and told him that walking together wasn't working out. Although we both desired to walk long distances every day, the way we would get to our destination was very different. It was best for both of us. Jerry was surprised, and I said I hoped he understood. I'm sure it was frustrating for him to wait while I took photos. I bid Jerry farewell. We had walked together for less than two days but it felt like a month. Time went by so slow on the Camino. There was so much to see and experience, I was often overwhelmed. I would miss walking with someone, but I had to remember, this was my Camino.

Similar to the end of any relationship that had run its course, I felt relief and a new sense of excitement. I had energy now and didn't need a break. The temperature was much warmer, about 15°C, and I wanted to change from my track pants into my shorts. I passed two women and just ahead of them, found a spot around a bend at the edge of a field. I figured I had less than thirty-seconds to change, and just as I finished, Jerry came by. We shook hands and said goodbye again before he raced off. I really thought I would never see him again.

The mud was terrible in sections, and I took extra care down the muddy slopes. Unlike earlier in Navarra, there was no trail maintenance here. In Villatuerta, I looked for a mailbox for the first time in Spain. I saw a yellow box labeled "Correos" and asked three Spanish woman who happened to be walking by. A pretty woman with dark hair spoke English and confirmed it was a mailbox. In front of the nearby church, the women asked me to take their photos, and then one took mine. The pretty woman who spoke English was from Madrid and referred to me as the "Canadian boy," which was a fine compliment, considering I'm not exactly a "boy." Let me rephrase that: I'm a boy, I'm just not that young. I don't think she was being sarcastic though. One time as we talked, I mixed up some French and Spanish and she gave a funny look and then laughed. The women were on an afternoon walk from Villatuerta to Estella. We walked at different speeds and stopped at different sites, but we crossed paths on occasion.

Past Villatuerta, the Camino followed a gravel road with flowers on the edge as it wound through wheat fields. I saw the eleventh century Ermita de San Miguel Arcángel from far away. The brick church was very simple and rustic; the opening of the main door had been permanently closed with bricks. Although it was only a short walk off the Camino, I was alone, and nobody else seemed interested in the little church. A short climb to an alto made me tired, and I began to slow. The Spanish women had passed me while I stopped at the church, and I saw them ahead at the bottom of the hill. After a short rest, I descended to a wide gravel road, rounded a curve, and met up with a cute, brown horse with a short mane. He was tied up in front of a bank of mustard flowers and posed for my photos. I was concerned he didn't have water and hoped his owner would return soon. I caught up to the Spanish ladies on the small bridge over the Río Ega, where they stopped for a break. I talked with the one who spoke English and again mixed up some French and Spanish. She asked if I was staying in Estella, but I said I had planned to get well past. I said goodbye to the pretty woman from Madrid and never saw her again.

I entered the outskirts of Estella and walked along a sidewalk to a park on the banks of the Ega. Across the road was the beautiful Iglesia de Santo Sepulcro, with a façade that had many ornate stone sculptures of religious figures and scenes. Perched on top of the hill was the Iglesia de Santo Domingo, a large, rectangular, stone building. The park looked popular, with many families relaxing and playing. Since it was late in the afternoon, most pilgrims chose to stay in Estella. The origins of the city were in the Romans' time, but it didn't flourish until the eleventh century, when King Ramírez focused on the Camino and pilgrim traffic. He also looked outside the region to parts of France and attracted people to open businesses. I didn't know much about Estella before my Camino. I had the pleasure of sipping Estrella Damm beer once or twice, but that was actually from Barcelona and spelled differently.

The rebuilt Puente Picudo had a steep span with a peak over a large arch that the Ega flowed through. Next, I found myself in the old city with narrow streets flanked by three- and four-story buildings. It was siesta time, and the streets were nearly deserted. I really needed some food and supplies, but every shop was closed. I also needed some money, and the only bank machine I saw didn't accept my bank card. The front of the town hall had colorful flags against the beige stone and ornate carvings under the overhang of the roof. A lone pine tree was perched on top of a rock bluff overhead. I stayed on the Camino but didn't realize until later that I had missed the convents and the main plaza that were a few blocks away. I found myself near the end of the city, facing a huge, modern sculpture of wrought iron. I had trouble determining what it was. I thought it was two large heads looking at each other with a maple leaf in the middle. It was Spain though, and I didn't think there were any maples. Then again, those may not have been two heads. Just outside Estella, the Camino entered a rural area, and soon, I saw a billboard for the Bodegas Winery over a large vineyard. A smaller sign stated that the *Codex Calixtinus*, the first guidebook for the Camino, had noted the excellence of wines in this area. The Bodegas Winery provided a fountain of red wine and water for pilgrims. Yes, a wine fountain, and it was free. I had prepared for this moment and carried a new, blue, plastic cup. I rinsed it out with water, placed it under the wine spout, and poured about a quarter full. The wine was okay and I'm sure not their best vintage, but the company should be commended for providing it. I can't imagine how much wine they supply in one day, let alone an entire year. I wanted my photo taken in front of the fountain and asked a woman for help. She and her friend had filled their glasses with wine twice in the few minutes I was there. They laughed and giggled loudly like intoxicated schoolgirls. I said goodbye and took a brief look at the Bodegas wine museum. The wine was inexpensive, with many bottles costing less than €5. There were informative displays, but most were in Spanish, and I could only pick out a few words. The clerk knew I wouldn't carry any bottles and didn't pay me any attention.

I needed a break and sat at a picnic table outside the museum. I faced the Monasterio de Irache and its large arched doorway underneath two detailed stone sculptures. My feet bothered me in the heat of the day, and I took off my shoes and socks to find my blisters were much worse. I couldn't imagine how my feet would be when I arrived in Santiago. I spread my wet clothes on the seats of the picnic table just as a tour bus parked and a group of passengers emerged. I hid my underwear but otherwise didn't care how I looked. I was exhausted and wished I found somewhere in Estella to eat. I wanted something different than nuts and chocolate. I looked at the plastic cup I brought for the wine fountain and determined it was no longer needed. I tossed the cup, used only once, in the garbage.

I felt a little better after a good break. It was six o'clock, and my goal for the day was Villamayor de Monjardín, over six kilometers away. I was nervous leaving a larger center in the evening. I never expected anything bad to happen, but I was alone most of the time. Past Irache, there was a forested area of oak and pine with many dirt roads crossing the Camino.

I thought if someone would attack me, it would surely be here. In these circumstances, I would hear Mom's voice saying, "Randall, are you sure it's safe? Be careful!" I would say, "Mom, if something is meant to happen, then it's going to happen." She hated when I talked like that.

I emerged safely from the forest but saw dark clouds heading my way. I tried to move faster, but my body wouldn't respond. The village of Azqueta sat on a hill above fields and trees. I tired from the small climb and stopped for a break outside the church. After Azqueta, the Camino wound through farmland, with the occasional vineyard. I stopped at the recently rebuilt Moorish fountain, an open brick shelter with a steep roof. A family, out for a walk, arrived at the same time as I did. A man gave a tour in Spanish to the adults while the children played outside. After a minute, they emerged, and I went inside, but it was only a pool with running water. I wondered what the site looked like when the Moors built it. My last climb up the hill was tough but soon, I saw Villamayor de Monjardín, with the church steeple rising above the village and the castle on top of the adjacent hill. For a moment, I watched an older man who sat on the ground at the side of the red dirt path sketching the village and surrounding landscape on his pad.

I was surprised to be greeted by Jerry outside the municipal *albergue*. He wasn't sure if there was a bed available and told me I had better inquire right away. I only had two choices for places to stay in the village. It was eight o'clock and too late to walk over eleven kilometers to Los Arcos. The French *hospitalero*, who spoke only a few words of English, said there was only a bottom bed of a bunk in a small room next to the washrooms. The room wasn't nice, and I told him I would think about it. I went outside and walked as fast as I could to the private *albergue*. The *hospitalero* there told me they were full, so I immediately went back down to the muni and took the last bed in the village. The cost was by donation, and the *hospitalero* took my pilgrim passport and told me I couldn't have it back until morning. Apparently, nobody was allowed to leave until 6:30 A.M.

My bed was in a terrible spot, next to the stinky boot rack and the stinkier washrooms. I greeted my bunk mate, Henry from Germany, who I guessed was in his late 30's. He carried a flask of at least one liter of the wine from the fountain. He seemed very proud of the free wine, but I only thought about how heavy it was. I badly needed a shower, but when I opened the door, it was so dirty, I couldn't go in with bare feet. I kept my flip-flops on the entire time. After my shower, I looked for dinner in the village. The only bar was jammed with men attending some kind of private celebration. The private *albergue* only served their guests, so I returned without any food. I sat in the kitchen while I talked and charged my camera battery. Although we didn't finish together, Jerry and I had walked thirty-eight kilometers, not bad, considering my bouts with sluggishness and all the time I took for photos. I severely lacked sleep and needed to address the matter soon. I had a feeling it wasn't going be different here.

After I nodded off at the table, I went to bed at nine-thirty. It was a night from hell. All night long, people farted, plopped in the toilet, and closed doors loudly. I was surprised how ignorant some people were, especially the ones who talked in our room while they waited in line for the toilet. And the smell. It was disgusting. I couldn't take this much longer. I needed a *me* night, which only included *me* in a private room. I had no idea where it would be, but it needed to happen.

SOMETIMES, IT ONLY TAKES ONE OR TWO PRICKS TO DO THE JOB

Day 4
Villamayor de Monjardín to Viana
30 Km

I woke up in the morning; it was not just another day. My head was aching, my body in some pain. You may not believe me, I don't care what you say, it's hard to walk all day when you don't get any sleep.

And I was so tired....

With only a few hours of frequently interrupted sleep, I got up in a bad mood. My head was in a fog as I got ready and ate a piece of bread with jam. Henry and I talked about the night so close to the washroom. He laughed it off, but I sure didn't. Maybe later, but not yet. I was the only one who spent more than a few minutes preparing their feet. Some people would watch and ask questions. My feet were worse with each day, and I had to make sure the blisters were drained, cleaned, and taped. I would need more supplies soon and realized the problem I had with stores being closed during siesta. Washing and drying clothes while walking long days in cool weather was also very difficult, and I had to figure something out. I was already down to only my supposedly quick-drying underwear, which I found uncomfortable and were causing a rash in my nether regions.

At six-thirty, the *hospitalero* brought the box of pilgrim passports into the reception area and allowed everyone to leave. My brain barely functioned, and I wasn't ready for another forty-five minutes. I put a small donation in the box and exited the *albergue* to a cool, over-cast morning. On my way out, the *hospitalero* gave me a *Buen Camino*, and I returned one right back. I finally got it, or at least a reasonable facsimile of one. I was the last pilgrim to leave the *albergue* and quite possibly, all of Villamayor de Monjardín. Although I had stretched, my legs had trouble moving. I was mentally and physically exhausted.

I knew better than to push myself and walked the best I could, which was slow. From the village, I followed a gravel road through rolling farmland of wheat, hay, and recently-plowed fields. There was the odd vineyard, and most of the hills were covered in low shrubs. The road was often lined with red poppies and other white and purple flowers. In one area, three-meter high wispy shrubs with light pink flowers decorated both sides of the path.

My pace increased as my legs and body woke up. At times, I could see dozens of pilgrims over a few kilometers ahead. The only pilgrim who passed me was a woman from a tour group who wore a day pack. I said *hola*, but she didn't even turn her head. I could have walked that fast, too, if my pack was only two kilograms and I slept in a private room every night. I hoped I wasn't rude like her when I passed someone. A pair of leather boots sat beside the road. One had its sole completely separated from the upper, while the other was filled with stones. I wondered if the owner had an extra pair of shoes, because it was still some eight kilometers to Los Arcos. And good luck finding boots in any of these villages. I caught up with Henry, who was tired and having a tough morning. We talked briefly, but I don't think either one of us was in the mood to say much. I kept my eyes fixated on a church or monastery, which sat on top of a hill a few kilometers to my right. The Camino wouldn't come close to it, so I took photos with various foregrounds, including flowers, bright green fields, and the ruins of an old pilgrims' hospital.

The temperature rose little during the morning and by the time I got to Los Arcos, I was cold and even crankier. My energy had depleted from the long morning walk without a break. I bought a Coke Light and two overpriced pastries and sat under cover outside the Iglesia de Santa María. A middle-aged couple from Québec, Canada saw my Canadian flag and came over to greet me. We talked about our impressions of the Camino and our experience so far. They were in the same *albergue*, and, not quite thinking, I criticized the people who kept me up during the night. He asked how long I had been walking and was surprised when I told him it was my fourth day. They had already spent a week on the Camino, and he asked me why I walked for so long every day. I told him, "I just want to get it over," an ignorant comment I later regretted. I was in a pissy mood.

The Québec couple entered the church, and I soon followed.

From the moment I walked in, I knew I was in a special place. The interior was simply gorgeous, with a beautiful *retablo*, or altarpiece (the structure above and behind the altar), murals, paintings, and stained glass windows. Soothing organ music played, and I looked around to find its origin. I glanced up and saw the player of the eighteenth century organ perched above the nave, or main hall. I immediately went to the mezzanine, where I watched and listened with enchantment. It was such a great thrill to visit the church, and I never expected such a beautiful one in the small town. It was a shame most pilgrims passed it by.

After I left the church, I felt better and had more energy. I walked along a good gravel path through more farmland and then joined a paved road with Sansol ahead. Henry had passed me while I visited the church and was sitting outside a bar in the village. We talked briefly, but it was too cold to stay outside. Instead, I entered the bar and ordered a very cold Magnum ice cream, which may not have made sense, but I needed a shot of energy. I also needed to take off my backpack. My shoulders were sore and even worse than the previous day. I looked at my guidebook and knew if I wanted to arrive in Logroño later, I needed to have a better afternoon.

The Camino dropped to a small bridge over the Río Linares and then climbed to Torres del Río. I sauntered up the hill, and by the time I arrived in the village, the energy I had gained from the ice cream was gone. A sign in the front window of an *albergue* advertised the internet, and I went inside. I caught up with news and emails and wasn't watching the time. When I checked, I couldn't believe I had spent over an hour on the computer. It was noon, and I had only walked a short distance from Sansol.

Now I had to climb about 150 meters of elevation gain on a steep trail to the alto at El Poyo. In front of the small monastery, Henry sat alone and meditated. We acknowledged each other, but I left him alone during his special moment. The grounds had piles of garbage that looked horrible. There weren't any trash bins, but that was no excuse. I couldn't understand why people couldn't carry out their trash. From the alto, there was an excellent view of the valley with Logroño and the region of La Rioja far in the distance. The sun peeked through the clouds and revealed the beautiful colors of the landscape.

A pleasant walk was ahead through farmland, vineyards, and trees.

As I descended, I stopped at a sign that advertised a hotel in Viana. My plan was to stay in Logroño, but I knew it would be tough with my slow speed. I would decide when I arrived in Viana. I recognized the small shrub, lithodora, from the gardens back home. It grew wild along the Camino and bloomed with bright blue, bell shaped flowers. I waited a few moments for the sun to come out and took some photos. Next to a vineyard at the bottom of a hill stood what I thought was a rustic farmhouse. I was so tired that if it had been a casa, I would have considered taking a room. Although the location was very peaceful, I discovered the building was a large storage shed for the vineyard. It was no longer enticing.

The sun emerged again, and it was the warmest of the day. I needed a good break and chose a spot under a pine tree overlooking the valley. I took off my boots and socks and discovered a new blister on my right foot. Henry rounded the curve and sat beside me, just as I was about to drain the blister. He looked as squeamish as if he was witnessing my colonoscopy. He said he couldn't watch and turned his head. I asked what he did with his blisters, and he said that he left them until they popped.

Believe it or not, the subject of feet and blisters is one of the most popular topics of discussion on the Camino. Everyone has their own way of dealing with blisters, but I was surprised how many people left them alone until they popped. Please understand that I'm not a doctor, and I won't profess to be some kind of blister or foot expert. This is only how I approach treating my own blisters. No advice is intended or given. Blister experts may want to skip three paragraphs. You've been warned.

I learned long ago the best care for a blister is to drain it yourself. The pain associated with draining the blister is much less than if it's left alone to split. I carried the necessary supplies, which included a sewing kit with needles and alcohol pads for sterilization. It was very important when walking over many days that everything was sterile so the chances of infection were reduced. Before I drained the blister, I made sure my hands were clean and wiped with an alcohol pad. My technique was to sterilize the needle and blister with the alcohol pad, then take the needle and make small pricks along the base. The fluid may not be all on one side of the blister, so it's important to go around. Sometimes, it only takes one or two pricks to do the job. Please, no prick jokes, thank you. I'm trying to be serious here. I used gauze or clean tissues to soak up the blister pus or goo or whatever it's called.

The skin flattens once the blister is drained, and I tried my best to protect it until it healed, in this case, likely not until well after the Camino was finished. I put a little ointment on it – not too much or the tape won't stick – and then covered the blister with gauze and tape. If there was a sensitive spot rubbing on the boot, I placed extra gauze on the blister as padding. If constantly protected, the skin should provide a natural adhesive strip and facilitate quicker healing. Often, I built up the area around the blister with gauze to alleviate some of the pressure and ease the pain. Sometimes on a small blister, an adhesive strip and some tape was enough.

Very importantly, I always took care of my feet in the evening. This starts with the presumption that the *albergue* floors weren't clean. Even if they looked clean, I assumed they were dirty. And some were disgusting. I would never walk with bare feet anywhere in the *albergue*, especially in the washroom. At times, I wore flip-flops while I took my shower. Blisters were drained after my shower, and once my feet were dry, I wiped the entire surface of both feet, including between the toes, with an alcohol pad. I certainly didn't want a foot fungus, and even wiped the top of my flip-flops every day. My feet were aired out as much as possible around the *albergues* and during extended breaks on the Camino. Of course, this was more difficult in cold weather. If I expected hot weather, I would consider taking a foot powder. After my feet were dry, I used a foot cream before bed. I know at this point on my Camino I didn't have foot cream yet, but I won't make that mistake again.

If you are still with me after my blister talk, I will continue with my Camino.

Henry and I enjoyed talking with each other on an afternoon when neither one of us felt like walking. He showed me his flask of wine again, which he had been carrying now for two days. He barely drank any, and I wondered how long he intended to carry it. Henry didn't seem to mind, he was so happy to get free wine. By now, the sun had disappeared, and it started to get cold. Henry pointed out the incoming clouds and wanted to leave. I told him to go ahead; I'd catch up. I packed up, stretched out my sore, tired body, and continued down through the valley. The path led to the main paved road where Henry walked ahead and Viana stood on a hill, at least two kilometers away. Dark clouds were now overhead, and I painstakingly tried to increase my pace. The temperature dropped considerably as I made the short climb into the old town of Viana. Above the portal was a sign commemorating five hundred years since the death of César Borgia, an Italian who had died defending Viana in 1507. The old town was beautiful, with much of it well-preserved. I stopped at the Iglesia de Santa María that had the best façades and tympanums I had seen. A crucifixion scene, among others, was depicted in rich detail. The town hall in the Plaza de los Fueros was an exquisite stone and brick building with a richly detailed, sculpted coat of arms, and oak glass doors.

I contemplated but had to make up my mind quickly. I still had time to get to Logroño but didn't feel like walking over nine kilometers in the cold with the storm approaching. Henry was outside one of the *albergues* and asked me to join him. I hadn't made up my mind if I was going to stay in Viana. I really wanted to check out the hotel I had seen advertised a while back. A friendly man in his 60's, Charles from Scotland, saw my Canadian flag and wanted to talk. He had been walking with a friend who had developed problems with his feet and legs and stayed behind in Los Arcos. His friend only decided to join Charles a few days before he departed and wasn't ready for a long walk. Now, they were apart, and Charles had no way of contacting him. I enjoyed talking with Charles, but I was freezing and needed to find a place to sleep.

The hotel was across from the Iglesia de San Pedro, which, at first, I didn't realize was actually ruins. I had to look through the windows to realize there was no roof. I entered the hotel lobby and asked the clerk for the price of a room. I had no idea how much a room in Viana could be, but I must admit, my budget gradually increased as the day wore me down. The clerk quoted €50 including breakfast, which I thought about for a moment. I looked outside and watched a white plastic bag being blown through the air by the wind, and that made up my mind. I was lucky the hotel accepted credit cards, because I didn't have enough cash. The clerk checked me in and told me that since it was a holiday, the shops in Viana were closed. My shopping would have to wait for another day.

It was only six o'clock, the earliest I had turned in so far. I had walked only thirty kilometers, by far the least of the four days. At that moment, I didn't care and would worry about it later. The room was clean and certainly the nicest I had seen so far in Europe. The bathtub had glass doors, gold-colored faucets, and a sense of cleanliness. Considering my experience in the *albergue* the night before, it was heaven. I washed clothes, hung them out around the bathroom, and hoped they would be dry by morning. I was hungry from not having a proper meal for two days. The downstairs bar was very smoky, so I ordered a ham sandwich with a Coke Light and ate in my room.

After dinner, I tried to use the internet, but the computer ran Windows 2000 and was very slow. Then, without warning, it stopped completely. I went back to my room, but it was still early. I turned on the television and found a regional hiking show. The hosts drove and hiked around Navarra and featured the natural beauty and historical ruins. The program was in Spanish, which was a shame for me, because I wanted to know exactly where they were. Sometime around nine o'clock, I fell asleep with the TV on and didn't wake until six in the morning.

DID I JUST ASK FOR VIAGRA?

Day 5
Viana to Ventosa
29.5 Km

A good sleep. That was all I needed. I felt so refreshed. I was ready by seven-thirty and went downstairs for breakfast. Initially, I sat at the bar with the other patrons, but when I told the waitress I was a hotel guest, she motioned me down a back hallway. I opened the door to a modern dining room, very similar to one I would find in North America. A large, continental breakfast was spread out on many tables, with a selection of breads, eggs, meat, cheese, fruit, and cereal. Only three other guests sat in the large room, and everyone kept to themselves. In the past, I purposely stayed away from a big breakfast, fearing it would upset my wimpy stomach or make me tired and slow my pace. I made an exception for the first time but must admit, if the breakfast wasn't included in the price of the room, I wouldn't have tried it. I ate until I was stuffed and even made a chorizo and cheese sandwich for later.

The breakfast made me sluggish, and I sauntered up the stairs to my room. I couldn't believe my socks and underwear still hadn't dried. I tried the hairdryer, but it wasn't enough. Without dry hiking socks, I was forced to wear a light pair that I had intended only to wear with my trail runners. I taped my feet, put my boots on, and immediately knew my feet would have an uncomfortable day. By the time I left the hotel, it was ten o'clock, and I had been up for almost four hours. I wanted a better day than the previous one. Leaving this late wasn't going to help.

The clouds threatened rain, and the bitter cold wind rushed through the narrow streets of Viana. I bundled up and wore rain pants for the first time. After taking photos of the church across from the hotel, I passed through a portal and headed down a hill and into a rural area. It was a little warmer below, but soon, I felt the first rain-drops. I took off my backpack and put on my poncho just as the rain stopped. I took off my backpack, put my poncho away, but moments later, the rain started to fall, and I went through the procedure again. I was already frustrated. A few minutes later, the sun poked through the clouds, and I brought out a pair of hiking socks to dry. It was the first time I walked while carrying socks, and I felt a little embarrassed. However, I knew it was a necessity if I wanted to walk long days. I still didn't know how I was going to dry my underwear and didn't want to be seen carrying it. The sun only shone for minutes at a time. It was too cold, so I put the socks away.

As my legs awoke, I walked faster along the paved path. At one point, I heard yelling and realized I had missed a turn on the Camino. I had only walked a few steps off but was grateful to the three women who called out. After a small climb to an alto, I crossed the border from Navarra into the region of La Rioja, one of Spain's most important wine-producing areas. Just outside Logroño, an old woman with long gray hair, dressed like a gypsy, sat at a table in front of a small house. We exchanged greetings, and she asked if I wanted my passport stamped. I had no idea who she was and declined. I had seen other pilgrim passports covered with stamps from restaurants and every other place that offered one. However, I wanted to keep mine clean and reserved for places where I had stayed. Nevertheless, the old woman probably thought I was a jerk.

Logroño is the capital of the autonomous community of La Rioja and has a population of 200,000 in its metropolitan area. It was founded by the Romans and since the early years, had an economic and military importance in the region. Logroño was the site of many battles through the centuries and was taken and retaken by various peoples and kingdoms. Its courts held trials for witches in medieval times and for Basques who were controversially tried during the Franco years.

I arrived at the stone bridge over the Río Ebro and put on my poncho and pack cover, just as the rain began to pour. The Ebro was wide and required a long span with eight arches. After I crossed, I picked up a map from the nearby pilgrim information center and entered the old city of Logroño. Inside the Iglesia de Santiago el Real, a small group of parishioners waited for midday mass. The church was lovely, with an ornate *retablo* that featured a crucifixion scene below another one featuring Mary. I was careful not to disturb anyone and took a few photos before I left.

I needed some supplies, but there were few shops along the Camino. A few rough-looking characters stared as I walked by, but there were always other people around, including the odd police officer. I'm sure I looked pretty rough myself, so I wasn't one to talk. I arrived at the palace and museum buildings at the end of the old city and went off the Camino to the Calle de Portales. It took me to a more lively area with shops, restaurants, bars, and the cathedral.

I entered the cathedral, the Iglesia de Santa María la Redonda, during its midday mass. Many people were inside, with pilgrims and tourists comprising at least half. A separate chapel was toward the back, with a beautiful *retablo* featuring Mary and Child in the center. I sat and looked around – it was so peaceful and serene. I couldn't get close to the main altar and didn't want to get in the way of the mass. I went back outside and walked around the cathedral. The dome and façade were beautifully sculpted and ornate, as were the two magnificent bell towers.

I wanted to look around the modern area of Logroño, but first, I went into a pharmacy – the one with the green cross that was prominent throughout Spain. These pharmacies were very different from what I was accustomed to back home. Most items were behind the counter, and with my limited Spanish, I had difficulty explaining to the three female clerks that I needed foot cream. They chuckled and seemed entertained by something I had said. I had no idea what was so funny. Did I just ask for Viagra? Yeast infection cream, or whatever it's called? Finally, one clerk admitted she knew some English and understood what I needed. The foot cream cost €10, which I considered expensive. However, my feet were burning, and I needed something badly.

Now I had only €20 left, which made me uncomfortable, especially if I needed a private room later and credit cards weren't accepted. I took out some cash from one of the nearby bank machines and walked back along the Calle de Portales. I heard my name called from behind and turned around to see Henry waving at me in the doorway of a doner kebab café. He had just been served a huge dinner and asked me to join him. Still full from breakfast and not really interested in a doner, I settled on fries after studying the menu for too long. The waiter couldn't understand my rendition of *papitas fritas*, and it took a few tries until he nodded his head and smiled. Henry asked if I got the passport stamp from the old woman before Logroño. I said I didn't, and he seemed disappointed that I didn't know who she was.

He became excited and told me she was mentioned in a book that was very popular with pilgrims in Germany. He told me the title in German but I didn't know what he was referring to. I later found out the book was *I'm Off Then, Losing and Finding Myself On the Camino de Santiago*, by Hape Kerkeling. It had sold millions of copies, but I had never heard of it.

Henry insisted that he pay for my fries and drink, which I didn't expect. I knew he had been out of work for a while, but I lost our little argument. After lunch, I took Henry to the cathedral, but it was closed for an afternoon break. I told him to make sure he toured it before he left. Henry already had a bed at an *albergue* and asked about my plans. I told him I needed to continue and get well past Logroño for the night. He understood, and we walked a few more blocks to a plaza, shook hands, and said goodbye to each other in the pouring rain. I never saw him again.

While the Camino in Pamplona left the city through the University grounds, in Logroño, it exited through a thriving, modern retail district with all kinds of shops, cafés, and other businesses. It was here I had my first encounter with something that would become very important to me – my favorite supermarket in all of Spain – Mercadona. While many stores so far on the Camino were small and often expensive, Mercadona had a good selection at reasonable prices. It reminded me of the supermarkets back home, and it was open during siesta. As if I had never been in a supermarket before, I went crazy and loaded up on food and medical supplies. For my tummy, I bought bananas, nuts, salami, a giant chocolate bar, chips, and Coke Light. For my feet, I bought insoles, tape, gauze, and alcohol wipes. I left Mercadona with a heavy shopping bag, and few of the items would fit in my backpack. The only thing I didn't find was hiking socks. My blisters were sore and getting worse.

The sun came out, and I tried to pick up my pace while eating a bag of a corn chip-like substance. After the retail and business section, the Camino entered the Parque de San Miguel, an open city park with a few modern sculptures. Except for one older man, there was nobody around. I pulled out a pair of hiking socks and carried them while I walked. From Logroño, the Camino veered onto a flat, paved path that went on for many kilometers. Walking was easy, and I made excellent time. At one point, I looked down and realized there was only one sock in my hand. I couldn't believe it. How could I lose a sock? I looked back and couldn't see it. There was no way I was going to backtrack for a stupid sock, so I kept walking. It could have been two or three kilometers back. Although I was pissed off at myself, I couldn't help mustering a little laugh. Now, I had three hiking socks, and none were dry.

The mix of natural parkland and farmland was a pleasant escape from the city. A group of at least twenty high school students on bikes passed me. One girl said *hola*, and I was lucky not to get run over by the others. The rain started again, and I stopped to put on my rain gear. I hadn't seen another pilgrim since Logroño until I saw a young couple huddled together in a small shelter. They looked cozy, and I didn't want to bother them. At the reservoir, Pantano de la Grajera, I watched a group of men fish for a moment, until the rain became too heavy.

Nearby, I took shelter inside a café, which sat in a wooded area beside the reservoir. I chose a table away from the smokers at the bar and ordered a Coke Light and an ice cream. The students who had passed me earlier entered and the café became loud and lively. On the television, the evening news showed the weather in Spain was about 10°C cooler than normal for this time in May. They showed a clip of snow on the mountains and then something I didn't want to see – a forecast of more rain and cold for at least a week. Not good news for this fair-weather pilgrim.

I checked my map and realized I hadn't walked far from Viana. It was past five o'clock and my realistic choice to stay for the night was in Ventosa, over twelve kilometers away. Once the rain subsided, I emerged from the café and took advantage of the public washroom. It may sound funny, but during my walk on the Camino, I became very thankful for the public washrooms. This is a world heritage site that attracts well over 100,000 pilgrims a year, with only a few along its length. I'm not referring to washrooms in a bar or an *albergue* where I was a customer or felt compelled to buy something. I'm talking about free, clean washrooms in public areas. There were times I would have gladly paid a few coins to use a toilet instead of taking a dump in the elements.

The park had camping spots under the trees in a very pleasant setting. As I left the reservoir area and park, I realized the path from Logroño, about five kilometers long, was all paved. I had made excellent time, even with my break. A small climb on a gravel path was my first test of the day. My feet were sore, but otherwise, I felt fine. The alto was next to a field of mustard, with the reservoir below and Logroño in the distance. The scene would have been far nicer without the dark clouds. The temperature became colder with wind gusts as I walked towards Navarrete. Along the way, there were many vineyards and the odd winery. I stopped at the ruins of Hospital de San Juan de Acre, a twelfth century hospice. There wasn't much left, only a foundation and jagged walls that were no more than two meters high. Behind the ruins was the huge Rioja Don Jacobo Crianza Winery.

Navarrete was situated on the side of a hill, and I tired from the small climb. The village was clean and well-preserved, with narrow streets. It was late, and I didn't have much time to visit. The church, Iglesia de la Asunción, was open and similar to the one in Los Arcos, the interior was more beautiful than I had expected. The *retablo* was incredibly detailed with statues and featured a crucifixion scene in the center with another of Mary above. I bought a Coke Light and found some cover outside the church where I could eat my sandwich. I fitted the insoles into my boots and hoped it would provide a little extra comfort for my poor feet. I don't know why I never bought them before I started. With a cold wind blowing in my face and over seven kilometers still to walk, I stopped momentarily in front of the *albergue* in Navarrete. Surely there would still be a bed available in Ventosa. I hoped I wasn't making a mistake.

After Navarrete, the Camino followed a highway and then veered onto a gravel road. The entrance of the cemetery had the façade that was moved from the Hospital de San Juan de Acre many years before. The sun poked out briefly before the clouds returned and it began to rain. The little climb and the weather were wearing me down. I hadn't seen another pilgrim walking since Logroño, and it felt odd to be so alone at times. Sure, the Camino between Navarrete and Ventosa had a freeway basically paralleling on the right-hand side, but it wasn't the same as seeing others. The simple interaction of a *hola* or *Buen Camino* was always comforting. Here, if I got lonely, I would have to wave at cars.

The rolling landscape had wet, reddish-brown soil that glistened with brilliant colors during the brief moments when the sun came out. However, I became annoyed with patches of reddish-brown mud that stuck to the bottom and sides of my boots. No sooner did I stomp off a layer of mud, then another patch to walk through would appear. Walking with heavy feet and skirting around muddy sections not only made me tired, it wasted time.

I finally saw another pilgrim, a lone cyclist who was determined to stay on the Camino. Most pilgrim cyclists in this area chose to ride along the freeway, by far the easier route. When the cyclist passed me, his bike, legs, and back were covered with a layer of red mud. I said *hola* and smiled. He didn't look happy and only nodded. At the bottom of a hill, the mud was so bad, he gave up and carried his bike across a ditch to a rough construction road. He mounted the bike, and as he rode on a surface meant for excavators and dump trucks, his head shook like a bobblehead. I watched him intently as he finally made it to the freeway and disappeared. It was funny; after he left the Camino, the mud wasn't that bad.

Besides the mud, the consistency of the markers or waymarks along the Way began to bother me. There were a variety of markers. Some depicted the scallop shell mounted on cement, stone, or brass. The hand-painted French flags were prominent earlier on. Most common, though, were the hand-painted yellow arrows which were often simple and unobtrusive. However, on some parts of the Camino, marking was often left to anyone who could operate a can of yellow spray paint. Sometimes, these arrows led in two directions. One spot on the way to Ventosa did just that with one arrow pointing straight and another pointing to the small path to the left. In this case, I could tell the proper route because of the footprints. However, I could see how some people could get led astray. I understand that some business owners off the Camino want pilgrims to patronize them, but to do so in this manner is unfair. I don't want to waste time or energy trying to figure out which arrows go where, especially when I'm walking late into the evening.

I saw a village ahead and was glad that I would soon be in Ventosa. Although I really needed a break, it was so cold, I didn't dare stop. The Camino veered away from the village, and I couldn't understand why it didn't take a direct route. I checked my map and realized I was looking at Sotés. Ventosa was most likely the village I saw another two kilometers away. I arrived at the *albergue* in Ventosa just past eight o'clock, cold and dead tired. The comforting Dutch *hospitalera* sensed my condition and patted my shoulder. She stamped my passport and showed me the dorm. The first person I saw was Charles from Scotland, who I had last seen on the streets of Viana. He still didn't know where his friend was and had chosen to keep walking without him.

The *albergue* was a vast improvement over the one in Villamayor de Monjardín. The washroom was clean, and I had a shower without my flip-flops. I hung up my wet clothes in the outside laundry, but it was so cold there, I didn't think anything would dry.

The communal room had a group of Dutch and German women who sat and chatted around the main table. Apparently, men were not welcome, so I joined Charles and Ted, an English man, on chairs placed against the wall. Ted was rotund and by far the largest man I had seen on the Camino. He was very cheerful and lent me a pen so I could write a postcard to Sarah. I checked my map and realized I had walked less than thirty kilometers during the day and less than sixty over the previous two. To complete the Camino in three weeks, I had to average almost forty kilometers a day. No offense to Charles, who had had an excellent day, but I knew if I saw someone two nights in a row, I was having problems.

The men talked, and the women kept to themselves. I nodded off, which was my signal to go to bed. The *albergue* had a well-stocked store, or *tienda*, and I bought a chocolate bar and some nuts for the morning. I asked the *hospitalera* if she had socks for sale. She didn't, but offered me a used pair of clean, wool socks for free. I declined and said I didn't wear used socks. She looked a little insulted, and I felt bad. I wished her a good night and hoped at least two of my three hiking socks would be dry enough to wear in the morning. I didn't care if I wore a black sock with a gray one, I just wanted a pair. Maybe I should have accepted her kindness.

FRÍO, FRÍO

Day 6
Ventosa to Redecilla del Camino
41.5 Km

At six o'clock, I woke up to the sounds of chanting. At first, I thought I was dreaming, until I realized the voices were coming from the overhead speakers and not from inside my head. The volume gradually grew louder before I pulled my tired body off the bed. As everyone in the room awoke, we exchanged "Good mornings" in various languages before rushing to the washroom.

Again, I had lain for two hours listening to various noises before I fell asleep. The dorm had the typical snorers, except for Ted, the large man from England, who snored the loudest of anyone I had heard so far on the Camino. Yes, louder than the French woman in Uterga. Even Ted's breaths were as loud as most other people's snores.

I looked out the window and watched the pouring rain for a moment — it was an awful day. I went downstairs and ran through the cold to the laundry room. As I expected, my clothes had not dried. A German woman smoking near the entrance said hello, and we talked briefly — mostly about the weather. She wasn't looking forward to the day, either. Now, it was time to get my feet ready. Each foot had blisters in similar locations, but the severity was different. The top of my left big toe, above the joint, had an area that was raw. I never had a chance to pop the blister before it split, and the skin tore away. I built up a thick layer of gauze around it, hoping to relieve some pressure. My feet took half an hour to get ready.

The *hospitalera* tended to her store, and I thought about asking for the pair of used socks. However, I remembered her disappointed look the previous night and didn't bother. On the counter, a package contained a bright, orange poncho. The photo on the front showed a man wearing a backpack and the poncho covered down to his knees. It was a thin vinyl or similar material, but I hoped it would last for a day or two. My own poncho was better quality but didn't fit right, or, at least, I hadn't figured how to wear it properly with a backpack. The new poncho cost €2.50, but back home it would have been in a dollar store, for most likely a dollar. I hoped it was money well spent.

Downstairs, I opened the door and looked outside. The weather was worse than when I first woke up. It was cold, windy, and pouring, and I really didn't want to go out. As I closed the door, a smiling, older German woman came down the stairs and asked how the weather was. I said, "Sunny and warm with a slight chance of showers." Obviously, she hadn't looked outside yet, and her face brightened with a big smile. Then I opened the door to show her it was a disgusting day. I don't think she was impressed with me or the weather.

It was a day that required almost all the clothing I had. I wore a T-shirt, fleece sweater, gloves, sun hat, wind jacket, rain pants, and gaiters. The *hospitalera* helped me put on my new, flimsy poncho. I think the model on the cover was a midget because my poncho didn't even cover my backpack. I said goodbye to the wonderful, friendly woman and finally stepped outside at seven-thirty. I immediately knew my poncho experiment wouldn't work. The wind gusted into my face, and the lightweight material flapped and pulled all over. The hood wouldn't stay on my head, and there was no way to tie it. I don't remember too much about Ventosa. I spent the entire time fighting with the poncho. About one kilometer outside of the village, I asked a German woman to take my photo. She laughed for some reason, probably because I looked like such an idiot. A bright orange, fucking idiot. Soon, I found a small shelter, took off the poncho, and put on my rain jacket and pack cover. Just like I should have done in the first place.

With the rolling countryside of fields, vineyards, and wineries, on a better day, it would have been a pleasant walk. However, this day was not pleasant at all. Not only did I have to contend with the weather, there was the thick, gooey mud that built up on my boots, which again made my feet heavier and which I constantly stomped off. I passed Ted who had left half an hour before I did, and he was obviously struggling. I couldn't believe he actually wore shorts on a day like this. We talked briefly, and he asked me if I had seen Charles. Charles left an hour before me, and I assumed he was in Nájera by now. I said goodbye to Ted, the nice man from England, and never saw him again. In fact, I never saw Charles again, either.

There was a short climb to an alto, but a light fog ensured I didn't see much. I stopped briefly at the ruins of the Monastery of San Anton for a photo and continued. The temperature wasn't more than 4°C, and I shivered with the wind. My sun hat didn't provide much warmth, but I adjusted the drawstrings on the hood of the rain jacket so only my eyes down to my mouth were exposed. Even better would have been a balaclava and a tuque or woolly hat, but I had left those at home. My hands were warm, and I was glad I brought the Eddie Bauer gloves. Descending from the alto, one steep hill was covered in mud, and I had to be careful with my footing. I saw the skid marks where someone fell and slid down the hill. Considering the problems I had washing and drying clothes, I didn't need to go flying through the mud.

In a hamlet before Nájera, a Spanish man in his 70's walked up to me and wanted to talk. He motioned for me to come with him, and of course, being my paranoid self, I hesitated. He seemed innocent enough, and I was sure, if necessary, I could outrun him, even with my backpack on. He pointed between two buildings, and we could see, in the distance, the hills covered with snow. He seemed very excited and kept saying *"frío, frío"* (cold, cold). He knew absolutely no English, and we tried to talk, but with my weak Spanish, we didn't get far. I really wished I could converse in Spanish instead of just getting by.

The rain stopped as I entered Nájera and I saw a small patch of blue sky to the west. However, it was still cold, and the wind continued to blow into my face. A serious-looking woman who spoke feverishly in Spanish approached me. From what I understood, she told me to go straight when I enter the town and don't turn right. Or maybe it was turn right and don't go straight. I thanked her for the information and hoped I could figure it out. As I left, she warned someone else behind me. She was either very nice or evil. I walked to the spot where I thought she meant and found two roughly painted yellow arrows that pointed to the right, down the hill, and into an alley. I thought that would be a good spot for a bandit to wait for a poor, cold, wet, lonely pilgrim, hit him over the head with a pig's femur, and take away his precious iPhone. Well, I fooled them and continued straight into the business district.

Here, I found something I really needed, a euro store. It was similar to a dollar store back home, but many items cost over a euro. I bought two pairs of cheap wool socks. They weren't my first choice for quality but were desperately needed. Really, I had needed them two days before. I also picked up two rolls of tape and extra gauze. I figured if I continued using tape the way I was, the length of the tape would equal the eight hundred kilometers of the Camino. Outside the euro store, I put on a pair of the wool socks over my light hiking ones and my feet immediately felt better in the boots.

At a bakery next door, I picked up a Coke Light and a cherry pastry before rejoining the Camino. I entered Nájera's historic district and at first, was amazed, not by the buildings, but by the magnificent red cliffs that towered over the town. From my vantage point, most buildings extended almost to the edge of the cliffs, and there didn't look like much room for backyards. I don't think I would feel comfortable with a giant cliff of earth and rock over my home.

Although the monastery, the eleventh century Santa María la Real, was somewhat plain from the exterior, the interior was truly beautiful. I almost didn't go inside. Initially, I walked into the lobby and saw backpacks left unattended in the hallway. The attendant, who knew some English, told me the admission was €3, but I had to leave my backpack with the others. I didn't want to leave mine unattended so I went back outside. Again, I thought about the monastery and decided I couldn't pass it up. I talked with the attendant, and she said I could leave my backpack in the souvenir store with her. It was very warm, and I spread out my gloves and hat, hoping they would dry. For a moment, I thought about taking out my wet socks and underwear, but the smell would have been unholy.

I opened the door and went outside to a beautiful, richly detailed cloister – the open courtyard and covered passage. In the walls and under the walkway were numerous tombs of notable clergy and monarchs. Inside, the pantheon held the tombs of some thirty monarchs of Navarra, and I had never seen so many in one room before. Within a cave, a copy of the statue of the Virgen de la Rosa stood at the same spot, where, according to legend, King Garcia III found the original and then ordered the church to be built onsite. The *retablo* of the nave was beautiful and adorned with a crown above a crucifixion scene. There was so much gold, and each sculpture was elegantly detailed. I sat, leaned back, and thought how lucky I was to be here. I toured the monastery for about forty-five minutes but could have stayed for two or three hours. It was a wonderful stop. I picked up my backpack, my nearly-dry clothes, and went outside to the pouring rain.

While I looked for a post office box, I found something else I desperately needed – an outdoor clothing store. Immediately, I went to the sock section. The two pairs of wool socks I had bought earlier would do in an emergency but weren't good enough for the long days

I was walking. I picked up two pairs of hiking socks, and they had cushioning on the spots of my feet where it was needed. I asked the clerk if she had a tuque but she didn't understand. I pointed to my head and said, "hat," I forgot the word in Spanish. First, she showed me baseball hats but finally understood and showed me a fashionable blue tuque. I hated to spend €16 on a tuque, knowing I had so many at home. I never envisioned walking during the Spanish springtime in temperatures close to freezing.

My bill came to €35, which was money I never had expected to spend. The clerk thought I knew more Spanish than I actually did. I said partial or short sentences in Spanish and she would follow with a few sentences of which I only understood a few words. I nodded my head a lot, which made her talk more. She opened a box and offered me some local walnuts. I ate a few and we talked some more before I bid her farewell. I left wondering if I had received my change back from the €50 bill. I hope the clerk didn't entice me with her scrumptious walnuts to keep the €15. Never mind, I'm sure she gave it back.

I never mailed my postcard to Sarah, but I was very happy with my new hiking socks, and the tuque was a welcome addition to my attire. By now, it had stopped raining, and overhead was a small patch of blue sky. It wasn't much warmer though, and as I climbed the hill out of Nájera, the rain and wind started again. I put my rain gear back on and then continued with the Camino in view for many kilometers ahead. Two civil police cars, each with two officers, drove by and seemed to be looking for something or someone. I hoped nothing had happened to any of the pilgrims.

For about six kilometers from Nájera to Azofra, the Camino wound through a gently rolling terrain with many vineyards, wheat fields and hayfields. The red earth was so prominent and rich. The last stretch before Azofra had an aqueduct, almost two meters high, beside the road. Few pilgrims were around in the early afternoon. I only stopped for a drink and continued walking. Just outside Azofra, a medieval stone column marker, La Picota, rose from a field beside the track. The gray and weathered marker had stood for centuries, while a new information sign in front had already fallen down.

Although I complained about mud earlier, the nine kilometer stretch between Azofra and Cirueña was by far the worst I had seen. It was disgusting, with thick red mud in large patches, at times fifty meters long and across the entire width of the path. I hated, really fucking hated, walking in that mud. The heavy rain stopped and then continued as showers. As I walked, the number of vineyards decreased, and the landscape was dominated with fields of wheat or hay. Patches of mustard flowers often flanked the Camino and looked brilliant against the red soil and the bright greens of the fields. I slowly climbed to the alto near Cirueña and looked all around. The tops of the surrounding hills were covered with snow.

Cirueña was in the middle of siesta, and I walked through the streets for ten minutes and never saw anyone. The town had some unsightly housing subdivisions and nothing much of historical significance that I saw. The Camino was marked with more hand painted yellow arrows than were necessary. One turn had five ugly arrows when one ugly arrow would have done just fine. I was tired after the long walk from Nájera and took a brief break at the edge of the town. A bar, 150 meters up the highway, was too far for me to walk. I had to save myself for the Camino. Four women sat quietly nearby, the only pilgrims I had seen for over an hour. My feet were sore, but otherwise, I felt good. I had so much energy, my shoulders felt better, and I could continue for a long time.

After Cirueña, I walked fast on a wide gravel path with much less mud than before. The edge of Santo Domingo de la Calzada had a dirty industrial area, and some spots had yellow arrows all over the place making the actual Camino a little difficult to follow. Santo Domingo de la Calzada had many well preserved buildings with descriptive signs in Spanish, English, and French. The English text was a welcome surprise. The town was originated by Santo Domingo de la Calzada himself, who, in the eleventh century, built the first pilgrims' hospice. He had also built bridges, cleared many kilometers of paths, and helped rid the nearby forests of lurking bandits.

It was after five o'clock, and I hadn't taken a good break since Nájera. I stopped at a bar, but when I opened the door, there was so much smoke, I didn't bother going in. I thought there would be another place in the town. Many houses along the narrow street were decorated with elaborate coats of arms, although I didn't know what they represented. The top of the bell tower of the cathedral was detailed and ornate, but it was difficult to get a close look. There were windows halfway up, and I would have loved to go and look out from them. Sadly, the doors of the cathedral were closed, as were the monastery and the old pilgrims' hospital. I headed out, past a small church, and crossed over the Río Oja on a stone bridge. I never had a break.

The Camino followed a gravel road through more farmland, with the only landmark, a modern black metal cross, on a hill next to the path. As I approached the village of Grañón, a fork in the road had a marker with yellow arrows pointing in both directions – not something I wanted to see at seven o'clock in the evening. I chose the route with the most footprints and soon saw the flags marking the French Way. Nearby, I stopped for a photo of the church steeple that appeared to be emerging from the bright green field.

Along the Way, I enjoyed entering churches and cathedrals, even for a moment. I tried many doors and was grateful when I could enter. When I arrived at the church in Grañón, the door was difficult to open. It creaked, scratched, and clunked, but I finally managed to squeeze inside. Immediately, I knew there was a problem. The pastor and the entire mass were staring at me with piercing, dirty looks. Apparently, I had opened the old door that was no longer used and failed to see the adjacent one that was. An old woman, who had just entered through the proper door, jabbered at me loudly in Spanish. She pointed to the door, then pointed at me, and then pointed to the door again. *"Lo siento, lo siento,"* (I'm sorry, I'm sorry) I said to the woman and everyone inside. I backed up through the old door and closed it as it creaked, scratched, and clunked again. The old woman came out, glared at me, and said something before going back inside. I had no idea what she said but had a feeling it wasn't very nice. I never saw much of the interior of the church, just the angry faces.

I was a little unnerved as I walked the one, long street through the center of Grañón. I didn't see anyone else and kept looking behind if the group of church people led by the old woman were following me. It was getting late and my stop, Redecilla del Camino, was still four kilometers away. As I climbed a small hill, my last for the day, my feet really bothered me. At the top, a large, new information sign stood on the border between La Rioja and the region of Castilla y León. I hoped the sign was an indication of a better maintained and marked Camino. I quickly descended to Redecilla del Camino and was greeted by another new sign that clearly stated where I was. The old narrow street was dead quiet, and I never saw anyone as I walked to the *albergue*.

There was no one in the front lobby either, and I waited for a few minutes before going to the dining room where a pilgrim dinner was being served. It was eight o'clock, and the *hospitalera* told me she wasn't expecting anyone that late, but a few beds were still available. The fee was by donation, and she told me to pay when I left in the morning. I declined a dinner, although it would have been great to have some company. She showed me to my bed, a top bunk above Anita, a pretty young, German woman with long blond hair. We exchanged greetings, and I unpacked my gear. I was surprised; there was only one toilet and one shower for all the men in the entire *albergue*, at least twenty of us. I couldn't imagine what kind of lineups there would be in the morning, and had to ensure I got to the washroom before the others.

After a quick shower, I went downstairs to the smoky bar and bought some chips and a Coke Light. I took my "dinner" upstairs to the small kitchen and ate while I charged my camera battery and read my guide book. During the day, I had walked over forty-one kilometers, which made me happy. I was back on track. My clothes still hadn't dried, and I hung them in the reception area. I threw away the odd sock whose mate was lost on a sidewalk somewhere on the outskirts of Logroño. That was soon followed by the expensive, supposedly quick-drying underwear that was giving me a rash in places where I didn't desire one.

By nine o'clock, I was ready for bed. Anita tended to her feet, and I told her about the merits of my new foot lotion, although I still hadn't tried it. I squeezed a bit in her hand and watched her slowly massage the lotion on her feet. Our talk about feet, blisters, and the Camino was honestly the highlight of my evening. That, and being lectured in Spanish by the old woman at the church in Grañón.

HEY BUDDY, YOU'RE NOT AT HOME!
Day 7
Redecilla del Camino to Atapuerca
43 Km

I wore my wind jacket and wool socks to bed, and I lay for at least an hour before I warmed up and fell asleep. Sometime in the middle of the night, I overheated and had to take off my jacket. Again, I stayed up at least another hour before I fell asleep and then woke up at six o'clock for good. Everyone in the room was still sleeping. There were more young people here, compared to the other *albergues* I had stayed at. Generally, younger pilgrims tended to sleep in later than older ones. In some places, older pilgrims began their mornings at five o'clock, often with no consideration for others. Nevertheless, sleeping past 7:00 A.M. was rare and difficult in any *albergue*.

I rolled off the bed and headed straight to the washroom. I had the lone sink to myself while someone used the single toilet. I was next and waited, and waited, and waited while a line up formed behind me. Finally, after fifteen minutes, the guy emerged from his sabbatical on the toilet, smiling, with a book in hand. Hey buddy, you're not at home! Now, it was my turn. I really didn't have to take care of business but was hoping to take care of at least a little business. On the Camino, the next washroom could be one hundred kilometers away. I went in the stall and fumbled with the lock that didn't seem to work. Just as I was about to sit down, the door flew open and barely missed my head. Another guy looked at me and apologized. Didn't he see the lineup? I was lucky, because if it was a microsecond later, my peepee would have been hanging out, for all to see. Unnerved, I sat down for a while but knew nothing would happen. I sadly left the stall without taking care of any business at all.

A few people still slept as I grabbed my gear and went downstairs to the reception area to get ready. Long days with constant pressure and friction on my feet gave them little time for recovery. I was concerned with the area above my left big toe, which was now the size of a five cent euro coin. It was raw and bright red, and it looked terrible. I taped my feet and hoped for a good day. I would always expect some pain. Some days, my blisters would bother me for hours at a time, while on others, barely at all. But then, all I would have to do is step on a sharp rock, and a shot of pain would remind me that they were still there. My clothes had hung overnight near the entrance, but it was too cold for them to dry. They had been wet for too long and would have to be washed again. I gave a small donation and went outside at seven-thirty into the rain and cold, another miserable day.

Despite problems with the weather and washing clothes, by now, I had found a good rhythm and felt more comfortable on the Camino. I knew my body better – what times of the day I was stronger, how to take care of my feet, when to take a rest, and the length of rest I needed. I better understood where to shop and where and what to eat, and I had an idea of the *albergue* life, although no two were the same. Each day was different – people, scenery, buildings, and towns. Each day had different challenges, but they weren't only from the weather, trails, and terrain. They came from within – sluggishness, lack of sleep or motivation, and pain. However, much of my initial nervousness was gone, and overall, I certainly felt stronger.

Redecilla del Camino had one long street with a small church and old houses. After the village, the path gently descended through farm-land to Castildelgado, another rustic and quiet village. Anita caught up as I looked at the church, and she took my photo in the front. We walked together for a while, but I stopped for more photos and told her not to wait. I had a short climb toward Viloria de la Rioja along a secondary road and saw green farmland for kilometers ahead. The Camino markers in Castilla y León were already clearer and more aesthetically pleasing than the majority of the ones in La Rioja. The entrance to Viloria de la Rioja had a sign that stated, "Santiago 576 km." At that point, the distance seemed so far – almost impossible. There wasn't much in the hamlet, but I stopped at a Pepsi machine outside the *albergue*. Instead of getting a Pepsi Max, the machine gave me a Kaz apple drink, which I found refreshing and a nice change from the colas. On the way out, empty cans littered the side of the road and looked really bad. Why was it so difficult to carry an empty can to the next village?

The Camino followed a secondary road until it reached the highway, and a sign indicated fifty-two kilometers to Burgos. I looked forward to the city and especially the cathedral. The rest of the way to Vilamayor del Río was along a gravel path parallel to the highway. This path, known as a *senda*, would be a prominent feature on the Camino in later days. There wasn't much to see, and I made good time. I only stopped in Vilamayor del Río to talk with Anita, who was taking a break in front of a rustic, stone house with vines clinging across its façade. Although Anita smiled, I could tell she was very tired. We talked briefly as the rain started, and I let her be.

I walked over five kilometers of similar farmland until Belorado, a well preserved town, rich in Roman and medieval history. The first features I noticed were the brown limestone cliffs that towered over the Iglesia de Santa María. Caves, once used by hermits, dotted the side of the cliff. One was made into a home, complete, with a door, oak-framed window, and patio. The church's bell gable, or *espadaña*, had four stork nests, one of which was huge. I saw the head of one and waited for it to stand. After a few minutes, two stood up at the same time, and I was happy to get the photo. The El Corro district of Belorado was picturesque, with small bridges that spanned the stream that flowed between old streets and rustic buildings. I saw Anita, but we only said hello and smiled.

I had walked twelve kilometers in two and a half hours and was hungry and needed to get out of the cold. The first bar I entered was too smoky, and I couldn't find anywhere that was better. Instead, I went into a pharmacy and, on impulse, bought a bag of six Mars bars that was on sale. It wasn't an exciting meal, but at least I would have energy for a few days. The rain stopped, and I sat on a bench in the plaza. I gazed at the heavily pruned trees that circled the grandstand, with the Iglesia de San Pedro behind. Few people were around, and half of those were construction workers who were busy on various projects around the plaza. It was cold, even with some sun, and when I started to shiver, it was time to leave. The walk out of Belorado was uneventful, and I only stopped to view an old, stone bridge over the Río Tirón.

Outside Belorado, I had my first encounter with a Repsol gas station. Repsol and a few others were always a welcome sight. They were open during siesta and had a store with a good selection of energy food at reasonable prices. This station had a washroom on the outside, and

I didn't even have to buy anything. After the joy of relieving myself somewhere that didn't involve hiding behind a bush, I went into the store and bought a Coke Light to show my appreciation.

I felt great as I walked through rolling farmland of wheat and hay and didn't stop until Tosantos. One hour where I just walked and took photos. It was during these long stretches with little to see that I wished I had someone with me. Sure, I greeted pilgrims but it was just in passing and rarely lasted more than a few words. I did have the opportunity to think. The Camino gave me many opportunities. Sometimes, I would think about Mom, Sarah, life, or work. Sometimes, I would think about different features on the Camino. Sometimes, I was just too damn tired to think at all. I arrived at Tosantos as patches of blue sky emerged, along with a few rays of sunshine. Now in need of a good break, I found a bar at the end of the village and sat down for a drink. It was noon, but the temperature outside was no more than 6°C. No matter how much I complained about the cold, the weather was still much better than the previous day.

In the hills just north of the village, the Ermita de Nuestra Señora de la Peña was built into the steep, tan-colored cliffs. The church had a small façade, with a bell tower, windows, and a double door. An open area was carved from the cliff and furnished with a bench. Nobody was around, and I would later find out the church was rarely occupied. In Villambistia, the church had a simple stone construction with the top of the bell tower finished in white stucco. A modern clock on the tower showed the wrong time. Just past the church, I stopped for a photo with old trees in front of the façade, which I thought would be haunting at night. Someone had painted a yellow arrow on the ruins of one building, which really bothered me. I had seen this before, but in such a small village with few buildings, the arrow really stood out.

From Villambistia, I had a quick one and a half kilometer walk to the highway and Espinosa del Camino, with houses that ranged greatly in appearance, from ruins, to large and well-kept. It was a quiet place, and soon I was back in the rolling farmland. From the distance, I saw what I thought was a pile of rocks in a field beside the track. I expected a monastery in this area but wasn't sure what it would look like. As I got closer, I realized the pile was really a small stone building, all that was left of the ninth century Monasterio de San Felices de Oca. The building, about four meters high and three meters square, looked so solitary and peaceful. It was built and rebuilt with bricks and stone, although a few had recently fallen. Grass grew from the roof, and a locked iron gate covered the main opening. I wondered how much longer this tiny building would be here. I spent more time at the ruins of the monastery than I did at other historical landmarks along the Way. As I walked away, I would glance every couple of minutes to make sure the little monastery was still there. Once I got over the crest of the hill, it disappeared.

The Camino followed a narrow shoulder of the highway, but it was dangerous with many cars and large trucks. Instead, I joined a rough path through a farmer's field, and although muddy, it was far safer. Villafranca de Montes de Oca was the largest town since Belorado, and it was time for a break and some lunch. Ahead, there was a long stretch through the mountains without any services. I was tired and needed to get the backpack off my shoulders. The first bar was packed, and I continued up the hill to the Iglesia de Santiago, with its brick covered in peeling, gray plaster that looked shabby.

Near the end of the town was a hotel next to an *albergue*. The outside of the hotel featured a stone wall with a portal and a double oak door. I walked through it into a lovely courtyard with stone columns, flowers, and wicker furniture. No one else was outside in the cold. When I peeked inside at the lobby, at first, I was reluctant to enter. The hotel was far more upscale than I would have expected in the town. I knew I looked rough and probably smelled unpleasant, but the waitress was friendly and asked if I wanted something to eat. She sat me at a table with a pretty German woman, about my age, who looked a lot better than I did. Initially, I thought Nina was a regular tourist, but she was a pilgrim and had sprained her ankle on the Camino. She would be at the hotel for at least two more days. I said if I got hurt, I hoped it would be here too – that was, if I could afford it.

I ordered the special sandwich, a ham and cheese, which wasn't really that special. We talked while Nina drank red wine and I ate my ham and cheese sandwich. I was happy to be out of the cold and talking with the pretty woman. The waitress told me the rooms were €50 plus tax, which I thought was reasonable. Before I left, I had a visit to one of the best-decorated washrooms I had seen so far in Spain. Nina and I went outside to the courtyard. She limped, and I could tell she was in pain. I had sprained my ankle once, and it hadn't healed for over a year. I wished Nina all the best and a quick recovery. Now, I had a mountain to climb.

A new sign stood on the side of the path, with the pleasant valley of farmland as a backdrop. It indicated the distance to Santiago de Compostela was 526 kilometers. Earlier, another sign had stated 576 kilometers, and I knew I hadn't walked fifty so far during the day. Somebody had their figures wrong. It didn't matter, both were a long way. The Montes de Oca were less like mountains and more like large hills. They were notorious in medieval times for the bandits who preyed on pilgrims. After the little monastery and my lunch with Nina, I was in a good mood. I hoped I didn't come across any bandits, because they were also notorious for ruining a good mood.

Snow covered the mountain tops across the valley, and I hoped I didn't have to walk on any slush. Soon, small patches of snow were scattered on the side of the path, and I was glad I wasn't here two days earlier. The Camino climbed a wide gravel path through a brushy hillside with shrubs and grasses. Stands of oak, still without their leaves, looked spooky against the gray sky. That would soon change with the onset of spring. Since I hadn't used the internet for a few days and had been without Wi-Fi since St. Jean, I thought I should call Sarah and make sure she and Adam were fine. She was surprised to hear from me, and we talked for a few minutes. Calls from Spain were expensive on my overpriced cell phone plan, and I took advantage of the rare times I had Wi-Fi so I could use Skype. I promised Sarah I would call again soon. I missed her, and I hoped she missed me too.

At the first alto, I heard a rumble from behind and was passed by a pilgrim cyclist. He scared me, because I never heard anything until he was only a few meters behind. We exchanged greetings, and I was glad he wasn't a bandit. I walked under another wind farm but this time was less excited. The alto was a barren scrubby area with few trees. The hills had been logged many times over the centuries. Soon, young pine became more prevalent among the shrubs – one of which was heather in full bloom. The heather in the gardens back home were often dwarf, but here, some were two meters high and covered with purple and pink flowers. As I passed through the large patch of heather, the sun emerged at its brightest of the day and brought out the brilliant colors. I had never seen anything like it.

From the alto, I descended past a memorial for men killed in

1936 during the Civil War. Many bodies were dumped in the area by the Franco loyalists. I followed a good gravel road and could see the Camino for at least two kilometers ahead. It continued to a pine forest, but here, the road had horrible mud and puddles, which I skirted around. At one point, I had to walk through the forest to get around a huge patch of mud. A fallen pine became my seat as I took my break at the edge of the forest. The sun was out, and besides slightly sore shoulders, I felt good. Even my feet didn't bother me too much. I ate a chocolate bar and watched numerous songbirds perch and fly. The only pilgrims I saw were on bikes.

I had another short climb, the third, and although each had little elevation gain, the accumulation made me tired. When I saw the village of San Juan de Ortega, it was not on top of a hill, but below. San Juan de Ortega was a man; the village and church were named after him. He lived in the area in the twelfth century and was important to the construction of infrastructure along the Camino; he also helped rid the Montes de Oca of bandits. It was five o'clock, and I was surprised the church was still open. Inside was the tomb of San Juan de Ortega. This was the first church I had seen with only one tomb and dedicated to one man. It was intricate and carved out of alabaster, with San Juan laying on his back with his hands in prayer. His facial features were realistic and haunting. San Juan de Ortega, the village, was small, and I was glad I had eaten earlier, because there wasn't much available. I bought a drink, pulled out a chocolate bar, and sat on the bench next to the monastery. My energy was waning, and I still had over three kilometers to Agés, where I considered staying.

From San Juan de Ortega, I descended on a good gravel path through a pleasant, gently rolling landscape with oak and pine. My energy was replenished, and I walked at a good pace. Soon, I saw Agés at the bottom of the hill, surrounded by farmland. The sun disappeared, and the cold wind roared. Agés was a quaint village, and I never saw anyone until I stopped in front of the *albergue*. For a moment, I thought about staying, but it was still early, and I decided to continue to Atapuerca, two and a half kilometers away. The Camino followed the side of the road except for one short section where it led over a small stone bridge, reportedly built by San Juan de Ortega himself. Outside Atapuerca, a group of boulders were mounted with bronze plaques to recognize the earliest signs of man in Europe which were found in the nearby hills. The archaeological site is now a UNESCO World Heritage Site.

I arrived at the *albergue* in Atapuerca at seven-thirty, but there was nobody in the office. I waited outside in the cold and was informed by a Spanish man that I had to call the *hospitalera*. I had never come across this situation before and told the man I was from Canada and couldn't phone Spain. Well, I suppose I could have phoned someone in Spain, but it would have been a hassle and probably cost me a million dollars. He was friendly and called the *hospitalera*, who informed him she would be ten minutes. The Spanish man motioned two of his friends over and asked me to take their photos as they posed in various positions in front of the *albergue*. The *hospitalera* arrived and told me there was a bed available. At first, she asked if I would like a private room, but it looked very similar to the dorms, so I declined. A sign advertised free Wi-Fi, which I looked forward to. She showed me the clean room, and I chose a comfortable lower bed on a bunk with nobody above. However, when I tried the Wi-Fi, I was disappointed it wouldn't work with my iPhone.

In the kitchen, guests gathered around the table to talk and eat. They told me there was a café a block away, so I went to find something for dinner. The food there was expensive, but I didn't have any choice. My bill for two empanadas and a Coke Light was €9. I went back to the *albergue*, had my shower and then ate at the table. The Spanish pilgrims were interested in Canada, and the man who spoke English asked me questions which he translated to his friends. I was interested in Spain and asked about their people and culture. Earlier, I had eaten an apple and wondered if it came from Spain. He said the apple likely came from Italy and didn't know of any areas of Spain where they were commercially grown. I thought Spain would have excellent apple-growing regions. My tuna empanada was wonderful, but once I finished, I had to take care of my feet. I drained a large blister on the bottom of my right heel, while a French woman watched with interest. She didn't speak English so all I said was, "Owwwwww." That was as far as it got. I had walked about forty-three kilometers during the day and was happy, considering the cold weather and many ups and downs through the Montes de Oca. Exhausted, I was ready for bed at nine-thirty and quickly fell asleep while thinking about my next day, because, sometime around midday, I would be in Burgos, the city I had looked forward to the most.

I NEED TO LEARN HOW TO ROLL THE R'S

Day 8
Atapuerca to Hornillos del Camino
39.5 Km

It was only five-thirty, and although I tried, I couldn't fall back to sleep. I had a restless sleep, not only from listening to snoring, but from those who got up in the middle of the night. Who knows where people went? Maybe it was to the washroom, or possibly for a midnight snack. Maybe they went for a booty call, or out for a pack of smokes. I didn't care, but hated being disturbed three or four times a night. My body was still tired, and I lay for a while longer, contemplating my day and even my Camino. Some days, it was hard to get motivated. This was one of them.

After an hour, I grabbed my gear and went to the kitchen. In the midst of eating my delicious fruit empanada, I had a brilliant idea, "Why don't I wash my clothes by hand and throw them in the dryer." What a brilliant idea, indeed. It was still early, and I had to get ready. Surely, there would be plenty of time. I smiled while I washed socks, underwear, and a shirt in the laundry room sink. When I went to open the dryer door, I realized I had made a huge mistake. It was not a washer and dryer but two washing machines. Shit! Now I had to carry wet clothes all day. I wrung the clothes the best I could and hung them while I got ready. I didn't see many dryers in the *albergues* and wondered why. It would make more sense to have two dryers. It's easier to wash clothes by hand but more difficult to get them dry, especially in bad weather. Of course, this is advice coming from one of the very few pilgrims who walked almost all day long.

My feet were a mess and took a long time to get ready. The new blister on my right heel was in a bad location, and the spot on top of my big left toe continued to look terrible. By the time I was ready, most of the pilgrims were already gone. I said goodbye to the group of Spaniards I had talked with the previous evening and left at 7:45 to another cold, overcast day. I hated carrying wet clothes and cursed myself again for not looking closer at the machines.

As I walked through Atapuerca, I realized I had no idea how to pronounce "Atapuerca." It wasn't as if I knew how to pronounce many of the other villages, but for some reason, Atapuerca seemed like such a cool name. I tried various versions in my head and said some out loud when nobody was around. The tourist office was closed, and I was too shy to ask other pilgrims. On the outskirts, there was a modern sculpture of one of the early forms of man holding a spear, and then the Camino veered toward the hills where he came from. The path was rocky, and my new blister hurt with every step. I had little energy and struggled. I wasn't the only one who had trouble and managed to pass a few others who were slowed by the hill. One large woman stopped halfway and looked as if she was about to give up. Her partner waited a few meters ahead, and they jabbered in a language I couldn't figure out. The landscape on the hillside was a mix of scrubby brush and rough grassland, probably best suited for sheep. As I climbed, a barbed wire fence became prominent on the left side of the path. It was a military area, and a sign stated *"Prohibido El Paso Zona Militar."* I had no idea what went on there and couldn't see anyone. The fence of tangled wire was at times two meters deep, as if outside a prison. I sure wouldn't want to see a dog or an animal get tangled in that fence. Or a pilgrim.

My feet ached as I continued up the rocky trail. Thankfully, I saw a cross and knew the alto was near. Except for grass and scattered shrubs, the top of the hill was rocky and barren. The climb was only about one hundred meters in elevation gain but had felt much more. I hated struggling so early and needed to make better time so I could spend a few hours in Burgos and then get well past for the night. From the pilgrim monument, I looked through the haze at Burgos in the distance. I had a long walk ahead of me.

I descended the rocky trail onto a gravel road, where the pain from my blisters eased only marginally on the better track. The terrain at the bottom of the hill gently rolled through farmland which looked to be more fertile than on top. The Camino joined a paved road and passed through the hamlet of Villaval. Here, two French women in their 50's or 60's rested on the side of the road. I said *hola* as I walked by, but soon the French women were catching up while talking continuously. I had no idea what they were saying but the words, "Move your fat ass, Canadian boy" came to mind. They stayed right behind me for about five hundred meters, but I was determined I wouldn't let them pass. The younger one came within a few meters and stayed for at least five minutes while her friend languished behind. No, she wasn't trying to walk with me, she was trying to pass me. The older woman yelled something in French, and the other stopped. It was a bizarre experience, and I realize the passing drama may have only been my imagination. Whatever it was, at least it kept my mind occupied during a rather boring part of the Camino.

Cardeñuela de Río Pico was one of the few villages where the church wasn't on the Camino but farther up the hill. I didn't have the energy to climb and only glanced from the road. The flat road should have meant for a fast pace, but after being pressed by the French women, I had little energy. At the village of Orbaneja, I went inside the café for my first break of the day. The café was packed with pilgrims coming from Atapuerca and Agés. I ordered a Coke Light and a fruit pastry and sat at the only free table. Not only did my body need a break, I needed to get out of the cold; the temperature was no more than 6°C. I took off my right boot and found the bandage over my new blister had shifted. I knew there was something wrong, and if I wasn't so stubborn, I would have stopped earlier.

A Swiss man joined my table, and we talked about blisters and the cold. That was the extent of our conversation. We were both too tired to say much. When a pilgrim at the adjoining table lit up a cigarette and blew smoke indiscriminately, it was time to go. As I was leaving, I was surprised to see Anita walking into the café. She had stayed in Agés, and, although tired from the morning walk, she was far more cheerful than I was. She asked if I planned to stay in Burgos, but I told her I needed to get a few villages past before I found a place to stay. She never understood my determination. Sometimes, on days like this, I didn't understand it, either. She said her feet were better and again thanked me for the foot cream. I said goodbye to Anita – the pretty, young, German woman with long, blond hair – and never saw her again.

At the end of the village, a small stone church sat beside the Camino. The oak doors had fascinating, black, Gothic crosses, and the stained-glass tympanum was the first one I had seen. A crest, carved in stone, adorned the façade above the door. I had no idea how old the church was, and when I tried the door, it was closed. A few minutes later, I crossed over the A-1 freeway, which led to a stretch of the Camino that was unassuming at best, and at worst, unattractive. Burgos, like many other cities, had a large area on the outskirts of urban sprawl. It was over eight kilometers through areas of commercial and industrial buildings, row housing, empty overgrown lots, and the airport.

After the long walk along the road next to the fenced airport, the Camino joined a well-marked sidewalk all the way into Burgos. In the midst of all the sprawl, I came across something I really needed: another euro store. When I entered, the clerk immediately demanded I remove my backpack. Reluctantly, I complied, even though I would have most likely dislocated my shoulder if I tried to stuff something into one of the pockets with it on. I stocked up on tape, gauze, and something else I desperately needed, underwear. I had worn the same two pairs of underwear longer than I care to discuss here. I had never expected I would have such problems washing clothes or that I would have thrown away the quick drying pair. I bought two more pairs and hoped that would be enough for the remainder of my trip.

At the Burgos city limits, a modern sign next to a bed of yellow and purple flowers stated the temperature as 7°C, but it felt much colder with the wind. Despite my morning struggles, I was happy to arrive by eleven-thirty and to escape the urban sprawl. Burgos has a population of approximately 180,000 and is the capital of both the autonomous region of Castilla y León and the province of Burgos. It is historically rich, with many centuries-old landmarks, and it has always been one of the most prominent cities on the Camino. Most importantly, Burgos is home to a beautiful cathedral.

It began to rain as I walked around the outside of the Iglesia Santa María la Real. The sign outside the church had English, but much of it was covered by advertising flyers. It was a relatively simple stone church with a wide bell tower. In the front, an ancient stone *cruceiro* – the top bearing a cross with a depiction of who I believe was the Virgin Mary – stood in the middle of a lawn overgrown with clover. Someone had tagged the lower column in purple, which was unfortunate and sad.

The early part of Burgos had modern office and apartment buildings with cafés and shops on the lower levels. The older sections were easy to distinguish by their weathered stone walls and buildings.

Another stone *cruceiro* stood in front of the walls, the top bearing the crucifixion. Across the walkway, I admired a four-storey building with its top two floors refinished in pink stucco and its balconies with planters of small shrubs and red geraniums. On the ground level, a café patio sat empty in the inclement weather. Next, I walked inside the ruins of the Monasterio de San Juan and had to refocus to understand that the walls I faced were once the interior. The walls of stone and brick were well-preserved, considering that they were built in the eleventh century. A pigeon took off, and I snapped a photo as it flew against the gray stone. Many spotlights faced the monastery, which I imagined created a haunting scene at night. I didn't have time to visit the museum next to the ruins. It would have to be another trip. I only had time for one major attraction, the Burgos *Catedral*.

The Iglesia de San Lesmés and the adjacent plaza was my next stop. The church had been rebuilt or renovated over many centuries, and sections had bricks that looked new. The church was rather simple, but the entranceway was delicately carved in stone. I entered through the richly detailed main door and tried to open the second one, but it was locked. Next, I entered a busy modern area with many shops and cafés. A recent bronze statue in the plaza depicted a chubby pilgrim couple. I passed through a portal under an old brick building, the top floor brightly painted in orange. Ahead was the old city and narrow streets of Burgos.

Despite the cold and intermittent rain, the old city was crowded. Unlike the Camino through Logroño, Burgos was vibrant, with many cafés, shops, and other businesses. At the Iglesia de San Lorenzo el Real, a small group attended midday mass. I sat in the back row, careful not to disturb anyone, and I dared not walk around. The priest, dressed in white, stood out brilliantly against the gold *retablo* as he gave his sermon in Spanish. I listened but only understood a few words. Still, I was happy to watch and take off my backpack, even for a short while.

I walked outside and soon could see the spires of the Burgos *Catedral*. I stared at the spires as they got closer and was excited when I made it to the small plaza that overlooks the north and east façades. As patches of blue sky emerged, a French pilgrim arrived, and we took photos of each other. Construction of the cathedral began in the thirteenth century and lasted hundreds of years. The exterior was simply amazing, and there were so many intricate details that I can't possibly describe here. For a moment, I watched an old man have a drink on a balcony of one of the houses on the east side of the plaza. Each house had a different color – gray, yellow, faded yellow, and fresh, bright red. The Camino followed along the north side of the cathedral, and it was possible to walk around the entire complex. I marveled at the exterior and noticed the main building on the west side was even grander. In the middle of the plaza below was a beautiful fountain featuring Mary and Child. Considering it was midday, I was surprised to see so few people. The plaza was patrolled by a police officer on the far side, who was busy talking with someone. I walked down at least three flights of stairs to the plaza, and another French man took my photo in front of the cathedral. When he returned my camera, I was disappointed that he took more of the plaza ground than the building.

Admission to the cathedral for pilgrims was only €2.50, and I was grateful for the backpack lockers; my shoulders needed a break. The cathedral was far more beautiful than I could have ever imagined. There were many rooms, each rich in history and details. Since it was built over many centuries, numerous architects and artists contributed and ensured a wonderful ensemble of *retablos*, tapestries, paintings, carvings, and tombs. The alabaster and marble tombs had incredibly haunting facial details. The outside cloister had stunning architectural detail. I spent one and a half hours inside the cathedral, but I could have spent an entire day. It was incredible.

As I toured the cathedral, I looked for a washroom but never saw one. I asked the cashier, and she told me there wasn't any. I couldn't believe that this major attraction, a UNESCO World Heritage Site, had no washroom. I picked up my backpack and headed outside with three goals in mind – explore off the Camino for a while, find a washroom, and have a nice lunch. There would be no peanuts and chocolate for lunch on this day. I wandered the streets on the south side of the cathedral and looked at buildings and in shops and cafés.

A tapas bar had nobody smoking inside, and I chose a table by the window. Immediately, I went to the washroom for a pee. "That was close," I thought, and I felt better with the pressure of my bladder finally relieved. At the counter, I studied the selection of tapas but had no idea what most of them were. They all looked artistic, and the waiter, who spoke better English than my Spanish, helped me choose. He was interested in the Camino and told me, with a chuckle, the weather forecast was poor for several days ahead. It was easy for him to laugh, considering he didn't have to walk. I didn't really desire to hear this weather nonsense, so I changed the subject to tapas. My stomach had rumbled for the previous hour, but I wasn't sure if it was from hunger or because my bladder was about to burst. The waiter helped me choose five different tapas with various combinations of meats, cheeses, and vegetables. They were so good that, once I finished, I ordered three more. My tummy was happy but full, and I hoped I could still walk. I left the waiter a good tip for his service, even though his weather forecast sucked.

I arrived back to the plaza on the west side of the cathedral and walked around to the stairs on the east side to finish the circle. Once back on the Camino, I passed through the Arco de San Martín to an area with many businesses, which included my favorite store, Mercadona. Although I was full, I bought apples, chips, bread, chorizo, cheese, and Coke Light. I saw something I really didn't need. A box of six chocolate-covered ice creams bars was on sale, and somehow, I convinced myself that I couldn't pass up a good bargain. I also picked up alcohol pads and more tape, because I had doubts about the quality of the euro store tape. New insoles were something else I needed, and this time I paid extra for thicker ones. I left Mercadona with a large shopping bag, much to my chagrin and delight.

An old stone footbridge led over the Río Arlanzón, and I found myself in the pleasant Parque El Parral. I sat on a bench overlooking the river and tried to rearrange my backpack to allow a few items from the shopping bag. The sun peeked through the clouds, and the afternoon was much warmer than the morning. I wasn't hungry, but I had to do something with the ice cream bars. I opened one and ate while I walked. After I finished that one, I had another and another, until, somewhere past Burgos, I finished the entire box. I don't know why I did that. I really only needed one. At least I had enough sugar to get me through to my next stop.

The walk out of Burgos was far more pleasant than the one in the morning. The Camino passed through the grounds of the University of Burgos and its many modern pieces of art along the main road. Leaving the city was a long walk, and I was glad to arrive on a gravel road that wound through farmland and parkland. It was past four o'clock and although I had spent a good part of the day in Burgos, I could have stayed for a few days. Hopefully, I can visit another time.

As much as I liked Burgos, it felt good to get out of civilization, and I was thankful for some peaceful solitude. I was happy to see trees and hear birds singing. I pulled out my clothes to dry and kept a plastic bag handy to hide my underwear if I saw someone. On my right was the sprawling prison – the stone bell gable rose from the church in the center – once home to political prisoners during the Franco years. I hoped that no one had escaped, because I didn't need that kind of company. Well, maybe if it was a beautiful Spanish woman who hadn't been with a man for five years.

While I stared at a small church near a park, a Swiss pilgrim cyclist noticed my Canadian flag and called out. He was in the midst of a long-anticipated journey from Switzerland to Santiago and usually rode well into the evening. We talked briefly, and I continued on a gravel road through wheat fields with the freeway in the distance. I crossed the Arlanzón again, and here, the river looked peaceful and serene, as long as I didn't glance over my shoulder at the freeway.

The entrance to the village of Tardajos had an ancient stone *cruceiro* and a new stone monument depicting a map of the Camino in Spain. On the map, Tardajos appeared about halfway, but I knew it wasn't close. In the village, a Spanish pilgrim cyclist stopped to talk. He spoke English well and taught me to pronounce "Atapuerca." He was patient, and after many tries, I finally got it right. He was surprised that I had stayed there the previous night and was more surprised when I told him I was walking to Hornillos del Camino. It was sunny and by far the best weather of the day. Really, it was the warmest in many days. He agreed and said goodbye. I thanked him for teaching me how to pronounce "Atapuerca," although I lost it a few minutes later. I need to learn how to roll the R's.

An old man walked up to me and talked in Spanish. He didn't know any English and pointed to various homes but none seemed that spectacular. He took pride in his village and obviously tried to show me something that I didn't see or understand. Again, I wished I could converse in Spanish. I stopped at a pop machine outside a store and pressed the Coke Light button but received a regular Coke. I went inside and told my story to the clerk, who obviously didn't give a crap. After some convincing, he finally opened the machine and gave me a Coke Light. I thanked him with all my heart and left cursing him under my breath.

From Tardajos to the village of Rabé de las Calzadas, there was a two kilometer walk on the side of a secondary road. Beyond Rabé, I saw the hill I soon had to climb. I was happy to be basking in sunshine, but far to the west, the clouds looked dark and threatening. Rabé de las Calzadas was pleasant with a small rose garden in the plaza next to the church. I passed a smaller church on the outskirts of the village and joined a good gravel road. Now I had to climb to something I had heard about – and had even been warned about – the Spanish *meseta*.

After a short climb, I stopped on a grassy hillside overlooking Rabé de las Calzadas and had a sandwich. I thought if I ate something, it would reduce what I carried in the bag. I took off my shoes and socks and laid out my clothing to dry. It was after seven o'clock, and I had walked almost nonstop from Burgos. It seemed like days since I had left Atapuerca, but it was really only twelve hours. I was getting tired.

After a very dry sandwich, I got myself organized and continued the short climb. The *meseta* is land that is flat to gently rolling and dominated by various agricultural crops including wheat and hay, and grasslands for grazing sheep and cattle. In North America, we would call it a prairie. People have opposing views of the *meseta*. Some say it's beautiful, while others say it's boring. One thing is for certain: to make good time or to make up for lost time on the Camino, one of the best places was on the *meseta*.

At the alto, there was farmland as far as I could see. I walked fast to the edge of the bench, and then had a short descent and a two kilometer walk to Hornillos del Camino. I felt great in the warm evening and continued to carry my clothes, hoping they would dry. When I entered the village, I put away my clothes as I passed two men who tended their flock of grazing sheep on the side of the road. Nobody else was around as I walked through the streets to the church and the adjacent *albergue*. As I entered, I was greeted by the overly friendly French *hospitalera*. She laughed and, as a table full of pilgrims watched, attempted to inspect my bags. Yes, I carried two bags. One with food, and the other with damp clothes that included underwear. I felt embarrassed and quickly pulled away my bag of clothes and put them at my feet. The *hospitalera* laughed again and told me there were no beds in the main *albergue*, but there was space in the overflow area at the school gymnasium next door. A school gym, was she serious? The *hospitalera* led me to the gym and helped me with the rollaway bed, which I put far away from anyone else. She warned the gym would get cold, and I could use the available blankets, which looked dusty, like they hadn't been washed for a century.

The Swiss cyclist who I had met earlier entered, and we were surprised to see each other. His name was Vincent, and he could speak English well. I was devoid of much communication during the day and was happy to have someone to talk with. He warned me the shower didn't have hot water. Great! I persevered through a long day and had a cold shower to look forward to. I tried, but the water was too cold for a regular shower, so I sponged myself the best I could. It was not a pleasant experience after walking all day.

After I dressed, I hung my clothes outside. Just a little more, and they would be dry. Vincent used the only available electric outlet in the gym, so I went to the communal room to charge my camera battery. During the day, I had taken many photos and was well through the charge on my backup battery. My stomach was more than full, and I put my bag of food in the fridge.

I had walked about 39.5 kilometers for the day, which I was happy with, considering the amount of time I had spent in Burgos. My afternoon pace was excellent. I talked for a while but was extremely tired and went to bed at ten o'clock. The gym was freezing, and I reluctantly grabbed two blankets, hoping they wouldn't be needed. Along with my sleeping bag and liner, I wore wool socks, base layer pants, a long-sleeved shirt, and my wind jacket to bed. I was still cold, so I reached down and, with my thumbs and index fingers only, unfolded the blankets and covered my body, careful not to touch my face.

All night long, I had a chill on my face, and even with the filthy blankets, I took a long time to warm up. I lay in bed and listened to the snoring that echoed throughout the gym. To make matters worse, the musky smell of the gym and blankets clogged my nostrils. As I tried to sleep, I looked at the skylight, hoping to see the night sky through the layer of dust and grime. I tried to imagine that the spots I saw were planets and stars, and not splatters of bird shit on the glass.

I FELT NO STIRRING FROM MY PENIS WHATSOEVER

Day 9

Hornillos del Camino to Boadilla del Camino

40.5 Km

Before seven o'clock, the gym was bustling as everyone started to get ready. I, on the other hand, stayed in bed, still covered by stinky blankets. During the night, I had had a restless sleep and felt uncomfortable and cold. I looked up at the skylight and was disappointed to see rain and overcast skies. It was clear when I had arrived, and I had hoped for a fine day. I was the last one out of bed and washed up in a cold room with cold water. Vincent was ready early, and we talked briefly before he left.

Still groggy, I sauntered to the communal room, where I made a chorizo and cheese sandwich, which again, was very dry. I had only one foot taped up when the janitor came in and told the few of us who were left to vacate because he needed to clean up. I taped my other foot under the overhang of the church, which had a simple façade with a square bell tower that overlooked the farmland below. Next to it sat a small graveyard enclosed with brick walls and a dark wooden gate.

I was ready by nine o'clock and the last pilgrim to leave the *albergue*. My clothes were still not dry, but I was hoping this would be the day. Of course, I hoped that every day. The streets had few people, and I walked quickly through the village to a gravel road that pleasantly climbed through the *meseta*. As my body awoke, I felt better, and for once, I couldn't complain about the weather. The rain had stopped, and although it was only about 7°C, it seemed temperate, compared to the same time the previous morning.

Ahead, I saw many kilometers of *meseta*, and much of the landscape was similar. A wind farm far in the distance to my right broke the monotony. Although I tried, there wasn't much to see. I looked near and far, up and down. There were few birds and no wildlife, which brought a question to mind – where was the wildlife? It was my ninth day on the Camino, and besides a small lizard on the first and numerous birds, I never saw anything. I was in forests, grasslands, valleys, and now, the *meseta*, and not a deer, antelope or even a damn squirrel. A few pilgrims were the only ones who resembled wild beasts, although I'm sure I had my moments, too.

Except for a short drop and climb out of San Bol, the land was flat or had a slight incline. The ruins of the monastery in San Bol were about one hundred meters to the right of the Camino. Not much was there, besides crumbling walls and foundation. About two hundred meters on the left sat an isolated *albergue*. To say San Bol was a hamlet would be an overstatement.

I passed more pilgrims as the track climbed gently to an alto. Two walkers without backpacks went past, and I couldn't keep up with them. From the alto, it was odd to suddenly see Hontanas almost hidden on the near side of the hill, just above the valley bottom. As rain began to fall, I entered the village along a narrow dirt road with old stone walls almost two meters high. Before Hontanas, a sign had advertised a supermarket, but when I arrived, it was small and didn't have anything I wanted. One bar was closed, and the other had too much smoke, so I didn't enter. After walking almost nonstop for eleven kilometers, I left the village without taking a break.

After Hontanas, the landscape was more scenic as the Camino followed along the side of the hill through a valley with the river below. The rain didn't last long, and I took off my rain jacket so it could dry. The track started off as a good dirt road, slightly overgrown with grass. Beautiful dwarf succulents with red flowers in full bloom adorned one small patch on the side. I had no idea what they were and didn't see them again. I climbed a small hill to the ruins of an ancient village. There was only a six meter high narrow section of wall that had crumbled near the base. I couldn't see it standing for much longer, but someone may have said the same thing years ago.

After a short descent, the path led to a paved secondary road lined by giant deciduous trees. Soon, I arrived at the ominous ruins of the Convento de San Antón, which originated in the twelfth century and for many years was an important stop on the Camino. An *albergue* was still present around the corner, but I didn't enter. Many of the details of the individual sculptures on the archivolt were weathered and lost forever. Nevertheless, they were fascinating. The archway spanned about five stories high over the road, and the top of the main building still had the remains of spires. A group of pilgrims sat underneath and had their lunch. I felt like joining them since I had walked for about four hours without a good break but decided to stop in Castrojeriz, a few kilometers away.

In the distance, the ruins of a castle on top of a hill became prominent. As I entered Castrojeriz, the Iglesia de Nuestra Señora del Manzano, a large stone and brick complex, looked impressive below the castle. The church had a weathered exterior, with grasses and the odd small shrub growing from the side. The main door was closed, and I didn't realize until I walked around that there was a side door which led to a museum. The admission was only a euro or two, and I gladly paid and entered. The small museum had art and artifacts from the church and local area. The stained-glass windows, decorated with roses, alone made the admission worthwhile. Outside, it was much colder and starting to rain again. I stopped for more photos of the castle and zoomed in on its jagged walls. One day, I'll walk up there.

As it rained harder, I took cover in an *albergue* with an internet station in the lobby. I needed a rest anyway and caught up with news, emails, weather, and unimportant random browsing. If it wasn't for the internet, I wouldn't know what was happening in Canada. Really, besides the weather, I knew little about what was happening in Spain. I knew the country, along with others in Europe, were in the midst of a financial crisis that officials were attempting to rectify. I couldn't see any obvious effects of the economy as I walked the Camino. However, I'm sure some people were affected by unemployment or from the loss of social programs. What else? The weather would be unseasonably cool and unsettled for at least another week. Hey, Spain! When does spring start? There wasn't any heat in the lobby, and I started to get cold. I checked the time and couldn't believe I had spent, or wasted, an hour on the internet.

Outside, the rain continued, so I took shelter inside a tapas bar. I wasn't hungry and only ordered a Coke Light and a small bag of chips. I finished the chips quickly and looked outside to see it was raining even harder. The tapas selection behind the glass looked good, and with the help of the waiter, I chose two. I didn't fully understand what I was eating, but they were enjoyable.

At least eight other people were in the bar, including three young women at the table next to me. All eyes, including mine, were fixated on the television, which showed the midday news from Madrid hosted by two beautiful women. I had no idea what they said, but they sure kept my attention. The anchors introduced something and began to show a clip from a movie featuring two very attractive, fully nude women who kissed, groped, and caressed each other in ways I'm too shy to explain here. Normally, I wouldn't mind seeing such a show of affection, but I felt uncomfortable with all these strangers. The three women at the table next to me watched intently, and one looked at me and smiled. I didn't know what to do, so I just smiled back. It's not something I've ever seen on the midday news in Canada.

The clip lasted at least a minute and was interrupted abruptly by the anchors who were laughing. I went to the counter, bought a giant cookie, and sat down again. I anticipated another clip of two beautiful women making love, but the anchors introduced a boring news story about a murder or something in Madrid. I guess that was my excitement for the afternoon. Hell, that was my excitement for the last two weeks. Yes, I know the Camino in itself is fulfilling, but this was different.

It was 3:15, and I had spent almost three hours in Castrojeriz, much longer than I had expected. The rain stopped, and I had to move. I continued my walk through the town to the Iglesia de Santo Domingo, where outside, a large stone fountain had a coat of arms and an impression of a castle on the top. Castrojeriz was a true Camino town, with one very long, main street. From the town, I followed a road through flat farmland, and ahead was the hill I soon had to climb. My body was tired, but I moved at a fast pace to keep warm.

I didn't know if it was because I was on a stretch of unassuming landscape, but my mind began to wander and then focus on a very serious matter. Many pilgrims spend their solitude on the Camino with religious or spiritual thoughts, while others take advantage of the silence to meditate. However, at that moment, my thoughts were with my penis. Something bothered me while I watched the clip of the two women making love. I don't know if I had been so focused with walking the Camino or because I was so tired most of the time, but I had not had an erection since the night before I left on my trip, a period of almost two weeks. I never had an erotic dream or even a daydream, for that matter. In fact, during the entire clip of the lesbians, I felt no stirring from my penis whatsoever. I wondered if there was something wrong.

It was always a concern of mine as I got older that my penis would stop working. No, I don't mean taking a pee, although I suppose that should be first on the list. I'm referring to the ability to make love or have sex. Even if it was an erection only to partake in what the Scottish-American comedian Craig Ferguson refers to as "self-massage." In the previous three years, I probably had sex two hundred times – far more including self-massage – and only twice I had trouble getting an erection. Once was a few months prior when I was sick, and I sure heard about that incident for weeks after. The previous time was almost three years before when my then girlfriend surprised me with a visit right after a horrible stock market day during the U.S. financial crisis. I don't know what happened – probably the stress – but nothing happened, if you know what I mean. Again, I heard about that lone incident for weeks after. I didn't know if I had to worry, but luckily I saw something ahead that took my mind off my penis.

As I approached the Río Odrilla, a raised Roman causeway appeared above marshland parallel to the road. The causeway was about two meters high and one hundred meters long, with a series of arches and supports made of stone. After I walked across the causeway, I went back along the road and even stepped into the adjacent field for side views. It was amazing, and I felt so lucky to walk along it. I had never expected the causeway, and I think I was more excited to walk along it than I was watching the lesbians on the television. I must say though, the causeway didn't make my penis stir, either.

As I rejoined the gravel road and began a steep ascent, I felt my normal afternoon sluggishness and struggled. At the alto stood a pilgrim monument – a newer, cement marker with a scallop shell impressed on the top. I looked back at Castrojeriz, the valley, and the vast *meseta*. Now, I was higher than the ruins of the castle. Nearby, there was a new open, covered shelter, one of few along the Camino. The top of the hill formed a bench with flat, dry farmland. After a short walk, I came to the edge and saw the Camino for kilometers ahead. I descended the steep gravel road but stopped at a monument finished in bronze with pictures of Jesus and a female figure who I assumed was Mary. The inscription was in Spanish, referenced Málaga to Castrojeriz, and was dated October 2009. I couldn't tell if someone died here or if it was to commemorate a walk. By far, it was one of the most elaborate pilgrim monuments along the Way.

At the bottom of the hill, I walked through a rolling landscape with scattered red poppies and the reddish soil providing contrast against the bright green farmland. After a small climb, I saw a small isolated brick building in the valley near a river. It was the San Nicolás de Puente Fitero Hospital de Peregrinos, a hospice that had existed since the thirteenth century.

While I observed the exterior, a pilgrim appeared at the doorway and invited me inside. The interior was very rustic and charming. The *hospitalero* was in his 30's, very friendly, and spoke English well. As a group of pilgrims watched from the old wooden table, he told me not to be shy, to come in, and talk. He offered me food and wine and said he had one bed available. I thanked him, but it was only six-thirty, the sun was out, and I had a good evening walk ahead. San Nicolás would be a unique and interesting place to stay one day. Later, I found out that some pilgrims planned their journey so they could stay there.

Next, I crossed the muddy, slow-moving Río Pisuerga, lined with deciduous trees and shrubs. The bridge, originally built in the eleventh century, was impressive, with its nine arches, and had been recently restored. The river marked the border between the provinces of Burgos and Palencia, and an impressive cement marker with a coat of arms greeted me on the other side. The church in Itero de la Vega was one of the simplest I had seen on the Camino. The front façade looked old, but it was really only brick with a door and a modest bell gable. I walked through the village quickly and only saw two locals. I hadn't seen another pilgrim walking since Castrojeriz.

This was the bluest sky I had seen all day, and I felt energized. As I gently climbed a gravel road through farmland of wheat and recently plowed fields, I realized I hadn't had a photo of myself since Burgos. I positioned the camera on my backpack and took a few with Itero de la Vega in the background. I looked so rough, like a wild beast, with my messy hair, dirty black fleece, and grungy rain pants.

As the pain from my blisters became worse, I pressed on through the monotonous farmland and finally arrived at Boadilla del Camino about eight o'clock. Earlier, I had seen a sign advertising a private *albergue* which showed photos of the buildings and yard with a pool and I wanted to check it out. The first *albergue* I passed was another private one, but they were playing AC/DC loud and appeared to be having a party. I'm an AC/DC fan but didn't want to be around any loud music when I was so tired and trying to sleep. I bypassed the municipal albergue and when I arrived at my destination, I was greeted by Francis, the friendly *hospitalero* from Ontario, Canada. As a fellow Canadian, he immediately made me feel welcome.

He asked where I came from that morning, but I had trouble remembering.

"Castrojeriz?" he asked.

"No."

"Hontanas?"

"No."

"San Bol?"

"Ugh, Nope," I felt a little embarrassed.

"Hornillos del Camino?"

"Yes," I knew I would remember somehow. He seemed surprised I had walked so far. I was pleased to find out later it was over forty kilometers.

Francis said there were no beds available but he would find a spot for me somewhere. He told me to have a shower and relax. His lovely assistant greeted me and led me to the dorm area situated in a renovated old barn. I was surprised to see a full unisex washroom. After a long, refreshing shower, which, unlike the previous day, included plenty of hot water, I washed a few clothes and hung them next to the fireplace. I talked with a young couple from Australia who had started the Camino two weeks before I did but seemed happy to take their time. The guy carried the first DSLR camera I had seen on the Camino, and I think his kit weighed more than my tent, sleeping bag, trail runners, and water bottle combined.

I went to the reception area to read and charge my camera battery. I still had no idea where I was sleeping, but I trusted Francis. While I talked with a guy beside me, a pretty woman with short brown hair entered the room and sat across from me. Her name was Claudia, and she was from Belgium. She had arrived only half an hour before I did, which was surprising because I rarely saw anyone walking in the evenings. It turned out we both had a passion for walking long days and smiled as we exchanged stories. It was refreshing not hearing "You're insane" or "You're crazy," or receiving some kind of weird look. Although I was tired, and it was well past my bedtime, I stayed up talking with Claudia. The other guy at our table tried to be part of the conversation but soon left. I guess it didn't help that we tuned him out. Sorry, guy.

By ten o'clock, we were both exhausted and bid each other a good night. Now I had to find where I was sleeping. By the time I got back, the room was dark and everyone was in bed. Guided by the light from my iPhone, I found my backpack next to a mattress on the floor. It took a while to get organized, and I fumbled a little, trying not to make too much noise. The hard mattress was uncomfortable, and the room and adjacent dorm had many snorers. I knew it would be a while until I fell asleep.

I was still awake an hour later when a young couple came in. They had been drinking and whispered loudly, thinking nobody could hear them. Although I, as well as others, said, "Shhhhhh," they whispered for at least half an hour. They were ignorant and annoying. Then they started moving their mattresses together but a couch was in the way. They moved the couch and bumped into tables. Finally the moving stopped, and I sensed they were together. The guy whispered loudly, and I seriously thought they were going to have sex about ten feet from my head. Actually, I wasn't sure, but if they did, it only lasted about twenty-seconds. That's about how long the girl giggled for before there was silence.

TWENTY IS A NICE ROUND NUMBER
Day 10
Boadilla del Camino to Calzadilla de la Cueza
43.5 Km

The trickle of pilgrims started leaking out of the *albergue* at five o'clock, and by six, many had already left. It wouldn't have been so bad if my mattress wasn't near the boot rack. Most of the early risers were over fifty years old, and they talked and slammed the door; one idiot even turned on the light. Many left while it was still pitch black outside. In the past, I had been criticized by certain people for walking late. At least I hadn't walked in the dark, yet.

After falling asleep past midnight and waking up early, I was still tired and just laid in bed or in this case, on the mattress. When I rose, I looked over to the young couple who had kept me awake and proceeded to make enough noise to ensure they didn't sleep in. I did nothing out of the ordinary – only bumping into furniture, dropping a boot, dropping a boot again (I am so clumsy), coughing uncontrollably, and singing the Spanish National Anthem, although I didn't know any of the words or melody. Okay, I'm exaggerating here, but I did rustle and bang enough to partially pay them back for being so fucking ignorant. The sounds of everyone getting ready and walking out the door was enough to keep anyone in that room awake. I grabbed my clothes from the rack and they were finally dry. Hallelujah!

I packed up and went to the reception area to work on my feet. Francis and his staff hustled around and ensured everyone was well taken care of. Claudia entered, and we talked briefly as we got ready. Francis allowed me to use his laptop, and it was the first time I had used the recent version of Windows so far in Spain. Until now, the latest version I had used was six years old. I had a slow morning and wasn't ready until after eight o'clock. I was among the last to leave and bid farewell to Francis. The *albergue's* large backyard was accented with flowers, shrubs, and a metal statue of two pilgrims. It was a kind of place where I could spend a sunny afternoon, but for some reason, I always seemed to be preoccupied on the Camino.

The morning was cold and windy, but at least it wasn't raining. The church was immediately across from the *albergue*, and in the middle of the adjacent plaza stood a fifteenth century *rollo* or *picota*, a stone column with an intricate top. The *rollo* was an important monument and was once used to hang people who had apparently done something wrong. For a brief moment, I thought of the young couple who had kept me and the others awake. Again, it was only a thought. I shall make no further comment.

I walked around the church and followed a road but soon realized there weren't any markers. I stopped for a photo of a cute horse with a long brown mane who posed for me in a field between houses. Once back on the Camino, I saw Claudia waiting for me. We walked out of the village together, and she wanted to meditate, so I told her to go ahead. I had to work on my audio journal anyway. Claudia was fast and soon disappeared while I languished behind. My blisters were sore, and I was already tired.

From Boadilla del Camino, I followed a gravel road on top of a dike with the Canal de Castilla along the right and farmland on the left. It was a pleasant walk, with trees scattered along the road and numerous birds singing. A small bird that looked like a sparrow followed me for a while, and I wondered if it was my mom. She often said she would come back as a bird but never told me what kind she would be. As I walked along the dike, the land on the left gradually became lower than the water level on the right. The irrigation system in Spain intrigued me, and I knew it had been integral to the nation's agricultural industry for centuries. The canal ended at an impressive lock just before Frómista, where water cascaded down the cement slopes on the downstream side. By now, the level of the farmland was four or five meters lower than the level of the canal. While I admired the lock, I talked with the Australian couple one last time before saying goodbye. Claudia was wandering off the Camino and looked lost. I waved for her to get back on track and continued into the town.

The Camino in Frómista only went through the edge of the downtown area. There were shops and cafés but not many historical features. The main church was a few blocks away, and I only glanced at it from across the street. The steady five kilometer morning walk tired me, and I looked for something to eat. The cafés were packed, and nothing else interested me. Another village was close, and I hoped to take a break there. I followed a sidewalk that led through a residential area until the freeway overpass, where there was a monument of a pilgrim cut from sheet metal. Ahead was the *senda*, a gravel path beside the highway. The *senda*, similar to the *meseta*, was excellent for making great time, and I knew I had to take advantage of it. It was Saturday, and by far the day with the most people I had seen walking the Camino. Many were Spanish families out for the day. They walked casually, and most seemed to enjoy themselves. I saw men in jeans, women with purses, young children with tiny backpacks, and babies in strollers. Once on the *senda*, my legs finally woke up, and I passed almost everyone ahead of me. The terrain was flat to gently rolling through farmland, and there wasn't much to see.

As I entered the village of Población de Campos, I and a group of walkers of all ages witnessed a peculiar sight for a Saturday morning. Less than a block off the Camino, an old man was facing us and taking a piss right in the middle of the street. Really, wasn't there a better spot? It was such a small village, how far could have he been from his home? Maybe that spot was the designated public washroom. Near the end of the village, I bought a Coke Light and a muffin from a bakery and sat outside on a patio. I couldn't stay long because it was so cold.

An old stone bridge over the Río Ucieza would be my highlight for a while, and I quickly walked along the *senda* to Revenga de Campos. The sleepy village had a wonderful metal statue of St. James commemorating the 2004 Holy Year. A few minutes out of the village sat an ancient, concrete cross in the middle of a field. It had weathered with time, and it was the first intriguing site I had seen along the *senda*. In front of another field, a man was photographing something, but I couldn't figure out what he was looking at. I glanced while walking slowly, but he gave me an unfriendly look and I moved on. I passed a young Korean woman and her friend, who I had met at the *albergue*. They were playing Asian pop music through external speakers, which I'm sure annoyed some of the pilgrims. It didn't bother me, but I went by them quickly.

It was sad but sometimes comical watching people scramble on the side of the *senda* trying to find somewhere to go to the washroom. There were no public washrooms and very few private spots. Land was mostly flat, trees were sparse, buildings were in the villages, and usually, there were many people around. Some went in plain sight, while others tried to hide their rather large asses behind a thin tree. To be honest though, it was only comical because it wasn't me.

I didn't stop in Villalcázar de Sirga as the wind picked up and gusted into my face. Back on the *senda*, I struggled as I climbed a tiny hill. I had seen signs posted for businesses in the upcoming town of Carrión de los Condes and would have my break there. After one more stretch with dark clouds above and wheat fields by my side, I arrived at Carrión de los Condes exhausted. It was one o'clock, and I had walked about twenty-five kilometers with only a minor break. Now, I was going to have a good rest and a good meal.

Carrión de los Condes originated during Roman times and later flourished from the area's rich agriculture and businesses that catered to pilgrims. At one time, it was an important center and had a far greater population than the 2,300 it has today. As I entered the town, I passed a two-story mural of either Jesus or St. James, I couldn't tell, next to a vacant rest area. I stopped at a statue of Carrión, the town's namesake, who looked either tired or pissed off at something. The town center had many tourists, and it wasn't only pilgrims and day-walkers from Frómista; some people had arrived on bus tours. A large group led by a guide was outside the Iglesia de Santa María. I listened in, but the talk was in Spanish, and like always, I only understood a few words. The interior was much more modest than I would have expected for a town of this size. There was a detailed miniature scene, which I thought was more appropriate for a Christmas window than a church.

Back outside, I passed an *albergue* that had a lineup of at least twenty pilgrims waiting for it to open. It was only one-thirty, and I couldn't imagine checking in so early. As I searched for a café, I wandered off the Camino and looked at shops and old buildings. Many shops were closed, and I thought it was too early for siesta. I only needed food and chose a small restaurant that looked like it served local cuisine. I didn't treat myself for lunch often, but after a good morning walk, I figured I deserved it. The menu was in Spanish, and I had trouble understanding most of the dishes. Sure, I understood "chorizo," but I had no idea how it was served. My waitress didn't know English and couldn't help much. She brought a plate of pasta with a red sauce covered with chorizo to another table, and it sure looked good.

Without consultation, I ordered my dish. At €6, it seemed cheap for a full meal, but when it arrived, I was surprised to see a plate with only eight small slices of chorizo. Apparently, I didn't choose the pasta or a full meal. Another waitress spoke some English and explained that this chorizo was a local specialty, mixed with pimientos, soaked in blood and red wine, and then aged. An entire page of the menu included different local chorizo recipes.

I wasn't used to eating anything soaked in blood and took my time. The chorizo was okay but difficult to enjoy; I kept thinking about the blood. I was also concerned how it would affect my wimpy stomach later and didn't want to make any emergency stops along the *senda*. Still hungry, I looked again at the menu. I didn't want to take another chance, so I only ordered fries, which turned out to be bland. I left the restaurant after paying €12 for my food and a drink without the meal I had hoped for.

Still sluggish and with my stomach rumbling, I continued through the clean and pleasant town. The skies had cleared, and it was the warmest of the day. I talked briefly with another pilgrim, who told me to visit the Iglesia de Santiago because it had a better interior than the other church. However, when I arrived, the doors were locked. I walked down the hill to the impressive stone bridge over the Río Carrión. Upstream, a medieval church sat proudly on top of the tan-colored hill. Parkland with trees and shrubs hugged the banks of the slow moving river. The Monasterio de San Zoilo soon appeared, as well as a surprise. I didn't expect to see another raised causeway in a park across the road from the monastery. I didn't know how old it was, and it looked rebuilt, but I was happy to walk on it nonetheless. At the end of the causeway stood a stone marker with the crest of Galicia. I had no idea why it was here because it would be days until I crossed the border into Galicia. The exterior of the monastery was beautiful, with a detailed façade and many religious statues.

On the outskirts of the town, I stopped at a gas station and bought chocolate, nuts, and a Coke Light. I felt sluggish, my feet bothered me, and my left knee gave me periodic pains. Even my shoulders were sore for the first time in a while. I had at least fifteen kilometers left to walk and needed some quick energy. When I emerged from the gas station, I was surprised to see Claudia outside, checking her map. She was equally surprised to see me, and we began walking together. Soon I realized, I couldn't keep up with her fast pace and told her to go ahead. I explained that if I continued walking that fast, I'd surely pass out.

I enjoyed walking with Claudia and hoped she wasn't offended. She took off on the paved road through seemingly endless flat farmland, and eventually disappeared. I honestly thought that I would never see Claudia again.

Although I struggled, I enjoyed the scenery of the afternoon walk much more than I had that morning. It was good to get off the *senda* and away from the hordes of people. Other than Claudia, I didn't see anyone else all afternoon. I enjoyed looking at trees, birds, natural areas, and different irrigation systems. I was amazed to see aqueducts with water flowing well above ground level. I knew they had been used for centuries but still couldn't understand how they worked. The paved road joined a gravel one, and although the temperature was cool, the sun was shining, and I didn't feel the need to rush.

At a pilgrim's rest area, I took off my backpack and sat at a picnic table. As I looked at my map, I noticed I hadn't cut my fingernails since I had left home. It was hard to believe how I let myself go during the Camino. It wasn't just my fingernails. I had worn some pieces of clothing longer than I cared to think about. My hair, my feet, and my entire aching body in between – nothing had the care it was accustomed to. Even my pubic hair was unclipped, left to grow like a Chia Pet on steroids. I read, cut my fingernails, and managed to spend forty-five minutes resting until I felt a chill. Dark clouds from the west were coming my way. The wind picked up, the sun disappeared, and I quickly got ready. I still had about ten kilometers to the village of Calzadilla de la Cueza and had to move.

I felt the first raindrops at the crossroads of another country road with seven kilometers left to go. By now, dark purple clouds were overhead, and I put on both my rain jacket and poncho. For the next hour and a half, I walked through cold and gusting wind with driving rain, often straight into my face. The storm wasn't bad, it was fierce. I scolded myself for taking such a long break earlier. As opposed to previous days, I wouldn't have a sunny evening walk.

I finally arrived at Calzadilla de la Cueza at six-thirty, which normally would be early for me to find a bed. I bypassed the *albergue* and looked for some shelter where I could think and wait out the storm. The only spot was an overhang at the entrance to a hostal. The storm wasn't letting up, so I went inside and asked the clerk for the price of a room. She showed me a private room, which was clean, but I thought €30 was a little expensive and told her I would think about it. I went back outside, and the storm was much worse, with howling wind and raindrops driving into the pavement and bouncing off. My decision was made, and I took the room.

I still had some food, so I bought a Coke Light from the bar and went to my room around seven o'clock. After a long shower, I washed my clothes and then completely dumped out my backpack to reconsider everything. I was tired of the chorizo from the Mercadona and tossed away the last piece. There were too many socks, and I left a new pair of the wool ones on a night table, in case anybody needed them. I had a few little bits of garbage that had made their way to the bottom of the backpack, but really, I didn't manage to create much room at all. I had everything well-organized though. I still didn't know if I would ever use the tent. It took up a lot of room, but I wasn't leaving it behind.

Although I had struggled at times and finished in the storm, I still had a good day and walked over forty-three kilometers. I had about 404 kilometers left to Santiago, and barring any unforeseen difficulties, twenty-one days seemed easily attainable. Twenty days was another matter. Twenty is a nice round number, though. I had never even thought of it until that moment.

That evening, I took advantage of the Wi-Fi, which I hadn't used since St. Jean, and checked emails and the internet. I called my aunt and my cousin, and then I talked with Sarah for over an hour, until I couldn't stay awake. Although I considered Wi-Fi as a bonus to a room, it always meant going to sleep later. Before bedtime, I looked at myself closely in the mirror for the first time on the Camino and noticed I was in better shape, with less fat. I was happy but found it disconcerting that the only way I could lose weight was by walking forty kilometers every day.

It was Saturday, and, although I could hear sounds from the bar below, I fell asleep soon after I laid down at ten-thirty. I woke up once in the middle of the night to the sounds of driving rain against the window but quickly fell back to sleep. I had made a good choice; I needed a private room more often.

FUCKING WIND
Day 11
Calzadilla de la Cueza to El Burgo Ranero
40 Km

Before seven o'clock, I looked outside at the pouring rain and immediately went back to bed. My mind and body were still tired, and neither wanted to get up. The long days and many kilometers were catching up with me. I checked the internet and talked with Sarah, but after half an hour, I told her I needed to get ready. At nine o'clock, someone pounded on my door. I didn't know why, unless they thought I was part of the tour group. Maybe since no one had seen me for so long, they thought I had died.

Outside, it had stopped raining but the cold winds gusted harder. I waited under the cover of the hostal entrance and attempted to get psyched up. Another day of bad weather was disheartening, almost sickening. A van full of pilgrims and gear stopped in front of the hostal. These vans would normally transport pilgrims who were behind schedule, tired of walking, or wanted to skip stretches of the Camino. The two Korean women from the *albergue* in Boadilla del Camino got out, and when I mentioned they were cheating, they barely smiled. The hostal didn't allow check-ins before noon, so they had a long wait. I talked, checked the internet, and made one last phone call to see how my aunt was. She found it hard to believe that I called her from Spain. Thanks, Skype. What would I do without you? Soon, it was a late ten o'clock, and I had to face the disgusting weather. I took a quick walk around the quiet village and then joined the gravel *senda* with the appropriate sign, "*Senda de Peregrinos.*"

The wind was incredibly harsh and constantly blew in my face with cold gusts that made my eyes water. I started off slowly; my blisters bothered me more than normal. I had even managed a new one the previous day; I didn't know how it found an empty spot in between the others. As I walked, I ate the last of the chocolate and nuts. Now, I was out of food and needed a store soon. Focusing on eating for energy was probably why I lost weight. That, and the little forty kilometer walk every day.

Except for the wind, the walk was pleasant through a rolling landscape with bright green fields and reddish-brown soil. Trees were scattered, and the wind bent the young ones almost forty-five degrees. I didn't know if I was in some kind of wind belt, but I thought it would be a great place for windmills. Raindrops fell for a few minutes before the clouds lightened, and for a moment, I saw my shadow, albeit a very light one. I patted my shadow's head, and it quickly disappeared. It was a cruel temptation of sun because soon, the rain poured and pelted my face. I swore at the wind many times, but it just blew harder. I'm sure it was a constant fifty kilometers per hour, with gusts over seventy. I didn't stop in Ledigos, a village on the side of a hill, with houses built with adobe or pressed earth bricks and a small church above. Outside the village, the wind gusted, and I had trouble staying on the path. I even shot some video of me trying to walk as a reminder. The minor climb to the village of Terradillos de los Templarios was difficult. The tough morning had already worn me down. I was frustrated and cranky.

A new private *albergue* looked inviting, and I stopped for shelter and some food. The interior was clean, and I could tell the staff took good care of the place. It had one of the cleanest washrooms of any *albergue* I had seen in Spain. The cafeteria was empty and only served by a man in his 60's. I bought a muffin and a Coke Light and sat at a table by the window. The man's wife or partner entered the room, and they began arguing in Spanish behind the counter. He yelled at her, and she at him. At first, I thought their argument was a little funny, but as it went on, I felt sad for them. It was uncomfortable sitting there by myself, so I quickly ate and left the cafeteria. They didn't notice and continued fighting. I visited the lovely washroom one more time. I didn't really have to go, but I thought I would take advantage of the facilities and drain every last drop of urine I could manage. I had concerns with taking a pee outside on a day like this because the wind would most likely freeze my genitals. It was too bad I didn't have to take a dump. I think I would have really enjoyed one there.

The architectural style of the church in Terradillos de los Templarios was different from what I had seen. It was long and narrow, with orange-brown bricks and a bell tower that was charming with its simpleness. A huge nest sat on top, and I waited for the stork to show, but it never did. From the village, I followed a good gravel path with a large buffer from the highway. Few pilgrims were walking, and I supposed most were hiding in a bar or taking the day off. Those were the smart ones. The terrain continued to roll, with large patches of mustard on the edge of the bright green fields. Finally, a wind farm appeared, and I'm sure on this day enough electricity was generated to power all of Spain for a year.

In the hamlet of Moratinos, a hill covered in tall grass had many doors and chimneys. I trusted they were used for storage but wouldn't be surprised if somebody lived in one. I was quickly back on the path through farmland, but by now I was losing my patience with the wind, which gusted the hardest of the day. If I mentioned it was bad earlier, it was far worse now. As I reached the crest of a hill, I was blown to the side of the path. I screamed, "Fuck you, you stupid fucking wind. FUCK YOU!" Actually, I had a couple of more "Fucks" in there, but I thought I would clean up my rare potty mouth for anyone reading this book. It was funny – or more likely, not – that that was one of the few quotes I noted on the entire Camino. Honestly, it was my eleventh day walking, and it would have been so nice to get one full day of warm, sunny weather. I don't mean 10°C. I wanted it fucking warm!

During my little tirade, I didn't realize there were three women on the other side of the hill, farther up the Camino. I hoped they didn't hear me, and they probably didn't because the stupid wind blew all my words behind me. One woman had her pants down and was taking a pee right on the edge of the path. When I first saw her, she smiled and I uncomfortably half-smiled back. She wasn't a slight bit embarrassed, but I sure was. I guess she never drained her last drops of urine at the clean washroom earlier. If she had, she wouldn't have been forced to go on the side of the path in full view of others.

Again, all my yelling at the wind didn't make it slow down. I needed a break and stopped at a bar in San Nicolás del Real Camino. It was packed with pilgrims who didn't dare go outside. There were no seats available, so I picked up a chocolate bar and a Coke Light and continued. About two kilometers past the village, I left the province of Palencia and entered the province of León. I could see the town of Sahagún a few kilometers ahead. Lucky for me, over Sahagún there were small patches of blue sky. The weather looked far worse to the south, with dark, purple clouds and heavy showers. For the first time on the Camino, I saw a pilgrim with a horse. I didn't know if there was a problem because the man was off the horse and leading it down a small hill. I walked fast and had almost caught up to them when the rider mounted and they galloped away.

The Camino veered off to the right, across the highway, and over the Río Valderaduey. The stone bridge with two small arches was originally built by the Romans but had been rebuilt over time. I couldn't believe someone had spray painted a yellow arrow on the side of the bridge. The path was obvious, and the arrow wasn't needed. Near the bridge was the Ermita de la Virgen del Puente, which was very similar to the style of the other churches in the area. It was being renovated, and the entire area was fenced off, but I didn't see anybody working. Nearby, red poppies and other flowers decorated a field, and I took photos as the sun came out. After a short walk, I arrived in Sahagún, one of the most unique towns on the Camino.

Sahagún's roots date back to the fourth century. The agriculture industry has always been important, and the area has been a frequent site of battles through the years. In the ninth century, it was occupied twice by the Moors and retaken by the Christians both times. The architecture of Sahagún is important because it's in *Mudéjar* style, named for the Moors who stayed in Christian territory but didn't convert. I noticed the churches of the last few villages also had architecture in this style, but in Sahagún, they were more elaborate.

Sahagún was the largest town I had been in for days, but when I arrived at three o'clock, it was in the midst of siesta. This town took its siesta very seriously. Since it was Sunday, almost everything was closed. I saw few people or cars and couldn't believe how quiet the streets were. First, I stopped at the Iglesia de la Trinidad. It was in the *Mudéjar* style but was rather drab on the outside and had some huge cracks in the brick. I went inside but was disappointed; it was now an *albergue* and had little resemblance to a church. The *hospitalera* kept asking if I was staying the night, and I told her every time that I wasn't. Across the street was another church, the Iglesia de San Juan. The façade was recently painted in white with light brown trim, and it stood out brilliantly compared to the nearby buildings.

Although it was still cool and windy, it was more bearable in the sun, which I was happy to see. It was a tough morning. I had walked twenty-one kilometers through trying conditions, and I was hungry, tired, and desperately in need of a rest. My late start put a forty kilometer day in jeopardy. I bypassed a bar that had few patrons but enough smoke for a few dozen. A bakery near the town center looked good and smelled better. A group of older men stood in front of the television and watched, with keen interest, not lesbians, but F1 racing from Barcelona. I picked two pastries and a Coke Light and sat at a table with a view of the TV. The men watched intensely, blurted out, and cheered. Not being a racing fan, I had no idea what all the excitement was about. I would have preferred to watch a hockey game, but it was a sport I never saw or heard mentioned in Spain. The pastries were huge and delicious. One had chocolate icing on the outside and chocolate filling on the inside. The other had a light icing on the outside and cherry on the inside. They filled me up, and I hoped they would give me enough energy for the afternoon.

I followed Camino markers with metal poles and a scallop shell on each as the sidewalk wound down the hill. At the bottom, I faced the magnificent Arch of San Benito, with its huge coat of arms with two lions on either side. The arch was once the façade of the Monasterio de San Facundo, which lay in ruins, with its jagged walls. Also in the historic area were the Iglesia de San Tirso and the Convento de las Madres Benedictinas, both in the *Mudéjar* style. I walked through the arch where the monastery once stood and saw the remainder of interior motifs and walls. The Iglesia de San Tirso originated in the twelfth century but had been rebuilt over the years, including recently. It looked in good shape and had a grand bell tower with many small arches supported by columns. I sat in the sun on one of the many benches facing the arch. I didn't have trouble getting a bench; there was no one else around. Because it was Sunday, I had hoped the church was open. Sadly, it was locked so I moved on.

After a short walk, there was the beautiful stone bridge with five arches that spanned the Río Cea. The view upstream looked so peaceful, with the banks of the slow-moving river adorned with trees, shrubs, and grasses. It was a real park-like setting, and I admired the willows that wept over the river. A fisherman wearing chest waders was in the middle of the river, but I never saw him catch anything. After the bridge, the Camino followed a tree-lined *senda* beside the highway. The terrain was flat, the track was good, and this would be where I could make up time, mind and body willing. The wind constantly blew into me, but thankfully, the gusts had ceased. Soon, the trees that lined the *senda* disappeared, and there was farmland as far as I could see.

The Camino arrived at an option, and here I had a tough decision. On the left was the *Real Camino Francés*, and on the right was the Roman route. I would have liked to take them both. Although I really enjoyed the Roman roads and architecture, I wanted to walk as much of the entire French Way as possible. It was a shame; I missed out on thirty-five kilometers of the Roman route, an entire day of walking. It would have to wait for another time. The area of the option had hand spray-painted arrows and words written on the pavement and the highway barrier. A sign depicting a cartoon character of a pilgrim was on the ground in a grass field away from the road. Someone had driven into it and sent it flying. A newer sign showed a map of the area, but overall, the signage was sloppy.

The French Way veered on what would be a long stretch of *senda*. I had energy and felt the best of the day – except for the bottom of my feet, which felt like they had coarse sand rubbing against them. I craved some chocolate or ice cream and regretted that I hadn't picked up two extra pastries from the bakery in Sahagún. I stopped briefly at a rest area in front of the Ermita de Nuestra Señora de Perales, a small church also in the *Mudéjar* style. Next to the *senda* was a Gothic cross mounted on stone and cement. The church was isolated and looked lonely with no other buildings around.

After walking over ten kilometers from Sahagún with no more than a few moments' break, I was tired and stopped at a bar at Bercianos del Real Camino for a drink and a little rest. I tried an empanada with some cheese-like substance, but it wasn't as good as the ones from the bakery. It felt great to get off my feet, but when someone started smoking at a table next to me, I had to leave. It was six-thirty, and my goal for the evening was El Burgo Ranero, still over seven kilometers away. I hoped there would be a bed available, a thought which increased my walking pace. I was back on a gravel *senda* through more unspectacular farmland. To the north, the mountains had snow, which helped explain the cold wind. With the sun in my eyes, I put my sunglasses on for one of the rare times I really needed them.

When I arrived in El Burgo Ranero just before eight-thirty, a group of pilgrims sitting outside the municipal *albergue* looked at me in disbelief. They gave the typical, "You're fucking crazy!" stares, and I smiled and went inside. The *albergue* was full, so I went to the private one on the far edge of town. The *hospitalera* there said her *albergue* was also full, but she had private rooms available for €30. For some reason, I didn't believe her *albergue* was full. The photo of the private room didn't look special and certainly not worth €30 so I politely declined and went back outside. The *hospitalera* followed me back to the muni, where I asked again if they could find a spot. They told me it wasn't possible, so I went to the main street, while the *hospitalera* from the private followed me again. It was odd for her to watch me so close, and I almost turned around to tell her to get lost. I thought my last chance in the town was a hostal. When I asked the clerk about the price, she said there were beds available at the adjacent *albergue* that she also managed. I went outside, and sure enough, I had missed the sign for the *albergue*.

Not only did I have a bed, I had an entire room to myself. Chances were, there wouldn't be any other idiots checking in so late. I gladly paid the €11, went to the bar, and bought some chips and a Coke Light. Across the street, a flock of sheep were tended by two men. It was a peaceful evening, and the bleats were carried gently by what was now only a breeze. The *albergue* was an old house, with only one washroom on the top floor. After I waited a few minutes for my turn, I had a quick shower and got ready for bed. The next day would be critical in terms of timing. I had another major historical center, the city of León, but it was about thirty-six kilometers away. If I was to get there in the early afternoon and spend the time I desired, I would need a spectacular morning of walking. For the most part, the terrain would be relatively flat, but there was a large hill before León to contend with. Despite my late start, I had walked forty kilometers and had a brand-new giant blister at the base of the toes on my right foot to show for it. My feet were sore, but my body felt good, just tired.

As I went to bed, I looked outside and saw a beautiful clear night, with stars that shone brightly. Without a doubt, this was the best night I had seen so far in Spain. Hopefully, it would be the same in the morning. Mentally, I had suffered through a tough day from walking so long into such a cold, strong wind. I didn't like being frustrated or angry at the weather. I didn't like swearing at the wind. I just wanted to be drenched in warm sun. As I went to bed, I had one final thought before I closed my eyes. It was a good thought. Earlier this morning, I had passed something very important – the halfway mark on the Camino.

I HATE TO LET YOU GO

Day 12

El Burgo Ranero to La Virgen del Camino

45.5 Km

With no heat, I woke up shivering at some point during the night and spread two blankets on top of me. At five o'clock, I woke up and just lay in bed for an hour until I was ready to get up. I felt rested after a good sleep. Having an entire room in an *albergue* had really helped. I was out the door by seven o'clock, my earliest start so far. It was a crisp morning, no more than 4°C, and the sun was yet to rise. The skies were clear, and it looked to be a fine day. I picked up an empanada and a Coke Light at a bar and headed out.

A pond and marshy area at the edge of El Burgo Ranero looked so peaceful, with yellow tufts of grasses protruding from its grayish-blue water. A bright orange building behind the pond caught the morning's first rays of sun. The gravel *senda* was lined with pilgrims as far as I could see. So this was what I missed every morning when I left at eight or nine or even ten o'clock. I walked fast to keep warm, but my body preferred to go slower. My mind and body chose a happy medium – a warm but comfortable pace.

The sun peeked over the horizon, and I couldn't remember the last time I had seen my long, morning shadow. Dazzling colors emerged, with greens from the fields and golden-browns from the recently plowed soil. The land was flat, with farmland in all directions. A Gothic cross stood prominently on top of a white pillar on the side of the road and glowed in the morning sun. With the warm sun on the back of my neck, I was in the best mood since I had started the Camino.

For the past few days, I had periodically sung in my head the rock band Seether's *6 Gun Quota*. It's such a cool, up-tempo song that makes me feel so alive. For the first time on the Camino, I brought out my iPhone and put in my earbuds. In the past, I had been reluctant to walk while listening to music, concerned what other pilgrims would think. Right now, I was in too good of a mood to worry. I listened to *6 Gun Quota* and felt energized and passed almost everyone. After the song was over, I played it again.

Then I played Shinedown's *If You Only Knew* because the lyrics of the chorus made me think of Sarah. When I had trouble sleeping in the *albergues*, I would picture her lying next to me. I hoped she knew and understood how much I missed her and how I cherished the time I spent with her and her son. And I hoped she was being good.

Next, I played *Otherside* by the Red Hot Chili Peppers, one of my absolute favorite songs. It may seem a little immature, but since the second or third day on the Camino, every time I would cross one of the beautiful stone bridges, I would sing, to myself, part of the song. Of course, it isn't about crossing over medieval bridges. However, I thought of it in the sense that across each bridge on the Camino was a new adventure, something unexpected. I would approach and take on whatever was waiting for me on the other side.

Next, I listened to something very special. Before I left home, I chose the Pat Metheny Group's brilliant instrumental *To The End Of The World* as the unofficial theme song for my journey. It was appropriate because Finisterre, my eventual destination, was on the Atlantic coast. In medieval times, Finisterre was considered to be at the end of the world. I can't explain how good this music makes me feel. When Pat Metheny plays his guitar solo at the six and a half minute mark, it never ceases to send a shiver down my spine.

After that, I played a few of my own songs, the first time in many months – well before my mom got sick. I have been an aspiring song-writer but remain unpublished. The last group of demos I made, I couldn't get anyone in a music or publishing company to listen to them. I never even got a chance to be rejected. It's a difficult business – not that I expect publishing a book to be much easier. One of my songs was written about someone once close to me who I cared deeply about. The person, who will remain nameless, brought me so much pain and grief, and after many years, I couldn't go through it any longer. For my own sanity, I had to make a tough decision and let go. It's difficult trying to help those who won't help themselves. Although it may not have been clear, all along, I was suffering too.

SUFFERING

Written by Randall St. Germain © 2006

Spend my days in disbelief
You lead a life of mystery
Always seem to lose control
And wonder why you're still alone
As your past starts to unfold
With each lie that you have told
Your voice is cracking from the strain
Years go by but you never change
Now you're suffering

I tried to warn you but you don't understand
Take another sip and there's no turning back
But I hate to let you go
When you're suffering
These habits you have weigh on my mind
With each day you're on borrowed time
But I hate to let you go

Troubled life that's incomplete
So much pain and misery
Fade away if you could
Tell me why you're misunderstood
Cover up hoping I won't find
Every little mess you leave behind
Breaks my heart when I look in your eyes
You're breathing still but dying inside
Now you're suffering

I tried to warn you but you don't understand
Take another sip and there's no turning back
But I hate to let you go
When you're suffering
These habits you have weigh on my mind
With each day you're on borrowed time
But I hate to let you go

Frozen in my mind is the message I hear when I won't answer
your call
Realized I'm wrong but now it's too late 'cause I don't know where
you are
And now I'm suffering

I tried to warn you but you don't understand
Take another sip and there's no turning back
But I hate to let you go
When you're suffering
These habits you have weigh on my mind
With each day you're on borrowed time
But I hate to let you go
When you're suffering

Anyone who has had a loved one go down a path of self-destruction can understand my lyrics. A woman with a beautiful voice sang on my demo of *Suffering*, and it always brings a tear to my eye. I have only played this song for my mom and a few friends. I will leave it there. Onward with my Camino.

Energized by the sun and music, I walked the thirteen kilometers to Reliegos at a fast pace, only slightly bothered by sore feet. On the outskirts, single-level homes and storage buildings had roofs covered in dirt and grass – I believe it was to conserve energy. The temperature dropped as dark clouds approached from the west. My pleasant, sunny morning was about to end. I began to feel sluggish and hoped that my fast pace of the morning wouldn't be a detriment for the afternoon. There was still a long way to León. After a brief break on a patio outside a bar, I left town on the gravel *senda* through fields with splashes of purple and yellow flowers and scattered red poppies.

I arrived at Mansilla de las Mulas just after eleven o'clock without a good break all morning. I wasn't expecting much from the town but was pleasantly surprised with the number of interesting sites. The entrance of the town had a pilgrim monument I had seen in photos but forgotten where it would be. It was a modern cement sculpture of two young, tired pilgrims sitting beneath a cross. The male, his head slumped, looked down toward his backpack. The girl looked over her right shoulder at the guy and was either tired or angry at him for being such an out-of-shape wimp. A group of pilgrims posed for photos, and I waited my turn. A French woman took my photo and then I took one of her and her two male companions. While I smiled in my photo, I didn't fully realize the theme, which was tiredness. The threesome all gave exhausted looks as if they couldn't go on anymore. I'll get it right next time.

A short walk away was the impressive Iglesia de Santa María, with its extremely bright burgundy and cream paint. It looked magnificent and was one of the best preserved or rebuilt *Mudéjar* style churches I had seen. It was closed, so I moved on to a café and picked up an empanada with beans and cheese enclosed in a wonderfully light pastry. The Roman option joined the Camino, and I couldn't help wondering what I had missed. I crossed the Río Esla on a stone bridge and marveled at the twelfth century city walls across the river. A few sections had crumbled, but surprisingly, much of it was intact.

On a gravel *senda*, I followed the left side of the highway besides a long stretch of flat farmland. The walk should have been easy, but I struggled even more. Progressively slower, I continued for almost an hour, until I saw a Galp gas station across the highway. I went inside and bought my favorites – Magnum ice cream, chocolate, mixed nuts, and a Coke Light. Outside, I sat next to a man from Slovenia who was also having his bout with tiredness. I gobbled my ice cream, hoping it would give me enough energy to fly to León. The man ate a sandwich that wasn't from the store, which looked much better than anything I had. With his limited English and my nonexistent Slovenian, we didn't have much to say but tried our best. When he was ready, he asked me to join him, but I needed more rest and told him to go ahead.

After my break, I continued but my feet, legs, shoulders, brain, and everything else were in some kind of discomfort. I didn't know how I was going to get through the day. There was still about fourteen kilometers to León, plus more in the evening. The *senda* ended at Villamoros de Mansilla, and the Camino followed the shoulder of the highway. Vehicles often raced well over the speed limit, and I hugged the edge every time I saw a truck approach. Besides the Slovenian, who was just ahead, there were few others walking. I didn't know what had happened to everyone. Without stopping, I passed through Villamoros de Mansilla and its one long road with two-story houses, empty overgrown lots, and flower and vegetable gardens.

Just before the town of Puente de Villarente, there was an impressive bridge with at least fourteen arches, with the Río Porma flowing through only two. The remainder spanned a park that included a playground and a football or soccer pitch. Two lanes of the bridge were for vehicles, with only a narrow sidewalk. The on and off ramps for pedestrians were only the width of my body. Again, I was concerned about the large trucks. Many of the old bridges in Spain had barely enough room for two-vehicle lanes, let alone a sidewalk.

Much of Puente de Villarente looked modern, with many businesses and apartments along the Camino. It was a long walk through the town, and I never stopped until the Repsol gas station on the far side. I bought a Coke Light and then crossed the highway and followed a gravel path through grasslands. Large construction vehicles working on the nearby highway had torn up small sections of the path, creating patches of mud. I was the only pilgrim around, so I draped my wet shirt on my backpack and carried my socks and underwear. The skies lightened up only briefly, and when it started to spit rain, I put everything away. A group of pilgrim cyclists rode by and all gave a loud *Buen Camino*, which I returned.

The Slovenian was sitting at a picnic table next to a fountain in Arcahueja. He looked beat and told me he couldn't walk anymore. He was going to see if there was a bed available at the small *albergue* nearby and asked me if I wanted to join him. For a brief moment, I thought about what he said, but I didn't think he meant "in the same bed." I explained that I wanted to get past León for the night, and he understood. We bid farewell, and I continued through the pleasant village, comprised mostly of single houses, before joining a gravel path, with the alto less than two kilometers ahead. The sprawling town of Valdelafuente was unique because the Camino didn't follow the main street but stayed in the field on the side of a hill. I struggled with the small climb to the alto that overlooked León – the sprawling city partly obscured by haze. A newer pedestrian bridge crossed the freeway, and there was a Brico Depot that looked similar to Home Depot back home. Entering León was different from the approach to Burgos because the Camino didn't wander through a lengthy commercial and industrial area.

When I entered Puente Castro, a suburb of León on the southeast side, two men stared at me from a street corner about fifty meters ahead. No one else was between us, and I only saw a woman walking about half a block past them. I became defensive and shifted on the street away from the sidewalk where they stood. One of them, a balding man in his 40's, leaped on the road and walked toward me. I quickly moved back onto the sidewalk but he changed course, and approached me with his right arm extended to shake my hand. He said something in Spanish, but I walked around him as fast as I could. I'm sure he only wanted money and was most likely harmless, but for a moment, I felt threatened. It was the first such encounter so far on the Camino, so I couldn't complain much.

The Camino followed a sidewalk through Puente Castro and its continuous buildings with businesses and homes. A church's bell gable had a large nest on every available spot, with each occupied by a stork. One nest was on the steep slope at the top, and I wondered how it stayed in place. At the Río Torio, the medieval bridge was reserved for vehicles, with a newer footbridge for pilgrims. The old bridge had at least twelve arches, but most spanned well manicured parkland. The entrance was flanked by two stone lions with evil expressions. Overhead, there was a Mercadona billboard, and I looked forward to visiting my favorite store, assuming I could find it.

When I entered León, it was three-thirty and later than I had hoped. I had walked thirty-six kilometers, and the last ten were very challenging. I was happy to arrive and wanted to make the best of my time. My goal for the night was the suburb of La Virgen del Camino, about ten kilometers away, and I had to allow enough time to get there. I always thought the origins of the city name, León, referred to a lion but was surprised to learn it was derived from the Latin word "Legio," meaning legion. León was once part of the Seventh Legion of Roman soldiers that guarded the city. In the first century, León was a major center for the gold trade. It has been an important Camino city for centuries and once had many pilgrim hospices. Today, León is the capital of the province of León and has a metro population of about 206,000, with tourism and services being the most important industries.

Through the modern section of León, I looked around and took photos. I thought I was paying attention but was shocked when I arrived at the municipal *albergue*, two kilometers off the Camino. What went wrong? The sidewalk was well-marked with yellow arrows, so I wasn't lost or wandering. I was pissed off and had to find a way back to the Camino. I thought about backtracking but wanted to see something different. The Plaza de Santa Ana now would be my destination, but my map didn't show most of the city streets. A man in a business suit was eager to give me directions, and I followed his lead but soon realized I was headed back to the *albergue*. I turned around, and after walking many blocks, I arrived at the Plaza de Toros, not where I had intended. However, I was happy to find the plaza, which had a new monument celebrating León's anniversary. It was constructed with wrought iron, with the years 910 to 2010 circumventing the inside of a roundabout and a large lion in the middle. Across the road was the León Arena, built in the 1940's and famous for bullfighting. I wondered what the arena looked like inside. In North America, most old arenas have long been replaced with large, modern buildings.

By now, it was raining, and I still had to find my way back to the Camino. I followed the Calle de la Corredera toward the San Francisco Jardin. It was a delightful walk, even in the rain, with interesting old and modern buildings. A shopping district had expensive designer shops and elegant buildings with lots of glass. I didn't see other pilgrims, but the streets were busy with tourists and people leaving work. San Francisco Jardin and the adjacent plaza had beautiful sculptures and fountains with gardens that were pleasantly planted with spring flowers but not overwhelming. My favorite sculpture was of a bearded shepherd with his arms outstretched as he looked toward the heavens. A sheep and a dog sat at his feet above a bed of white flowers. I sensed I would be looking toward the heavens too, if I didn't find the Camino soon. I didn't know how much extra I had walked, but I was exhausted.

Magnificent Roman walls appeared in a modern part of the city; however, they looked out of the place amongst the newer buildings. Maybe better said, the newer buildings looked out of place amongst the Roman walls.

Finally, I arrived on the Camino in the old city, with its wonderful, narrow streets. Cafés, bars, and shops were on the lower levels, with houses and offices on the upper floors. I had missed at least two kilometers of the Camino and proceeded to walk back. When I made it to the junction, as expected, I found yellow arrows that led both ways. I never thought it would have been so easy to go off course, but it wasn't all bad. I had seen a part of León I never would have otherwise. For two hours, I had constantly walked around the city but still hadn't seen the León Cathedral. I turned around and walked back along the Camino. Despite the pouring rain, the old city was bustling with pilgrims, tourists, and residents. I looked at old churches, buildings, and shops, until I arrived at the Plaza Regla in front of the cathedral. I was excited and called Sarah, but we had a bad connection. She couldn't understand where I was. I repeated "Leon, Leon" without the Spanish accent, but I think she heard something else. I bought her a postcard so she knew where I had called from.

Although the León Cathedral was not as extravagant as the one in Burgos, it was still one of the best on the Camino. My highlight of the interior was the nave with the beautiful stained glass windows, each one a piece of art. I arrived at the cathedral late in the day, and I was very tired. It was difficult for me to thoroughly enjoy myself, and I didn't stay long. Added to that, after the Burgos Cathedral, I had set my expectations too high.

I went into the old city and looked for a place to eat. It was six o'clock, and I still had more sightseeing plus the walk to La Virgen del Camino. If I had had more time, I would have chosen one of the many tapas bars. Instead, I ate a chicken sub and fries at a café until I was stuffed. Again, the lack of washrooms was an issue in León, and I made sure I used the one in the café. I headed back to the plaza and took one more look around the cathedral before leaving. After a pleasant walk, I arrived at the Plaza San Marcos. Here, the former monastery and adjacent museum had a beautiful façade with many intricate details. It dated to the sixteenth century and was used as a monastery until the nineteenth. Today, the former monastery is an upscale Parador hotel. In the middle of the plaza stood an ancient *cruceiro* and a statue of a tired, worn-out pilgrim leaning against the base. The plaza, with its gardens, monuments, and art, was alone worth the visit to León.

Near the plaza, I crossed the Río Bernesga on an elaborate sixteenth century stone bridge, reserved for pedestrians only. In front of me, four men in their late teens wrestled a man in his 30's to the ground. They didn't steal anything but roughed him up well. The older man was accompanied by an elderly woman, who began yelling at the young men in Spanish. The teenagers took off, followed by the older guy yelling at them. The elderly woman was left standing alone on the bridge. It was a crazy sight, too much for my tired mind to handle. The old woman wasn't hurt, and there wasn't anything I could do anyway, so I did what I did best – I kept walking. The suburbs of León started on a cobblestone walkway, with a park on one side that led to an area with many businesses of all kinds. I found Mercadona and bought my normal assortment of food and supplies. Again, I left with a full shopping bag.

Along a sidewalk, I climbed steeply through a shabby area with older houses before a stretch with an industrial area on the left and grass fields to the right. The sun came out, and it was the warmest part of the day – cold rain to warm sunshine in one hour. On the main street of La Virgen del Camino, I stopped at a Repsol station for a Coke Light before continuing up the hill toward the *albergue*. A hostal was farther down, but I didn't want to take the chance of it being full or too expensive. After walking many blocks up the hill, I couldn't find the *albergue*, which didn't seem to be where it showed on my map. I asked a man for directions, but he didn't know what an *albergue* was. Thinking I somehow missed it, I walked halfway down the hill but didn't even see a sign for the *albergue*. Flabbergasted and exhausted, I looked again at the hostal below. After contemplating for a moment, I decided to take a chance and hoped they still had a room. I didn't have the energy to walk back up again and would have most likely spent the night in a dumpster if there was nothing available. I was lucky. The small but clean room was reasonable: €24, including Wi-Fi. I checked in at nine o'clock, had my shower, washed my clothes, and collapsed on the bed.

The distance I had walked along the Camino was about 45.5 kilometers, but with my extra wandering around León, I'm sure it was over fifty. It was certainly my toughest day so far. Most of the afternoon, I had persevered with little energy. Before I went to bed, I thought I'd give Sarah a quick call to say good night. She was lonely, and we talked well past my bedtime. When I saw it was midnight, I told her I had to go to bed. I laid my iPhone beside my pillow and immediately fell asleep. It was the third night in a row I was by myself, and I knew I would have a tough time sleeping in a room with others again.

I MISSED ALL THE SNORING AND FARTING

Day 13
La Virgen del Camino to Astorga
44 Km

It was only six o'clock and certainly not my intention to wake up so early. I checked the internet and called Sarah, talking until it was well past seven and time to get ready. My feet were awful, with a huge new blister in a terrible location on the back of my heel. At the Mercadona, I had made a mistake and bought elastic bandage, instead of tape. Now I had to conserve tape until I could buy more. There was no point in wasting the elastic bandage, so I experimented with double and triple layers to cushion older blisters. Still exhausted, I moved slowly all morning and never stepped outside until after nine o'clock.

My backpack was extra heavy, with the large chocolate bar and two bags of mixed nuts from Mercadona. The washed clothes were only half-dry, but I had a warm, sunny morning ahead of me, and they wouldn't take long to finish. I stretched my tight and sore muscles and knew I would be taking it easy for a while. Now, I had to cross the busy highway to get to the gas station. I suppose I could have walked up the hill to the stoplight, crossed the road, walked back down the hill, bought my pop, and walked back up the hill. That would have been too much, so instead, I ran across the busy highway and jumped over the median with my backpack on, which is something I don't advise. As a reward for my efforts, I bought two Coke Lights, and then walked back up the same hill I had the previous evening.

I looked back at León and hoped I could visit the city again when I had more time. Maybe I would have appreciated the cathedral more if I hadn't been so tired. From León, a steady stream of pilgrims walked up the hill in La Virgen del Camino. Most looked happy, although some were tired with the steep climb to start the day. The hills that I had to contend with would be later in the afternoon. La Virgen del Camino had many businesses, including cafés and stores, but most were closed. It was a modern suburb with a newer church, and I didn't see much along the Camino that looked historically important. The *albergue* ended up being two blocks away from where I had stopped looking. Oh, well, everything worked out fine with the hostal. Across from the church, I veered down a small hill, past an old murky fountain, and to an option. It was another mess of yellow hand-painted directions and arrows on the pavement, with two crudely written signs. However, the directions were clear, and I took the left route toward Villar de Mazarife.

My legs loosened, and I began to find my pace on a reddish-brown dirt and gravel road through flat, overgrown fields. I crossed two highways in close proximity and then had a short walk to Fresno del Camino, a small suburb of León with playgrounds and modern houses. From Fresno del Camino, I followed a secondary road up a short hill. On the way, I took off my fleece sweater and wore only a T-shirt for the first time since the third day. Not wearing so many layers created a packing problem, and I had difficulty stuffing my backpack with clothing I normally wore. I thought about changing into my shorts but still couldn't trust the weather. It had to get cold and rainy at some point during the day. It always did. The track pants were a nice change from the rain pants that I had been wearing every one of the last eight days. It was hard to believe; before I left, I thought I would wear rain pants for maybe five days at the most.

I ate chocolate and nuts as I walked along the road through a scrubby hillside, which led down a hill to the Río Oncina. The village of Oncina de la Valdoncina had pleasant two-level houses, many with bright colors of orange and pink with white porches and an abundance of flowers and shrubs. It was a place where people could live close to a city without any sign of a city. Two friendly men greeted me as I passed by. We tried a little conversation, but an older woman on the porch of a home yelled, and the men became preoccupied with whatever she was saying.

From the village, the Camino followed a long stretch of orange gravel road through a flat, dry landscape of grassland and farmland with scattered trees. The temperature was about 10°C, certainly not hot, but excellent for walking. My shirt was hanging from the side of my backpack, and I brought out my socks and underwear to dry. Pilgrims were spread out, but I always hid my underwear when I got close to anyone. I felt great and passed many people, hiding my underwear every time. I was long past the embarrassment that carrying my socks brought, although I'm sure it looked strange.

As I passed a young man, I heard, "Hey, where are you from?" I put my socks in the bag and shook hands with Steven from Alberta, Canada. For days, I had talked little with other pilgrims and was happy for some company, especially a fellow Canadian. Steven was in his 20's and had traveled in South America before he arrived in Europe. On sort of a whim and short notice, Steven decided to walk the Camino, and his religious family was proud of his pilgrimage. He had an obvious limp and wasn't sure what was wrong with his foot. I don't think Steven understood the stress his body would endure from walking so far. When he asked how long I had been walking for, instead of telling me that I was crazy or a similar response, he said he had met someone else who walked all day like I did.

Her name was Claudia from Belgium. I couldn't believe it. Steven had met Claudia at an *albergue* in León. She had injured her foot, and the doctor told her to rest for a few days. Although we were sad that Claudia was hurt, Steven and I both smiled at the thought of meeting the same person among thousands of others.

We walked and talked through the village of Chozas de Abajo and back on the same flat road through the same grassland. We discussed the Camino, hockey, and Canada. Steven's limp got worse, but he didn't want to stop. However, when we arrived at Villar de Mazarife, he said he couldn't go on. We stopped for photos of the large mural dedicated to pilgrims and walked into the village. Two *albergues* were on opposite sides of the road, and one advertised a physiotherapist, the first I had seen at an *albergue* or even a village. It was a coincidence – possibly a blessing – and we both laughed. After walking for about two hours together, I bid farewell to Steven; it was a shame to lose his company. I never saw him again.

At the edge of the small plaza, a store was surprisingly well-stocked and had good prices. The owner was a friendly woman who coaxed me to try a fruit pastry. I took one, and she encouraged me to take another. Then I added tape, chocolate, nuts, a Coke Light, and a Magnum ice cream. My bill was over €10, but I had so much good stuff.

The early afternoon sun was out, and I needed a break. I had already walked about fifteen kilometers without stopping for more than a few moments. A small park near the end of the village was perfect, and I chose a bench in the sun. Being able to remove my boots and socks in the middle of the day always felt great. These were the breaks I enjoyed. Not the "hide in a bar to get out of the cold" breaks. Outdoor breaks in the sun were all I needed. I wasn't alone in the park. A weary pilgrim sat on a bench while another was sprawled out on the lawn. A local woman tended to her two children as they laughed and played. I savored my ice cream as I wrote a postcard from the León Cathedral to Sarah. I could have stayed in the park all afternoon, but as much as I enjoyed walking with Steven, we were slower than my usual pace. Astorga was still thirty kilometers away, and I would have to move my Canadian ass if I wanted to arrive before dark.

The Camino followed a flat, paved road through fertile farmland, where the soil was worked by large tractors and loaders harvesting crops of giant potatoes. At least, I thought they were potatoes, because some of them were the size of cantaloupes. It was incredible for this city boy to see large dump trucks carrying away heaping loads of potatoes. As the trucks pulled away, the odd potato would bounce off the load and crash on the road. Along this stretch, an elaborate irrigation system became evident. Old cement and stone aqueducts along with wider, modern ones carried large volumes of water to the fields. Many of the narrow aqueducts were a meter above ground, and again, I couldn't understand how the water got so high. Where did it even come from? Was there a pump? Does water climb? I had no idea.

After Villar de Mazarife, I only saw three other pilgrims in front of me on the long stretch of road. I passed one, and two were far ahead. Cars sped by, and the drivers apparently liked the flat, straight road with no police around. I thought about the police; beside a few officers in the big cities and the two just past Nájera, I hadn't seen any. Not once had I seen a police officer in a village. Was there no crime in the villages? Do people police themselves? What happens if the neighbor's dog takes a dump on your lawn, you take a dump on your neighbor's lawn, and then your neighbor comes over with a shotgun; do you call 911? Was there a 911? I had many of these questions. As I walked, I would think of something, only for that thought to soon be replaced by another. Many of my questions are still unanswered. Most of my questions are long forgotten.

The road I had followed for over an hour ended, and the Camino veered onto a gravel road near a small stand of trees. The two men who were in front of me rested beside a wide aqueduct. I said *hola*, and one of them mumbled something back. The other didn't even look up at me. I sensed I was interrupting something very private between them, so I let them be. I descended a small hill and saw Villavante ahead, its church tower rising against the darkening skies to the west. Now only separating me from the village were large, recently plowed fields and about two kilometers of country roads. Villavante had an attractive *Mudéjar* style church, with a recently renovated façade and tower. The orangey-red bricks and peach-colored trim stood out brilliantly against the last patch of blue sky. It was three o'clock as I sat outside a bar eating another Magnum. My new blister was killing me, and I took off my boot to relieve some pressure. The afternoon was warm, at least 12°C, but there were clouds rolling in, and it looked like the fine weather was about to end. I wanted to get as far as I could before the rain started. I nicely folded my dry clothes and stuffed them in the backpack. Dry, somewhat clean clothes equal happiness on the Camino. At least, for me they did.

After the village, I walked beside train tracks, past another giant pile of giant potatoes, and back on another flat gravel road through more farmland. The road ended, and the Camino followed the side of a paved secondary road, crossed the highway, and entered the town of Hospital de Órbigo. The *Mudéjar* church two blocks on my right had three huge stork nests on its bell gable and one on an adjacent house. Each nest was occupied by a stork standing on guard. I was lucky to have a good vantage point to see all four so close to each other.

After a short walk on a narrow, cobbled street, I arrived at the wonderful bridge for which Hospital de Órbigo was famous. Really, I had no understanding how magnificent it would be. The bridge had an amazing nineteen arches with the Río Órbigo flowing through only three. Similar to recent bridges, most of the span was over parkland. It was the width of a car but reserved for pedestrians only. The bridge itself was longer than many of the hamlets on the Camino.

The medieval bridge had been destroyed and rebuilt many times over the years. Many battles, including ones involving Napoleon, are part of the history of Hospital de Órbigo. The only problem, at least for viewing, was the scaffolding for a major restoration was required on the sides while a large part of the surface was being rebuilt. Photos that didn't show signs of the restoration proved difficult, so I accepted the bridge as it was. Maintenance is a necessity for the longevity of these old bridges. I was thrilled to walk along the span, and it was one of the highlights of my Camino.

The town was clean and had many cafés and shops, but after the bridge, everything else was anticlimactic. I had enough food for the day and didn't stop until the far edge of the town. My heel was in considerable pain, so I took off my boot and sock to find the blister had completely split. I re-bandaged the blister and cursed myself for not fixing it earlier.

A flat, gravel road led through farmland, and there was no one else in sight. My foot was better, but I still felt every step. It was almost five o'clock, though, and I had to keep a good pace. After the quiet hamlet of Villares de Órbigo, the Camino passed through a natural area with grasses, shrubs, and trees. After a short climb, a rough path led to a gravel road and more farmland, with the hamlet of Santibáñez de Valdeiglesias ahead. I felt my first raindrops of the day and reluctantly put on my rain gear. Couldn't I have one day without rain? Was I asking too much? By the time I arrived in the Santibáñez de Valdeiglesias, I was in the midst of a mighty, spring downpour. I suppose I was asking too much, after all.

There was an *albergue* in the village, but Astorga was where I wanted to stay. This was one of the first times I would really challenge myself. As I walked the Camino, I became stronger and faster. Normally around midday, I would have a few hours of sluggishness, through which I had to persevere. Once evening came, I usually felt great. Now, I had less than three hours of daylight with two altos and eleven kilometers ahead. I didn't think about the possibility of injury or bandits. I only thought about getting to Astorga before dark.

After Santibañez de Valdeiglesias, the landscape was beautiful, with vineyards, orchids, and brownish-red soil among the bright greens of the grasses and farmland. At times, the Camino marking was interesting. Instead of signs or markers, stones protruding from the path were splashed with yellow paint that sometimes had worn off. I had to be careful I was on the right route, since it was late in the day, and I didn't have time to waste looking for the Camino. The first hill tired me, but I walked at the best pace I could. The only people I saw were two men inspecting their vineyard. Nearby, a folk art pilgrim monument featured a young man with a fly-fishing pole next to a cross. Okay, I think the fishing pole was supposed to be a walking stick – a four-meter-high walking stick. After a short drop, a dirt path led through hayfields and ancient-looking vineyards. Other fields were more natural, with yellow and purple flowers among the young pine forest. I descended to a small stream, where oak trees stood in rows and were spaced equally apart. Old walls, once used to enclose livestock or someone's home, had crumbled to mere piles of brown earth.

Nearing exhaustion, I climbed until the terrain flattened. Ahead, an isolated long red brick building looked like it was used for storage or to hold livestock on a farm. However, there was no farm around, and I couldn't quite figure out what the building was for. A bowl of fruit and a jar of money sat on an outside table. A sign said the offerings were free or by donation.

With gray skies and no one else around, I did find this area a little spooky. At times, the markings were difficult to follow, and I had to be careful not to lose the Camino. Again, stones in the ground were splashed with yellow paint, but some had worn off. At one crossroad, there were only small stones shaped to form an arrow pointing the direction of the Camino. At least, I hoped it was the right way. I was happy to arrive at the alto and the Cruceiro de Santo Toribio. The city of Astorga was still a long way below.

I descended on a sidewalk along the steep road, past vineyards and homes. San Justo de la Vega was almost deserted. I stopped in front of a bar and mailed the postcard I had written earlier. A couple saw me and stared as if I was crazy to be walking so late. I peered through the window of a hostal and contemplated asking if they had a room. However, it was time I got back to the *albergue* life. I missed all the snoring and farting. How was I going to manage when I got back home? I would have to stay at a local hostel when I needed my fix of snoring and farting. With patches of blue sky overhead, I crossed over the Río Tuerto on an old bridge that had cracks and large pieces of stone missing. As I walked by, I waved to a man fishing on the river shore.

I wearily sauntered along a gravel road that glistened in the evening sun. On my right was green, peaceful farmland, while on my left was the backside of industrial buildings. On this stretch, I felt isolated and thought if I was going to be accosted, it would be here. I had felt that way before, and just like before, nothing happened. Past the industrial area, there was a small, rebuilt Roman bridge with three arches and a stream flowing through one, as well as through the foundations of a nearby home. Living with running water constantly underneath one's home would take some getting used to, I would imagine. Outside, a man cut logs while a Labrador cross dog intently watched me pass by. There was one unexpected climb over railway tracks on an elaborate pedestrian bridge. After at least two stories of stairs, my legs and mind pleaded, "No more!"

I had expected to stay in the main *albergue* at the top of the hill in Astorga. However, I was pleasantly surprised to find a new, private one that wasn't on my map. It was 8:45 P.M., and I was dead tired after another long day. I was lucky there were plenty of beds. The *hospitalero* wasn't very friendly and said few words. He signed me in, took my €6, and showed me the dorm. An older man from Germany was the only one there. I'm sure he thought he was going to be alone and never expected someone to arrive so late. He was friendly, and we talked briefly before I had a shower and something to eat. During the day, I had taken many photos and had to charge at least one camera battery. I had walked about forty-four kilometers and about ninety over two days. I couldn't complain but wondered if I could keep up the pace. Walking that much almost seemed insane.

As I sat eating nuts and chocolate, I thought about the next day, which would likely be the most difficult. I had to climb into the mountains, with two altos and the most elevation gain since the first day through the Pyrenees. I needed a good sleep to rest my tired body. However, even that wouldn't prepare me for what was upcoming – the absolute worst day on the Camino.

WHO ELSE WOULD I DREAM ABOUT?

Day 14
Astorga to El Acebo
39.5 Km

During the night, my roommate made a few trips to the washroom, and that, combined with his occasional snoring, ensured I had a restless sleep. He began to get ready at five-thirty, and although he tried to be quiet, he apologized when he saw I was awake. I told him not to worry, I had intended to get an early start. However, I was thinking more like eight o'clock and not six. He was ready quickly and said goodbye. Tired and sore, I didn't get up. If I had been in nicer accommodations, I might have lain there for hours.

The night had been chilly, and at some point I reached out and covered myself with one of the rarely-washed blankets at the foot of the bed. I assumed it wasn't pleasant outside, and when I finally managed the courage to look out the window, I was sad to see a gloomy, rainy morning. It reminded me when I left Ventosa, except this time I wouldn't have the relatively flat ground of La Rioja. Ahead, there were mountains and the possibility of snow, which I dreaded walking through. My new blisters looked bad, and I took extra time getting my feet ready. I put on almost every layer I had – gloves, tuque, fleece, wind jacket, rain jacket, rain pants, pack cover, and poncho – before emerging at eight o'clock to a harsh wind pelting my face with rain. Above, a layer of fog covered Astorga. I knew it was going to be a shitty day.

Astorga was once a Roman stronghold and has always been an important Camino city as a resting point before the trip west into the mountains. Not only were there Roman ruins and historical landmarks with beautiful architecture, it was a tourist city with modern services. I didn't read much about Astorga before I arrived; I only knew that one of the options from another Camino, the Via de la Plata from Seville, joined here somewhere. Along the streets were many cafés and shops, although most were closed at the early hour. The shops that were open catered to pilgrims and had clothing, food, and medical supplies. They also had Camino souvenirs that were sold mostly to tourists who didn't walk the Camino but pretended they did.

At the Iglesia San Francisco, I was more interested by the adjoining two-story building, which was dwarfed by the main one. It looked like a chapel and had an interesting, showy gable with nine bells. A sign in Spanish stood outside, but I couldn't understand much. In front of the church were the ruins of a Roman building covered with a glass roof. There wasn't much left to see, mostly crumbled walls and foundations, but a small area of tile or mosaics remained.

Across from the church, the main *albergue* had beds for over 150 people. I couldn't imagine staying there when it was full; I didn't think I'd sleep much. Hell, I wasn't sleeping much with one other pilgrim in the room. The elegant city hall had its bell-tower flanked by figures of a man and woman dressed in black above a giant stone coat of arms. Only one other man stood in the plaza on this dreary morning. I'm sure on a better day, it would have been bustling with people. The exteriors of the palace and cathedral were simply magnificent. I never thought the Astorga Cathedral would be so detailed and intricate, even comparable to the one in León. I would have loved to spend some time inside at the very least, but none of the buildings were opened. Astorga surprised me, and I never budgeted time for sightseeing. In the future, I'll spend a good part of a day there.

From the city center, I walked through a residential area and down an incline to a busy highway. I kept a good pace on the sidewalk and only stopped at the Ermita del Ecce Homo, a small, charming church with a welcome sign in nine languages. Other than the Ermita, the outskirts of Astorga was uneventful, with a rolling landscape mixed with farmland, scattered homes, and the odd industrial building. The rain continued, with no sign of letting up.

After I crossed over the freeway, there was a gravel *senda* and its large puddles that slowed me down. Thankfully, Murias de Rechivaldo soon appeared, and although I hadn't walked for long, I was already disgusted with the weather and needed to take cover, which I found at an *albergue* at the end of the hamlet. I didn't need a drink but felt obliged to buy something. The friendly *hospitalera* only had regular Coke, which I never drank, but she welcomed me to sit outside under the covered patio. I had planned to stay the night in Molinaseca, on the other side of the mountain, but it would be difficult because of the slow conditions. Soon, I felt a chill and couldn't sit outside any longer.

After Murias de Rechivaldo, the road climbed gently as the landscape changed from farmland to scrubby fields of grass and shrubs. Crumbling slate walls and the ruins of homes were scattered across the fields. A constant stream of wet pilgrims bravely headed toward the mountains, and I passed many as I warmed up. It was difficult to look around much, and if I did, I would often get a face full of rain. With the low clouds, I couldn't see the mountains ahead, and even the short hills nearby were obscured by a light fog. Two rough-looking, middle-aged men stood beside a pickup truck in the pouring rain and seemed to be looking for someone. They stared at everyone as they walked by, and I couldn't tell if someone was missing or wanted, but it was an odd sight.

With Santa Catalina de Somoza just ahead, I stopped at a barren rest stop with only a few picnic tables and benches. Sarah had asked for a photo with me wearing the florescent green 2010 Winter Games poncho, and with the camera timer, I took a few of myself adorned in drenched rain gear. The entrance to Santa Catalina de Somoza was gloomy, with hundreds of meters of crumbling stone and slate walls. The church tower rose in the fog above a puddle filled dirt path, the edges overgrown with grass and shrubs. I needed a good break out of the cold. Despite being small, Santa Catalina de Somoza had three *albergues*, but I was only interested in the bar. Although it did cross my mind, I wasn't planning to get drunk. I only needed some warmth, a little food, and a Coke Light.

I looked through the window at the busy bar, and there was only one small table left. Obviously, I wasn't the only one wanting to get away from the weather. As I maneuvered around the pilgrims who gathered under the small cover outside the bar's entrance, a woman who was leaving saw my poncho and asked me with a slight drawl if I was from Vancouver. Immediately, I knew she was American. To this point, I hadn't seen too many Americans on the Camino. I knew they were out there because I had heard about them. However, sightings were rare, at least for me, and I never saw one with an American flag. Besides the Americans in St. Jean and the one who took my photo in the Pyrenees, I didn't remember seeing another since.

Julie was from the state of Oregon and was very friendly and extremely talkative. She assumed I had attended many events during the 2010 Winter Games, but I explained that I was only at one, which wasn't really a sporting event. It was a medal presentation and concert by the Vancouver rock band, Theory of a Deadman. She gave me a blank look; I don't think she had heard of them. However, I did attend many of the festivities and saw the pavilions, but she wasn't impressed. Julie came to Vancouver to *see* the games, and she *saw* a whole lot more than I did.

Of course, the topic turned to the Camino, and she asked how long I had been walking. When I told her it was my fourteenth day, she gave me a look of bewilderment and said, "Please don't take offense, but that is simply crazy." By now, I had heard similar responses many times, and instead of being offended, I took them as compliments. Julie had walked ten days longer but developed foot problems, which forced her to take some time off. I could tell she would be happy when her Camino was over. If I had known we would talk in the cold for twenty minutes, I would have invited her to join me inside. We both shivered and had to go in our separate directions, Julie back on the Camino and me into the bar. We bid each other farewell, and I wished the American pilgrim a wonderful journey.

A table was still available in a warm spot away from the smokers and the front door. I was hungry and ordered an empanada with sausage and tomato sauce. I sat, ate, and drank until another twenty minutes had passed and I had to coax myself to leave. My poncho never dried and now was wet inside from condensation and being so close to other wet jackets. Between Santa Catalina de Somoza and El Ganso, the landscape opened up with much of it for grazing. I never saw any animals though, and it seemed they were inside somewhere and much smarter than me. A stretch along a gravel road took an hour, but I only remembered the fog, the cold, the puddles, and having my face pelted with rain every time I looked up.

Entering El Ganso, I passed more stone walls in various states of crumble and had my first exposure to what is known as *Maragato* architecture. The houses were typically one level and built with large slate stones. Originally, the roofs were thatched, but now, most had tiles or other materials. Homes in ruin would be missing all or part of their roofs. The church and many homes had been recently renovated or rebuilt, giving the village a sign of renewal. There was a lively bar, but I didn't stop. It was noon, and I had a long walk ahead.

As I left the village, the skies and rain lightened slightly, but dark clouds continued to obscure the mountains. I badly wanted to know if there was snow ahead. Most of the pilgrims walked on the shoulder of the road, while I stayed on the *senda*. After a kilometer of walking through mud and puddles, I couldn't take it anymore and joined the others on the road. The landscape was mostly farmland to start, but as I climbed, trees and short shrubs became more prevalent. The road was busy, and often, there was little or no shoulder to walk on. At times, I even jumped over the barrier when I was afraid of getting hit.

Once, there was so much traffic, with large trucks and speeding cars, I gave the *senda* another try. Ahead, a young woman walked through the mud and puddles with running shoes that were once white with pink trim. She had a tough time and often slipped. As I passed, I said *hola*, and she barely managed one back. At one point, the *senda* led through a pine forest. I enjoyed the patches of heather with pink and purple flowers but hated the mud, which was worse away from the road. When I emerged from the pine, I jumped on the road and stayed on it until Rabanal del Camino. Finally, I could see the mountains, and they revealed what I dreaded all morning. Snow!

The small church in Rabanal del Camino was recently rebuilt with bright stones and a new door. Many of the homes along the deserted main street were also recently rebuilt, while others lay in sad, crumbling ruins. Pilgrims packed a bar, and after walking twenty-two kilometers through difficult conditions, I decided to join them. I didn't want a large meal and just ordered fries and a Coke Light. Across from me, a man in his 30's tried to impress two women and managed to talk them into walking with him. He even discussed where they would stay that night. One of the women was interested, while the other looked at her friend in disbelief. I ate my fries and almost ordered another before I looked out and saw only sprinkles of rain. By the time I got outside, the rain had stopped, and the skies lightened. It would be a sunny afternoon. Or so I thought.

From Rabanal del Camino, a gravel road soon turned to a dirt path with mud and huge puddles. At one spot, a small pond had formed, and everyone walked a few meters through the grass to get around it. This was far worse than the mud earlier. I was desperate not to get my boots wet and walked as far as I needed around the puddles and mud. At first, the path was a gentle ascent through scrubby grassland. Then

I climbed a steep, rocky trail where I passed the two women and the guy from the bar. One woman struggled as the guy waited impatiently above and encouraged her to move a little faster. I didn't think he liked me passing them because when I smiled at him, he looked away. The women didn't have a problem and said *hola* back. I wished them all a *Buen Camino*.

After I crossed the road, there was a gentle climb to the village of Foncebadón. I looked up the main street and saw that half of the homes were in ruins, far worse than the previous villages. Foncebadón was once a thriving village, important during Roman times when they built a road for moving goods and travelers through the mountain pass. Many of the ruins had only large piles of stone or short jagged walls remaining. On the side of the main street, a rough gravel road, stood the Cruz de Foncebadón – a cross carved out of wood, stained dark, and mounted on a centuries-old stone and cement base. A sign stated not to place stones beneath the cross, and there were none. As I faced the village, to the right of the cross was a home in ruins, while on the left was an occupied one with an unsightly roof patched with numerous sheets of metal and other materials seemingly picked from the garbage.

I was tired from the climb and stopped at the *albergue* for a break. I bought a Kas orange drink and sat in the back of the communal area. A baby played on the floor in the hallway at the bottom of the stairs, and I had to be careful not to step on her. She laughed as she played, and the mother periodically checked on her. A woman came down the stairs and saw the baby at the last moment. I was just about to yell when she looked down. Seriously, I thought the sun would emerge at some point, but when I went outside, it was pouring rain. I was not happy as I walked through the rest of the village, past a lonely wooden cross and the ruins of the Hospital de San Juan. There wasn't much left but a two-story section, which looked like it was once a tower. The crumbling was so far advanced, I honestly couldn't see it standing for much longer.

The dirt and gravel path was muddy with large puddles. I climbed a scrubby hillside, and soon, the rain was mixed with snow. The valley below was encased in fog, and even the alto, which I assumed was close, was in the clouds. I passed a small stone church, which I thought was old but was surprised to find out later it was built in 1982. Finally,

I saw the alto and the highest point on the entire French Way, La Cruz de Ferro. Next to it, a white van was parked, and a man and woman stared at the cross from inside their warm, dry vehicle. How dare they drive up here? Better yet, maybe I should catch a ride with them off this damn mountain. By now, the snow was sloppy, falling in giant flakes. I felt a spot on my shoulder where water had seeped through, and worst of all, for the first time on the Camino, my feet were wet. What a shitty day! I couldn't even share my misery with anyone because, once again, I was the only one walking. I hadn't seen another pilgrim since Foncebadón.

A short section of the Camino next to the road was being worked on by three men. It was a convenient location and easy for the crew to access, but the work stopped once the path veered away from the road, leaving another muddy mess to walk on. Farther on, I passed an ancient graveyard overgrown with trees and shrubs. Ahead of me was the most haunting site on the entire Camino – more haunting than anything I had seen in my life – the village of Manjarín.

Almost every slate and stone building was in some state of ruin. Of the first twelve buildings I passed, I think only one had a roof and was occupied. There were some signs of life at a small *albergue* that existed amongst the rubble. Outside, a sign showed distances to various places, including 222 kilometers to Santiago. If I survived my time on the mountain, I would be past the three-quarter mark sometime during the next day. Across the road was a privy, one of the few washrooms on the Camino. It would have been a welcome sight on the *senda* a few days earlier.

Although I was wet and tired, I took my time in Manjarín. Each house, no matter the state, had a sense of character. Some houses sent shivers up my spine, and I wondered what had happened to the people who were once there. Did they abandon the village, or did the village die with them? I became particularly fascinated with a spot at the base of a tree on a bank above the road. Closely laid slabs of slate resembled gravestones but didn't have inscriptions or engravings. I walked up the stairs for a closer look but still had no idea what it was. Was it a graveyard? A play area? I couldn't figure it out. I looked back at Manjarín – an ominous, yet stunning site – and knew I might never see anything like it again.

I continued on the dirt path and came across the worst and potentially dangerous section on the Camino. Here, the trail traversed a steep hillside, but there was a huge puddle, at least a few inches deep and impassable. On the left-hand side was a military area protected by an electric fence. On the right was a steep bank covered in rock and shrubs. Now what? I had no idea if the electric fence was working and sure wasn't going to touch it with so much water on the ground. I preferred not to scramble up the hillside either. It was steep and wet, and the rocks were either jagged or slippery. I don't mean to rant, but this pertains to what I mentioned before. It's easier to repair or maintain a trail when it's close to a road but more difficult when a section, such as this, is isolated. Isn't it in everyone's best interest to have a trail that is at least maintained to a certain respectable and safe level? I would suggest that many of the officials who are responsible for looking after the Camino have never even walked much of it. Maybe in the city, but not out here, especially during wet weather.

I decided against testing the electric fence and grabbed a branch of a shrub and, with some slipping and sliding, pulled myself onto the bank above the giant puddle. With more slipping and sliding, I managed to work my way down to the other side. I was pissed off. This section was by far the worst of the day. The mud was horrible, and the puddles were large and numerous.

After one more climb, I was happy to see the radio tower and the observation post at the second alto – the Cruce Militar. My climbing was over for the day. I continued to fight the mud and puddles until I gave up and joined the highway for the last kilometer or so to El Acebo. Although it was seven o'clock and not late by my standards, I couldn't go on. I was wet, cold, tired, and broken. The mountain and weather won the battle for the day.

El Acebo surprised me. After Manjarín, I had no idea what to expect. What I found was a village that was well-kept and charming. It looked like it would be a good place to visit on a day when it wasn't pissing rain. The first *albergue* was full, but when I walked into the second, the *hospitalero* welcomed me with a comforting smile. He understood I was wet and cold. My stay was by donation, and I was expected to attend both the dinner and breakfast. Another pilgrim took my soaked boots and stuffed them with newspaper. It was a procedure I had never tried, but they assured me my boots would dry faster. I took off my rain gear and hung it in the entranceway. I only had a couple of small spots that had soaked through. My rain gear worked great, considering the conditions. However, the entranceway was cool, and I knew my boots wouldn't dry there.

The *hospitalero* showed me the dorm, with four well-spaced double bunks, and I choose a top bed near the window. The *albergue* was clean, and my bed looked comfortable. At least, comfortable for an *albergue*; don't get me wrong, I'm not comparing it to a Parador hotel. I immediately noticed four very attractive young women in the adjacent dorm, and I smiled and said *hola*. I had a quick shower because I couldn't be late for dinner. Already, I had been reminded by the *hospitalero* and another pilgrim not to be late. I didn't really have a charming wardrobe, so I chose a lovely ensemble that included base layer pants – that looked not all that different from long underwear – a wrinkled, Mexx long sleeve shirt, and my wind jacket that I had worn all day. In fact, I had worn that jacket every day. I put on some extra deodorant in case my jacket or any other part of me was stinky.

I was the last to arrive for dinner and found a spot at what seemed to be the older persons' table. I looked around and couldn't believe the number of attractive women staying here. There were six, and at least four of them were stunningly beautiful. Without a doubt, this *albergue* had the most attractive women so far on the Camino. I sat next to a man in his 60's from California who was traveling with his daughter and grandson. The boy, only eight years old, was the youngest pilgrim I had seen so far. I'm not including the day walkers on the weekends, I'm referring to the actual pilgrims with backpacks who stayed at *albergues*. I was very impressed because at his age, a big holiday for me was going to Disneyland. I wondered if I would have turned out any differently, had I walked the Camino so young.

Before dinner, the *hospitalero* asked us to stand and hold hands in prayer. Honestly, I don't know the last time I held anyone's hand in prayer and felt uncomfortable. The man from California was to my right, and we held hands in the way a couple normally would. The woman on my left held hands in a totally different manner, presumably the religious way. I was glad when that was over.

The dinner was simple and consisted of pasta or soup. I chose the pasta and was lucky to get some soup also because not everyone did. Of course, there was plenty of bread to go around. I enjoyed the dinner and company. The Americans had only started in León and were intent on making it to Santiago. A German couple who sat across from me knew little English, but we managed to talk anyway. Although I have some German in me, I don't know any words, but as with many other languages, I hope to learn one day. The main topic of conversation was the weather and conditions on the Camino. Everyone had a story and an opinion. I told my story about the huge puddle in between the electric fence and the steep bank as if no one else there had walked through the same spot. Of course, everyone had.

After dinner, I charged my camera battery and used the internet while talking with a pretty Asian woman. The *hospitalero* brought the clothes rack inside the communal area, next to the electric stove. I grabbed my wet clothes and found a good spot and later even managed to sneak in my boots. I wanted my boots at least dry enough so I didn't have that cold, clammy feeling when I put them on in the morning.

I had walked about 39.5 kilometers for the day, and considering the climbing and conditions, I couldn't complain. I regretted not having better conditions and enjoying the walk through the mountains, but the *hospitalero* mentioned it was typical spring weather. I hadn't taken my normal amount of photos, with the weather including driving rain or snow most of the day. The forecast was better for the next day, but I still had to get down the mountain. Outside, it was still foggy and pouring. As I went to bed, I walked past the beautiful women in the adjacent dorm and wished them all a good night. It was a beautiful close to an otherwise horrible day. I went to bed with dreams of.... my girlfriend, of course! Who else would I dream about?

WILD SPANISH LAVENDER

Day 15
El Acebo to Villafranca del Bierzo
40 Km

The recorded sounds of an oboe permeated the dormitory at six-thirty and within my head several moments later. It was a strict *albergue*, and we weren't allowed up until we had heard those sounds. I thought something would happen if I left early, although I had no idea what it would be. Since the communal breakfast was mandatory, there was no point in rushing. I had slept well and was only woken up a few times by snoring, the worst coming from the adjacent room. Could it possibly be that one of the pretty, young women snored so loud? It couldn't be. I'll blame it on the German man. Or the American. I was scared to look outside, but I finally lifted my exhausted body and went to the window for my morning weather check. Outside, there were dark clouds, rain, and fog. Oh shit no, not again!

Breakfast consisted of bread and various jams, but I wasn't interested. I talked with the others and finally coaxed myself to at least eat one small piece of bread piled with strawberry jam for some energy. I didn't stay long and went back to the dorm to take care of my feet. Because they had gotten wet the previous day, the new skin covering the old blisters was loose and required careful bandaging. By the time I was ready, it was eight-thirty, and I was the last guest to leave. I apologized to the *hospitalero* for my lateness, but he said not to worry and wished me *Buen Camino*. He volunteered at the *albergue* with his wife, and, although I made light of their rules, they were gracious and should be commended for the time and care they provided.

The rain had lightened to a few drops, but it was still cold. My boots, although not completely dry, were much better than I had expected. Placing them near the furnace all night really had helped. I wished I had seen El Acebo in finer weather. The village had a rustic charm, with its stone houses and slate roofs. The *hospitalero* explained how El Acebo, similar to the previous villages, once had many homes in ruins. In recent years, as tourism and popularity of the Camino increased, it had brought in money, and people returned to live. At the end of El Acebo, a monument for a fallen cyclist stood outside a tiny stone church and its adjacent graveyard. An old bike was mounted on a boulder, its front wheel high in the air. I descended along the road through a thick fog and could barely see one hundred meters ahead. Soon, the rain fell harder, and I cursed out loud. Fudgsicle or fiddlesticks, I forgot exactly what I said, but it wasn't very nice.

The Camino veered off the road onto a dirt and gravel path that descended, at times steeply, into Riego de Ambrós. The hamlet had rough stone houses, some with old wooden porches that looked ready to fall over. I passed through quickly onto a rough, muddy trail. Three Germans from the *albergue* were on a steep section, and one woman struggled with her footing on the wet rocks while her male companion watched from below. The trail flattened and led to one of my highlights on the Camino – wild Spanish lavender.

A favorite of mine in the gardens back home, I had never expected to see Spanish lavender in Spain – although the name should have suggested that it was a real possibility. By now, the rain had stopped, and the skies lightened. The hillside was brilliant with purple from the lavender and white from the broom. I passed the group from California and shared my excitement about the Spanish lavender, but I don't think they were too interested. They walked slowly, while I was energized. I said goodbye and descended below the remainder of the fog.

It was perfect timing for one of the most picturesque stretches of the Camino. The mountainside was covered with Spanish lavender and white broom at their peak blooming period. One hillside had a large patch of peonies, but only a few flowers remained. A group of pilgrims walked on the highway, apparently thinking the trail was a mess. It wasn't that muddy, but it was steep and rough, and I had to be careful not to slip on the wet rocks. This section reminded me of hiking in the mountains near my home. The sun emerged, and I was in a much better mood than the previous day. I sat on a rock outcrop, across from a mountainside covered with white broom that overlooked the valley below. Although I hadn't felt pain, I wanted to give my knee a rest from the steep descent.

A group of twelve pilgrims in their early 20's passed me at a feverish speed. The last was a man who saw my Canadian flag and wanted to talk. The group was from Utah in the United States, and they had been on the Camino for a few weeks. They enjoyed their experience, which I sensed had religious importance. He asked how long I had walked for. I told him it was my fifteenth day, and I had to repeat myself that I had started in St. Jean. He didn't believe me the first time. I told him to catch up to his group, since I couldn't keep up with their pace down the mountain. As I descended, yellow broom took place of the white broom, but sadly, the Spanish lavender disappeared. Although I never planned my trip to see the mountainside in bloom, I was lucky and will never forget it.

The trail ended just before Molinaseca, and I joined a sidewalk along the road that descended from the mountains. I met the young man from Utah on the medieval bridge over the Río Meruelo, and he insisted on taking my photo. I took one of him with his friend and bid them farewell. Molinaseca was pleasant, with a narrow street and old, well-kept buildings. Besides pilgrims and a Coca-Cola delivery driver, few other people were around. I bought a Coke Light and a chocolate bar and walked through the town. At a small plaza, I sat next to a fountain with a statue of who I believed was St. James in the middle of the pool. The Coca-Cola delivery van parked across from me; I raised my Coke Light to the driver, and he smiled.

It was warm, and I took off my jacket but really wanted to remove my rain pants. After a short break, I followed a sidewalk along the busy road that links Molinaseca to Ponferrada. After a section of mostly large, modern houses, the hillside opened up to fields and vineyards. After two kilometers, the Camino veered onto a gravel road past a group of large, newer houses, brightly painted in red, orange, and yellow. I stopped for photos of brilliant red poppies nestled among rock walls with a background of vineyards and green hillside.

When I arrived at a road that led to a Roman fountain, I felt great and didn't hesitate walking the extra two hundred meters. The brick and stone structure was rebuilt and didn't look like a fountain from the road. I followed the stairs that led underground, and sure enough, there was a fountain. Back on the Camino, I hid behind a tree and finally changed into my track pants. I had worn my rain pants almost every day for two weeks and had a large hole on the inside of each leg below the knees. I was disappointed and had expected them to last much longer. The rain pants were supposedly a good brand and certainly not cheap.

The hamlet of Campo was deserted, except for a black cat crossing the road ahead. Nothing unlucky or eventful happened, and I continued onto a long straight, unsightly stretch of paved road through overgrown grass fields. Ponferrada was still about two kilometers across the valley. I was looking forward to the castle, but otherwise, I didn't know anything about the city. Just before Ponferrada, the medieval stone bridge over the Río Boeza had one huge arch that involved a small climb to reach the peak.

The Camino markers in Ponferrada were among the best I had seen. After the bridge, a unique sign was finished in brass and clearly showed the direction of the Camino and the *albergue*. I tired from my first climb of the day but didn't care because in front of me was the Ponferrada Castle. I had never seen anything like it. In Canada, I had visited two castles but they were just over one hundred years old and resembled large houses.

The Ponferrada Castle was built in the thirteenth century and had great walls, towers, and a bridge over a moat. I walked through the portal and paid the €3 admission. Pilgrims left backpacks unattended, which I wasn't comfortable with. After some thought, I reluctantly carried mine. It was a shame because I had hoped to give my body a rest. I roamed the castle and visited everything, which required walking up a tight spiral staircase that I had to squeeze through with the backpack on. From the upper level, I looked across the Río Sil to the modern section of Ponferrada, with snow-covered mountains lurking in the distance. Grasses, poppies, and other flowers grew from the fields and the courtyard walls of the castle.

I had an excellent visit and spent well over an hour in the castle, more than I had expected. I was exhausted and needed some rest. A French woman took my photo in front of the castle, and I obliged with one of her and her daughter. I bought two postcards and chose a patio that faced the castle for a break. One postcard was for Sarah, and the other, my first souvenir, was for myself.

The door of the nearby Iglesia de Santa María de la Encina was open, and it was the first church I had been inside for a few days. The highlight was a realistic-looking statue of Christ lying on his back inside a glass coffin, his hands raised as if he were still alive. As I crossed the Río Sil to the modern area of the city, I took one last look at the castle sitting mightily on top of the hill. At a nearby store, I loaded up on food and supplies and left with a shopping bag. There was little room for anything in my backpack.

This area of Ponferrada had many modern art pieces, one of which depicted four women working on a homestead – a tribute to women, I believe. In the distance, an impressive, modern bridge with a single white arch spanned the Sil, and farther behind were mountains covered in snow. There were no other pilgrims as I left the city. For now, I was alone again. Many of the homes on the outskirts were large and gated. The city seemed prosperous. Mining was once an important industry that dated back to Roman times. Some mines had been depleted, and others were closed for long periods during recent recessions. Currently, Ponferrada is a service center for the region. Judging by the many vineyards, I'm sure the wine industry is also very important.

In front of the Iglesia Santa María in the quiet suburb of Compostilla, I sat on a bench for a quick break in the sun. The area was quiet and peaceful, with only a few people walking by. After writing a postcard to Sarah, I checked my map and realized I still had another twenty kilometers to my destination of Villafranca del Bierzo. It was three o'clock, and I needed to make good time. I felt great, and knew that if the weather stayed like this, I could walk well into the evening.

The Camino was well marked along the road with cement posts that were newly painted with a yellow scallop shell against a blue background. Toward the south, an odd-shaped, brown, modern building stuck out like a sore thumb. Really, it looked like a swollen thumb. It stood about twenty-five stories in an area dominated with houses. Although I thought the building was odd, I took a photo and stared again. I'm sure some would consider it brilliance in architectural design.

As I entered the suburb of Columbrianos, I stopped at a church on the hillside overlooking the valley. A large group of cyclists were having a race or a rally, and the parking lot was a rendezvous point. They had a catered dinner on a table set up next to a large van that carried their gear and supplies. For a moment, I thought it was the Tour de France, until I remembered where I was.

The other side of the church was far quieter with only two pilgrims having a siesta on a bench. They were trusting, with their belongings spread out around them. One never knows what they may find in a backpack. If someone stole a certain bag from mine, all they would get would be stinky underwear and socks. I made sure I didn't disturb the sleeping pilgrims and continued to the main street of Columbrianos.

The town was almost deserted, and I only saw a few people as I walked to the Ermita de San Blas. The small church looked recently rebuilt and had one side decorated with a colorful mural of St. James.

Soon, the Camino veered onto a narrow, paved back road through a flat area mixed with large homes and farmland. I had to be careful because most of the time, there was barely enough room for one car and far less room for a car and me. If I may be candid, I had been holding a dump since Ponferrada but never found a washroom along the way. It got to the point where I slowed down until I couldn't take it any longer. Finally, I found a semi-hidden spot in a very small patch of forest on private land and took care of my business. I emerged back on the road as two women out for a late afternoon walk approached. They gave me funny looks but didn't say anything. Maybe they thought I had a siesta. Maybe they thought I took a shit. I couldn't tell and wasn't going to ask. That's what happens when there are no public washrooms anywhere – uncomfortable situations occur.

Now, free of all burdens, I walked faster and made excellent time. The side road I had walked on for almost an hour joined the main one on the outskirts of Camponaraya. There were many shops and cafés along the Camino, but it was siesta, and most were closed. The town had modern art pieces, including one depicting a man and a woman to commemorate wine and pilgrims. The plaza had an odd sight, a bell tower rising from the roundabout. There was no church.

After crossing the A-6 freeway, the Camino joined a gravel path at a rest area. As clouds grew darker, I climbed to a rolling landscape dominated by vineyards, with red poppies and yellow mustard lining the path. I had no idea how to determine the age of vineyards, but these ones looked like they had been there for centuries. They were vast, and at times, a kilometer long. A wooden sign stated that Santiago was 195 kilometers, although I was sure it wasn't accurate. It was more like 195 kilometers from Villafranca del Bierzo, but whatever the case, I was getting closer.

A man in his 60's was the first pilgrim I had seen walking since Ponferrada. It wasn't raining, but he wore a bright red poncho that was easy to spot against the vegetation. I said *hola* as he talked to another man inspecting a vineyard. Once I got to the main road, I stopped for a quick break. The friendly pilgrim came up to me and spoke quickly in Spanish. I only understood a few words and said, "*Lo siento, No en-*

tiendo" (I'm sorry, I don't understand). I had used this expression other times on the Camino and never had a negative reaction. This man was offended though. He quickly lost his smile and walked away. I didn't mean to offend him, I just couldn't understand.

After a short break, I walked along the road into Cacabelos, staying a safe distance behind the Spanish pilgrim. There was no point upsetting him any further. I passed a small stone church, which reminded me of the ones in the hamlets on the mountain, and then the Camino veered onto a narrow street of shabby, old buildings, many with faded, peeling paint. The Spanish pilgrim stopped and looked at me. I thought he wanted to talk since we were the only two still walking. I wanted to say something and asked him how he was doing in Spanish. Now this was a simple expression, *¿Cómo estás?*, I was sure of and had the correct pronunciation. He glared at me and only said, "*No entiendo*," and looked away. He had completely lost his friendliness toward me.

A larger stone church with a single bell tower over a stained glass window proudly displayed a large sign of St. James with "Cacabelos 2010" written. I crossed over the swollen Río Cúa on a medieval bridge with a narrow sidewalk. The most elaborate church in Cacabelos also housed an *albergue*, and I greeted another pilgrim who stood outside. The Spanish pilgrim who was no longer my friend went inside, and it looked like I'd be alone again. The church had an interesting but unsettling statue outside of a figure who I presumed represented Mary holding a baby Jesus. However, in this case, Jesus had an adult face. It kind of creeped me out.

The rain started, and it was a real downpour that lasted ten minutes. The sidewalk ended and left a dirt shoulder to walk along the busy road. As I climbed the hill, I felt sluggish. I had felt great most of the day, but it was six o'clock and I had already walked a long way. After a large vineyard, I passed a winery where three women stood outside having a smoke. Soon, I arrived in the quiet village of Pieros and stopped for a moment at the small, peaceful plaza that had deciduous trees with green and burgundy leaves and a well manicured lawn. Just past Pieros, there was an option with yellow, sloppy, hand-painted arrows on the pavement. I chose the route to the right that climbed along the road for a short distance and then veered into a charming vineyard just as the sun emerged again. From the top of the hill, I saw an ancient-looking church just north of Pieros. It had a single black cross on top of a stone gable and was nestled at the bottom of a hill and surrounded by trees.

Although it didn't last long, I really enjoyed the walk through the vineyard. I took my time with photos of the old vines and reddish-brown earth. Two men were tending to the vineyard, and I waved to them. They smiled and said something back, although I had no idea what it was. After a short descent, I was in the hamlet of Valtuille de Arriba, which had a stream or an aqueduct running through the middle. I didn't stop and joined a gravel road through patches of brush and trees. From the forest, I emerged into a vast vineyard, one of many in the area. A sign in Spanish had been erected by the winery, and I understood that Cabernet Franc was grown here. After a short climb, I came across one of my favorite sites along the entire Camino. A white split-level house stood above the hillside at the end of a magnificent vineyard. Three giant trees, which resembled cypress, towered over the house and provided shade. That was one place I could have stayed a while – somewhere I could be creative.

The few small ups and downs were starting to wear me out. Another large vineyard had signs, this time in English and Spanish. The traditional grapes were Mencia and Godello, but the winery also planted new varietals, including Cabernet Sauvignon, Gewurztraminer, and Tempranillo. Near Villafranca del Bierzo, I was surprised to meet another pilgrim, a German woman who had family that lived near Vancouver. A construction crew blocked the road with a backhoe, and as we waited, we talked about Canada and the Camino. She normally didn't walk this late but had gotten a late start and was falling behind on her journey. The first view of Villafranca del Bierzo was impressive. The town was above the valley bottom, with the monastery, a grand stone building, perched on top of a hill.

Now, I needed to find somewhere to stay. After bypassing the municipal *albergue* without looking inside, I went into a private one and was immediately greeted by the *hospitalero*. He didn't know English well, and had trouble with my Spanish. I tried to tell him I wanted to see the dorm and bed first, but he didn't understand. I gave up and he signed me in, took my money, and led me to the dorm. There were at least twenty double bunks, with many pressed against each other, and I chose a lower bed along the wall because I didn't want to sleep beside anyone. The upper mattress was very close to the bottom one, which concerned me because it was so dirty. The washroom had curtains as doors, not only for the showers, but for the toilets, too. I couldn't remember the last time I saw curtains in front of a toilet. I washed some clothes and hung them out, hoping they would at least partially drip-dry before morning.

During the day, I had taken many photos and was well into my backup battery. Neither the dorm nor the outside communal area had an electric outlet. One outlet was available in the dining room, but dinner, which I had already declined, was soon to be served. I sat down and plugged in my camera, but after only a few minutes, someone announced that everyone had to be seated for dinner. If I wanted at least one battery charged, I had to eat.

I had a diverse group of people around me, with all ages and nationalities. We started with a prayer and then were served a tomato-based soup. There was plenty of bread and a simple salad before the main course, which consisted of a fried egg with a piece of chorizo on top. It was okay, but not what I expected for dinner. I'm sure if anyone was really hungry, they weren't happy.

Then the dessert arrived, and at first, I thought maybe it was some exotic type of fruit that I had never seen before. However, upon closer inspection, it was nothing less than rotting fruit. Yes, rotting apples and oranges. People looked in disgust and bewilderment. I didn't dare touch anything, but the man across from me peeled an orange and after taking one whiff, made a sick face, and put it back in the bowl. This fruit wasn't even fit for animals. After the culinary experience, I left, thinking I had just spent €6 to charge my camera battery and hoped I wouldn't have to get up in the middle of night with some kind of stomach ailment. I said good night to those at my table and finally got to bed at ten o'clock.

I had walked forty kilometers for the day, but the next one would be far more difficult. It would be interesting, a day I had been looking forward to. I would have a long walk, followed by a climb over a mountain into the wonderful, mystical region of Galicia.

A GRUELING DAY
Day 16
Villafranca del Bierzo to Triacastela
51 Km

All night long, I thought about the mattress above. The room was dark, and I couldn't see anything, but I knew the dirt was there. I envisioned tiny flakes of the filth coming off, slowly descending through the air into my open mouth. I would have slept on top if it wasn't for a stain on the mattress. It was a loud dorm; many of the others snored, and the old bunks made loud creaking sounds every time someone got up. By five o'clock, the early risers began to get ready and ensured that only the soundest of sleepers could get any more sleep. I lay there until after six, grabbed my gear, and went outside to the communal area. It was cool and rainy, and, considering that I had another climb into the mountains, I wasn't looking forward to the day.

By the time I was ready with my feet all taped up and dressed in a full compliment of rain gear, it was eight o'clock. Villafranca del Bierzo is located above the confluence of the Río Valcarce and the Río Burbia. It is important, not only for the Camino, but economically because of its strategic location in between mountain passes. My first stop was at a wide stone castle with towering walls. It was currently occupied by a family and not open to the public. I wondered how big that family could be. I'm sure there was enough room for a hundred people inside. Maybe their last name was St. Germain, and they were my distant, Spanish cousins. I wouldn't mind staying in a castle for a night or two.

Nearby, a new tourist sign in Spanish and English featured the gastronomical highlights of the area. As I discovered the previous evening, wine is very important, along with apples, pears, and pimientos. *Botillo*, a pork dish, is the representative food. I wished that had been part of the pilgrim dinner because it sure sounded appetizing. I thought back to the Spanish pilgrim at the *albergue* in Atapuerca who had told me there were no apples commercially grown in Spain. Maybe they didn't know or I misunderstood.

I walked down the cobbled street into the downtown area and went off the Camino to the Plaza Mayor, which was quiet on this rainy morning. After I saw the Iglesia San Francisco, I walked to the Iglesia San Nicolás, with its beautiful façade featuring a long staircase leading up to double doors finished in dark stain. Coats of arms, stained glass, and an intricate statue decorated the outside. Back on the Camino, I crossed the bridge over the wide, shallow Río Burbia. On the town's side of the river, there were rows of houses, each designed and finished differently. All around the town were mountains and hills.

As I left Villafranca del Bierzo, I thought about my distance to Santiago. I had just under two hundred kilometers, and at my pace, I could be in Santiago in five days, making it twenty days in total. It was hard to believe. As I progressed, I was in better shape, felt stronger, and had more confidence. Considering the awful weather most of the time, I had done quite well. That's enough for now. I still had a long way to go, including a big day ahead, which would include a climb of over nine hundred meters of elevation gain into Galicia. Most pilgrims planned to stay at O'Cebreiro, but I intended to get well past, perhaps to Triacastela, over fifty kilometers away on the other side of the mountain. Whether I made it would depend on the weather and trail conditions. I only hoped for a better day than my last venture through the mountains.

From Villafranca del Bierzo, the Camino followed a sidewalk lined with pilgrims, which climbed alongside a busy highway with mountains on the sides and the Río Valcarce on the left. After an hour or so, the Camino veered across the highway onto a secondary road into the hamlet of Pereje. There wasn't much there, so I didn't stop. Back along the highway, I saw a pilgrim with a large umbrella. Normally this would have made me laugh, but I had to think. It seemed to work fine at that moment, but if there was wind, it would be a problem, and his arms would get tired after a while. The umbrella would be a pain to carry when not in use, but I suppose you could use it to fend off dogs or bandits. However, I still preferred rain gear.

As I continued, the mountains shrunk to hills, and the valley bottom flattened. The landscape and vegetation had changed noticeably since Villafranca del Bierzo. Here, it was evident there was more rain, which created a fertile environment filled with trees and bright green pastures along the river. Again, the Camino veered onto another secondary road into Trabadelo, and not only did I have to be careful when crossing the highway, I also had to be careful walking alongside it; there were long stretches with no sidewalk or barrier. Some of the cars drove fast down the hills with little consideration for pedestrians.

I arrived at La Portela de Valcarce at eleven-thirty, after walking thirteen kilometers without a break. It was time to get out of the rain, and I went inside a bar with only three pilgrims inside. The bartender looked unhappy. There was a roadside station just before the village, with a café and a store that was more popular. Many pilgrims were outside his bar, but most walked by. In Ambasmestas, it dawned on me that not only had the landscape changed since Villafranca del Bierzo, but so had the small villages and hamlets. Homes and churches were generally small and simple. Usually, there were one or two businesses. Sometimes, there were none. These places took a few minutes to walk through at most.

Vega de Valcarce, however, was larger, with cafés, shops, and even a bank machine. An artesian bakery looked interesting, but I didn't want to walk the nearly one-hundred-meter-long driveway. Leaving the village was done by walking along a busy secondary road with barely enough room for two vehicles. The short walk to Ruitelán continued on the side of the road through a bushy landscape with mountains on either side. The valley along the river was picturesque, with stands of trees and lush farmland where cattle grazed. The only things disturbing the peacefulness of the hamlet were two giant freeway bridges that towered above.

I stood for a moment in front of the old stone church, which looked so spooky on such a gloomy day, and wondered what it would be like at night. I've said that before and need to somehow plan some of my next Camino either at night or before sunrise. I'm sure the near-ghost town of Manjarín must be even more haunting at night, especially during a storm.

Across the river, Herrerías looked eerie. It sat at the base of a mountain, with its stone church and other ancient buildings engulfed in a light mist. The approach to the village was through a forest on a narrow gravel road with old stone walls on either side. I crossed the small, calm Río Valcarce on an ancient stone bridge with one arch and black iron railings. Herrerías was long, with houses on the left side of the road and a large plot of pasture and trees on the right.

After the tiny hamlet of Hospital, the Camino began the steep climb on a paved road. Even on a dull day, the landscape was vibrant, with numerous shades of green. For some reason, there were few pilgrims on this stretch. A man and woman ahead were slowed by the hill, and I easily passed them. Farther up, a sign directed walkers on a trail while cyclists were to stay on the road. A walker who obviously remembered the previous mountain decided the road was a better choice. Cheater? Wimp? Smart? Maybe this man was a bit of all three.

The forest was pleasant, but the trail was often rough and steep. An exhausted cyclist walked his bike on a trail not meant for a road bike. I said *hola*, but he was so out of breath, I thought he was going to puke right in front of me. Soon, the rain stopped and the skies brightened. It was good timing because I was heating up and took off my rain gear. Another cyclist had a tough time pushing his bike, and I easily passed him also. When I finally emerged from the trees, I looked behind at the beautiful valley of forests and farmlands. The view didn't last for long because as I climbed, the clouds returned, but this time they were dark. I put my rain gear back on as the rain poured and the winds howled. As I continued into the fog, one of the pilgrim cyclists passed me, but he soon got bogged down by a steep hill and I went by him again. We smiled and chuckled every time we passed each other.

I wasn't tired; I was full of energy. It was a tough walk, but the only real pain was from the weather. Just before the hamlet of La Faba, I saw a woman with a Mountain Equipment Co-op (MEC) backpack. It's a Canadian company, so I assumed she was Canadian. She was from Winnipeg, Manitoba and had persevered on the Camino for over a month, and she was determined to finish. She walked slow and told me she had had enough for the day; La Faba would be her stop. It was good timing because no matter how bad I thought the weather was earlier, it got far worse.

I walked through La Faba quickly and soon was back on a muddy dirt and gravel path. Around me were vast areas of rich grazing land, with large patches of low shrubs. I'm sure the landscape was lovely, but the wind was so fierce, it drove the rain straight into my face, making it difficult to see. A man stopped ahead and appeared to be waiting for me. I couldn't see his face until I was up close. It was Victor from Belgium who had sat across from me at dinner the previous evening. He was friendly, and immediately we talked about our dessert. We both had a good laugh, far greater than the uncomfortable one we shared at the *albergue*. Rotting fruit for dessert, unbelievable! Victor and I talked about life in each other's countries, and he convinced me to visit Belgium one day.

I was excited when I saw the border marker as we entered Galicia. It was newly-painted with bright colors but also covered in graffiti. Victor and I took each other's photo, and despite the weather, I was happy to make it to Galicia, a region I had heard so much about. Galicia: a peaceful land with ancient stone churches, lush green pastures, and large dogs that roamed free. I saw my first concrete marker showing 151 kilometers to Santiago de Compostela; they would become an obsession and a distraction from this point on. Fog and mist covered O'Cebreiro and made viewing difficult. Victor had walked enough for the day and thought I was crazy to continue. We said our goodbyes and he headed to the *albergue* as I took shelter in a downstairs bar. It was three-thirty, and I had walked thirty kilometers. It was a good time for a break.

O'Cebreiro is an ancient town once occupied by the Romans but today has a Celtic feel. The town is also known for its homes, called *pallozas*, made of stone with thatched roofs. As I wrote this book, I watched Rick Steves' Europe 2010 show *Galicia and the Camino de Santiago*, where he visited O'Cebreiro on a bright sunny day. The village looked beautiful in HD, but when I was there, it was difficult to see across the street. In the entrance to the bar, I hung up my poncho, ordered a Coke Light and chips, and sat at the back table. The front door was open, and the bar didn't have any heat. After a few minutes, I started shivering and had to leave. The bar had character, with an old pub feel, but on this day, it was too cold and clammy. I had a walk around the town, but the weather didn't make it enjoyable. Taking photos was difficult, and the lens got wet every time I tried.

I left O'Cebreiro along a paved road that veered onto a gravel one beside a power line. There was some gentle climbing, but nothing like before. Few walkers were out, and I was passed by a group of eight horses and their riders who rode by at a gallop and disappeared around a bend. The cyclist I had passed twice earlier went by, and we both said a loud *Buen Camino*. He was soon followed by the other cyclist, and I realized they were together. I walked as fast as I could to the village of Liñares and only stopped at the old church. It was so foggy, I was right beside the church, and it still wasn't clear. The rain stopped as I left Liñares, and by the time I made the short climb to the Alto de San Roque, the sun had emerged to expose the true beauty of the mountains and valleys. There were vibrant shades of green from farmland, shrubs, and trees. The soil was a reddish-brown, although I never saw the red until the sun came out. The alto had a large, modern, bronze statue of a pilgrim, and one of the cyclists looked so happy and proud as he posed in front. As they left, we waved to each other and they quickly disappeared. I admired them for taking the more difficult route up the mountain because they didn't have to.

A gravel path led through lush grazing land with the odd patch or row of trees to Hospital da Condesa. I carried my poncho, and it had even dried by the time I reached the hamlet. The bar looked cozier and warmer than the one in O'Cebreiro, but my only stop was at the attractive church with gray stones and white grout. I thought the church was old, but I later found out it was rebuilt in 1963, which is a baby in these parts. It wasn't much older than me.

I left Hospital da Condesa on a pleasant gravel path while the clouds rolled back in. As I admired the small stone church in the tiny hamlet of Padornelo, there was one last burst of sunshine before the skies darkened, followed by rain and gusting wind. The short climb to the Alto do Poio straight into the wind tired me, and I thought it was time for a break. The alto had an *albergue* and a hostal, and I was surprised how large the buildings were in such an isolated spot.

While I stood in the doorway of the bar and contemplated if I should enter, I felt a sharp pinch on my left thigh. I turned around, and there was a large dog staring at me. I couldn't believe it. I was bitten by a fucking dog. He looked to be a Labrador Retriever crossed with a German Shepherd or something. Okay, he was kind of cute as he looked up at me as if he was expecting a cookie. He certainly wasn't going to get a cookie from me, not that I had one anyway. I yelled and scared him away only to watch him scamper across the highway and bite another man in his thigh. His female companion screamed so loud, the dog ran and disappeared behind a building. It was comical, and I think the dog only wanted some attention. My rain pants weren't ripped, and I knew if there was any damage to my thigh, it was only a slight bruise. I was a little shocked, though, because most of the big dogs I had seen before were on leashes.

At that moment, I decided to get off that mountain. That was my plan initially, but it was late in the day, and to arrive at Triacastela before dark would be tough. I descended the gentle slope through the fog at a good pace but was slowed by frequent large puddles and mud patches. The hamlet of Fonfría had an *albergue*, but I stopped only at the small stone church near the edge of a cliff where the views must be great on a clear day. The hamlet of Biduedo had a tiny stone church with a slate roof that was the most rustic of any I had seen on the Camino.

The rain stopped, and I took off my poncho. The valley below basked in the sun, and I really needed to get there. It was seven o'clock, and with no *albergues* along the way, I didn't have any choice. The trail got steeper, and I had to carefully balance between a fast pace and not falling flat on my face. The descent took its toll on the muscles of my legs, groin, and buttocks, which were sore with every step. My feet bothered me, and I felt at least one new blister come alive. Often when I'm hiking, I find the descent later in the day more grueling than the earlier climb.

After I walked through a large patch of purple heather on a steep hillside, I stopped for one of my favorite photos of a bull lying proudly on the grass near the edge of a cliff with a picturesque mountain behind. A town was far in the distance, and I knew if that was Triacastela, I still had far to go. After one more steep descent, I crossed the highway and entered the classic Galician track – a narrow gravel and dirt road with old stone or earth walls on either side. It was often peaceful and pleasant walking, except when there was mud or water, which had a tendency to pool. It could also be a problem if there happened to be a stubborn herd of cattle, such as the one I encountered.

At first, I didn't know what to do. It wasn't something I was accustomed to or wanted to see so late in the day. Five cattle, including two bulls with pointy horns, walked toward me. I didn't want to run back, so I clung against the dirt bank on the side of the road. They sauntered and didn't look like they would charge, but I felt uneasy especially when one cow started chewing the grass at my feet. After a few moments, a bull took the lead and headed up the road, while the others followed. I walked briskly ahead but there were more cattle, at least a dozen this time. These ones were on the move and brushed right against me.

At the end of the herd, there was a man with a small horse and a dog. I was glad to see him, but he was surprised to see someone walking so late. He didn't know English, but I asked in my rough Spanish if I could take their photo, and he obliged. Initially, the man, the horse, and the dog all looked at me. Just before I snapped the photo, the dog decided to follow the cattle and the horse decided he couldn't wait to eat a clump of grass on the side of the road. Nevertheless, it was still one of my favorite photos. I said goodbye to the man and the horse and saw more cattle, but they were spread out and easily passed.

The sun was out, and it was a pleasant evening walk through tiny hamlets that were difficult to distinguish. At the entrance to one, a giant chestnut tree stood with a brand-new sign in front stating it was eight hundred years old. Chestnuts are important to the Triacastela region, and there is a chestnut festival in November.

Then, something odd happened. As I walked through the hamlet, I heard someone yelling at me from above. No, I don't mean the Lord, but I looked up and saw an old man with his head out of a second-floor window of a house. At first, I thought I was off the Camino but looked ahead and saw yellow arrows. He motioned for me to stop and then disappeared. I had no idea what he wanted and wasn't going to find out. With a burst of energy, I took off only to see him yelling at me from outside his door. I didn't do anything wrong. Maybe, in his own special way, he invited me in for a drink. Then again, maybe he wanted to blow my head off with a shotgun.

After the experience at the *albergue* in Villafranca del Bierzo, I contemplated looking for an inexpensive private room. I needed a good sleep but didn't want to spend much because it was so late. I bypassed the large *albergue* at the edge of the town, made a quick stop to look at the church, and went downtown. Many people were around, but I was the only one with a backpack. The first hostal was full, and the second one wanted to charge me €40, which I thought was too much. The third hostal was also full, but as I passed a private *albergue*, a young man who was staying there said it was very good. It was almost nine o'clock, and I didn't want to walk another block. There was a bed available, and I chose a lower bunk in a small, mixed dorm with six people. The *albergue* was clean and had a full kitchen, a laundry, and a large communal area. After my shower, I washed clothes and feasted on some mixed nuts and chocolate before bed.

I was exhausted, dead tired. My entire body was sore, and my feet were the worst they had been in days. I had a new blister on my right foot, and even the ones that had begun to heal looked bad. A scab that had recently formed on the large, terrible blister above my left big toe ripped off, exposing the red flesh again. As I collapsed on the bed, I smiled. I had walked over fifty kilometers – a grueling day – but I did it. I got off that mountain.

LUSH
Day 17
Triacastela to Ferreiros
39.5 Km

Without a dirty mattress above, I didn't have to worry about flakes of filth finding their way into my mouth. However, my sleep was disturbed by the young man on the top bunk, who obviously had a bladder disorder and stumbled off so many times, I lost count. Once, he slipped, and his stinky foot just missed my face by inches. Except for me, everyone in the dorm was young, and there was little movement even after seven o'clock. From my bed, I looked out the window and saw rain. I was in no hurry to leave.

As I lay in bed, I thought about my important day ahead and my goal to get past the one hundred kilometer marker to Santiago de Compostela. The skies lightened, and I rose out of bed at seven-thirty, the first in the room. My sorry feet looked the worst they had in days and needed extra care. Like most mornings, I moved slowly and wasn't ready until nine o'clock. My clothes were almost dry, and I hung my shirt on the side of my backpack. I had carried a small net bag all along, and it finally dawned on me to use it for my underwear. That relieved the embarrassment of carrying them, although if someone looked closely, they could tell what it was. I stepped outside to patches of blue sky and the sun poking through the clouds.

Triacastela refers to the three castles that once stood here, but none remain. It's also the end of the last mountainous area on the Camino. The difficulty wasn't lessened because the farther I went, the more I was worn down, and even climbing the smallest of hills felt like climbing a mountain. Outside a shop, on the quiet main street, a bulletin board had a poster with a message for pilgrims who spoke English. It was from a teacher at a local school who asked for those with time to stay in town for a few days and help teach English to children. I would have if I was in Santiago or Finisterre because, barring unforeseen circumstances, it looked like I was going to have a lot of free time somewhere.

There was an option out of Triacastela, but I chose the slightly longer route to Samos so I could see its monastery. For about five kilometers, the Camino followed along the highway. It was a pleasant morning warm-up on a flat to slight descent through the Oribio Valley with the river on the left. After a short climb, I veered into San Cristobo, where I passed two women leading a flock of recently sheared sheep along the road. I said *hola* to one of the women, but she didn't acknowledge me. I think the sheep smiled more. The hamlet had old stone walls and buildings in various stages of ruin. A picturesque river with a short waterfall across the entire width ran next to the homes. At the edge of the hamlet, an abandoned stone house looked enticing. I went inside and joined a man and woman peering from the glass-less window. In the middle of a grazing field, a small waterfall appeared – seemingly by magic – and the three of us watched the amazing sight. I'm sure there was a simple explanation for why it was there, but I didn't try to figure it out.

Through farms, lush fields, and sleepy hamlets, I often followed a typical Galician track, with walls of dirt or rock on either side of a dirt road. Here, the mud was horrible, mostly to be found in large patches, and I often had no choice but to walk through it. I've already expressed my views on the problem with mud on the Camino. The same could be said for Galicia.

My short climb to Renche was a struggle, which concerned me so early in the morning. I was expecting an easy day but never thought there would be so many ups and downs on both sides of the streams. I was in need of some food and a good rest, but dark clouds were approaching, and I didn't want to stop. The rest of the way toward Samos was similar, through farmland and hamlets with their tiny churches. My first view of Samos was from the hillside directly above the monastery, a large, fortress-like, stone complex, which sat at the valley bottom, surrounded by buildings and trees. It was an incredible site, and I couldn't wait to get down there. I carefully descended the steep hill to the highway, and as I entered Samos, the skies opened up with a huge rainstorm. Before running for cover, I stopped briefly on the old bridge, which had a wonderful view of the monastery, and the Oribio Valley. The bridge had railings designed with scallop shells in black iron, and although newer, fit in well with the rustic stone.

A covered plaza facing the monastery would be my sanctuary from the storm. As I waited for the rain to let up, I talked with a very attractive French woman, about my age, who I watched somewhat sexually nibble on an empanada while looking into my eyes. She insisted I try it – I mean the empanada – but I declined, stating that I wasn't hungry. Call me old-fashioned, but I like to at least get to know someone a little before I try their empanada. She did have beautiful blue eyes though, the color of the sky. For a brief moment, I watched crumbs fall off the pastry, right into her ample cleavage. Dressed the way she was, in a leather jacket, a tight red sweater, and jeans, there was no doubt she was a tourist and certainly not a pilgrim. Maybe it was because I didn't go out at night, but to that point, I hadn't seen much cleavage along the Camino. This woman sure made up for it.

Soon, there was a group of tourists and pilgrims under the cover, but the rain didn't look like it was going to stop. After twenty minutes of standing and talking, I said goodbye to the French woman, put on my rain gear, and braved the storm as I walked to the monastery. The façade of the church was impressive, with stone columns and statues, stained-glass windows, and bells that hovered above a double staircase leading to the huge double doors. When I entered, a staff member explained in broken English to a group of tourists and me that the next tour wasn't for another hour and was only in Spanish. Entrance to the monastery was only with a scheduled tour. I had a long day ahead and didn't want to wait.

Samos was a small town, pleasant and very clean. Everywhere I looked, there were garbage bins. Cafés were along the main street, but none of them interested me. Outside one, a large sign advertised a hamburger. It had been weeks since my last burger, and I would have enjoyed a good one. However, I knew from walking through other towns, it was a stock photo shared by many cafés and restaurants. I looked in but decided against it. I possibly passed up the best burger in all of Spain. The only place left was a grocery store, where I bought tape, chocolate, nuts, and a Coke Light. I followed a sidewalk finished with paving stones to a pilgrim monument depicting a man leading his wife and young son on the Camino. The sidewalk joined a gravel path beside the highway, and I continued through the valley. The skies lightened, the rain stopped, and I shed my rain gear, much to my delight.

Along the river, there were interesting bridges and buildings, including an old stone house with a river flowing underneath. Fertile grazing pastures were situated in areas where the valley bottom flattened. Trees lined the river and were home to many songbirds. I always wished I could identify a bird from its song but only could with a few back home – one of which is a loon and not that difficult to discern. Garbage bins were spread out, even a considerable distance from Samos, and there was little garbage on the ground. Even though the walk was along the highway, I really enjoyed it, especially when the sun came out.

About two kilometers from Samos, the Camino veered off the highway, and for the next six, it would be a typical Galician track along a river valley. I walked through so many dairy farms and hamlets, I lost track. Initially, there was a gravel road which turned to dirt with huge patches of mud, far worse than the morning's track had been. My boots built up a thick layer, which I shook off, only to go through more. Again, there were many ups and downs, and I struggled with every hill. I was tired, possibly from not having a proper break, or maybe it was the daily grind taking its toll. My mind and body were telling me something – probably that they were exhausted. I kept telling myself, "Only a few more days." Maybe Sarah and the others were right. Walking like this was really fucking crazy.

The landscape was very peaceful though. A grove of giant chestnut trees in a field of purple flowers and grasses made me stop for a moment and marvel. The pastureland was thick and bright green. There was one word to summarize this part of Galicia. Lush.

The Camino arrived at the highway, and I followed a gravel path down the hill. I thought my break would be a few kilometers ahead in Sarria, but an *albergue* with patio recliners on the front lawn looked perfect. It was almost three o'clock, but there wasn't anyone else outside. I bought a Coke Light, took off my socks and boots, and reclined. It was great to relax in the sun. After I finished my drink, I bought another and reclined again.

I had some concerns about finding a place to stay later. I had intended to get well past Sarria, but unlike most sections on the latter stages of the Camino, there were relatively few accommodations until Portomarín, over twenty-two kilometers away. My goal was to get just past the one hundred kilometer marker and no farther. That was all I needed to be happy. However, I had to be careful. The *albergues* in the area were small, and I couldn't count on the odd casa or hostal. I also didn't think I could walk to Portomarín, especially after an elevation gain of 250 meters out of Sarria. After my break, I thanked the attendant for letting me relax in his yard and continued down the hill.

To obtain a *Compostela*, pilgrims must walk at least the last one hundred kilometers of the Camino. Since Sarria is about 120 kilometers from Santiago, it's a popular starting point. I crossed over the Río Sarria into a riverside area with a park across from a promenade with modern apartments, cafés, and shops. Next, I had to climb a few flights of steep stairs that took me into the old town. Along the Camino, there were many people, but few had backpacks. Most pilgrims who had arrived in the afternoon already had a place to stay for the night. The steep hill had exhausted me, and I stopped at a store and bought a Pepsi Light for a change. My climbing wasn't finished as I continued to the Iglesia de San Salvador, a small, ancient church with a towering gable.

I was looking forward to the castle and knew it sat in ruins. However, until I arrived, I didn't realize how much in ruins it was. The castle was destroyed in a medieval war, and only one tower stood. It had a weathered look, but I found out later that it had been reconstructed. A couple of small buildings resembled storage sheds, and I didn't think they were very old. The grounds were overgrown with grass, brush, and trees. The entire area was fenced off in the front, with stone walls along the back and sides. I wanted to look around, but the back was next to an industrial site, and I wasn't sure if I was allowed to enter. I did anyway and had a better look at the stone walls and tower. In the parking lot, two men were doing something in a car. I wasn't sure if they were exchanging something or were about to have some sort of encounter. Or maybe they were about to do a combination of both. I walked by quickly, just as a security patrol drove up to them. I had no idea what was going on and didn't care to find out.

Across from the castle, I glanced back at Sarria and the valley I had just walked through. I was always amazed at how much I walked. The hills where I was only a couple of hours earlier now looked so far. My climbing was over, but the reprieve wouldn't last for long.

The thirteenth century Covento de la Magdalena was a short walk away, and as I stared at it, I thought it looked far newer. The single bell tower had grey stone and looked old, but the façade had bright colors of various shades of brown and beige. The Covento was closed for siesta, or maybe someone saw me coming and locked the doors. I walked down the hill and over the Río Celerio on a beautiful medieval stone and brick bridge with four arches. It was for pedestrians only, and I envisioned ancient wooden carts traveling over it. Small shrubs, flowers, and grasses protruded from between the stones. A peaceful spot with no one else around, it was one of my favorite bridges on the Camino.

Although I didn't feel like it, now I had to climb. The Camino followed a gravel and dirt path with small plots of crops among stands of trees. An ancient chestnut tree, similar to the one before Triacastela, had a sign in front asking for it not to be mistreated. I can proudly admit that along the entire Camino, I did not mistreat a tree or any other vegetation. Maybe some blades of grass or a small shrub when I had to take a pee, but I'm sure everything lived. As I climbed, vast farmland emerged as far as I could see. It was the land of dairy farming, and there was a pungent odor to accompany it.

In Barbadelo, a large sign on a building advertised a store, but when I entered, I was surprised it only contained a dozen or so vending machines. I left with a Coke Light for my evening journey. By the way, if someone reading this book is counting the number of Coke Lights I had on this day or any other, you have too much free time on your hands. Seriously, I would also be interested in knowing, but I'm not going to count myself. Maybe I should run a contest of some sort. Anyway, I know I had a few. I don't drink tea or coffee, I drink alcohol casually, and besides water, I don't drink much of anything else. Diet Coke and Diet Pepsi are my main liquid vices, with Pepsi Max and Coke Zero my favorites. As I expected, they were one of my major expenses in Spain. However, the bottles were cheaper in the stores and machines than in the bars.

The church in the hamlet was twelfth century and very much looked like it. It had a unique design, with the square bell tower completely on the left-hand side of the front façade. Ancient stone crosses stood along a wall in the front. It was a pleasant evening walk in the warm sun, and I felt great wearing a T-shirt. I passed more farmland with stone fences and tiny hamlets with few houses. Cattle mooed, birds chirped, and roosters did whatever they do. Blue and yellow lupines with white daisies grew in large patches along the road. Oak and other deciduous trees provided shelter and dominated the ground along the streams. It was another lush landscape.

Past Barbadelo, I inquired about a room at a casa, an old two-level, brick farmhouse. I hadn't passed the one hundred kilometer marker, but I was close, and it could be difficult to find a bed later. The older woman didn't understand English or my Spanish but called her daughter, who did. The room was a good price, but there was a shared bathroom, which I didn't want. After thinking for a moment, I decided to continue and hoped I wouldn't regret it later. I climbed gently on paved and gravel roads, through farmland and forest, and on small footbridges over streams.

Finally, at seven-thirty, I made it. Not to Santiago de Compostela, but the one hundred kilometer marker. I was happy and wanted to make sure I had a good photo. I set up the camera on the wall across the road and took photos of myself standing beside the marker. It was covered in graffiti, which was a shame, but I'm sure it was an important spot for many pilgrims, especially those who started in St. Jean. While playing with the camera timer and posing for photos, I didn't realize a woman in her 80's had been watching me with apparent interest. It was one spot where I would have liked someone to share the moment with, and I guess I did, with her. As I passed, I smiled and said, *"Buenos Noches"* or good night. She gave me a big *Buen Camino*.

At 99.5 kilometers, the Casa Morgade featured a beautiful old farmhouse and a restaurant. There were no beds available, but if it wasn't so late, I would have stayed for dinner. Whatever they were cooking sure smelled good. The small *albergue* in Ferreiros didn't have a bed either, and I was a little concerned because the next one was also small and not for another four kilometers. It was past eight o'clock, and I was dead tired.

I lucked out just past the hamlet, near the 97.5 marker, where there was a new *albergue* not listed in my guidebook. I was relieved and went to the door of the charming farmhouse. A woman came out, but when I spoke English, she called her husband. They were French, in their early 50's, and introduced themselves as Claire and Alain. The friendly couple was surprised to see me this late and welcomed me into their home. They introduced me to the only other pilgrim in the large dorm, Sophia, who was also French. I hadn't seen this sort of situation, where an *albergue* was part of a home. The stay was by donation, and

I was required to have dinner and breakfast. I was hungry and didn't mind. I chose a bed far away from Sophia to give each of us privacy. The room was clean, and the beds rivaled the hostals' in comfort.

After I showered in the new bathroom, I washed my clothes in the laundry sink and hung them out to drip. Dinner was at a late nine-thirty, but since I had arrived at eight-thirty, it left little time. Upon my arrival in the kitchen, I apologized for my attire, which was my usual formalwear – the wrinkled, black Mexx shirt and wrinkled, black base layer pants. The country-style kitchen was large and featured a wood stove in the center. The four of us sat on stools around an island beside the stove. Sophia spoke English well and helped translate if needed. Oh, how I wish I could speak French and Spanish.

The first course was a traditional Galician soup called *caldo gallego*, with beans, potatoes, onion, and chorizo. It was very good and unlike anything I had tasted before. There were two other dishes, a salad, and I even tried a local sheep cheese. Alain didn't believe the animal that said, "Baaaaa" was a sheep in English. He got very animated with his impersonation of a sheep, complete with facial expressions and bleat-ing. We all had a good laugh, although I wasn't sure how much he intended to be humorous.

By the time dinner was finished, it was ten-thirty, and I didn't get to sleep until after eleven. It was an excellent dinner experience, but the late night wasn't necessarily good for my Camino. One night wouldn't hurt, I supposed. The dorm was cold, and I wore my formalwear to bed. Even with my sleeping bag and liner, I still couldn't get warm. At the foot of the bed sat two thick, neatly folded quilts and I spread them on me and soon warmed up. As opposed to other *albergues*, Claire's quilts were clean and looked new. As I fell asleep, I heard sheep faintly bleating somewhere under the night sky. Or maybe it was Alain.

WITH A HUGE GRIN, HE BEGAN TWIRLING HIS STICK LIKE A BATON

Day 18
Ferreiros to Casanova
42 Km

After a good sleep through a quiet night, I woke up at six o'clock, ready for a big day. Breakfast wasn't until seven-thirty, so I lay and thought about my remaining time on the Camino. I had walked about 39.5 kilometers the previous day, and had about one hundred kilometers remaining, which I thought should take three days. I preferred to arrive in Santiago during the early afternoon on the third day to find suitable accommodation. My plan was to stay near the cathedral, instead of the large *albergue* at Monte de Gozo that would require about five kilometers of backtracking. Roughly, I had two days of forty kilometers each, which left twenty on the last. That was all the planning I needed.

I went into the kitchen for a simple breakfast of bread and jams. Claire placed a large bowl of hot chocolate in front of me, which I wasn't sure how to consume. I politely took spoonfuls, savoring each as I put it in my mouth. When Sophia received her hot chocolate and drank directly from the bowl, that was all the guidance I needed. As the four of us drank, we talked, and between the slurping and language issues, I didn't understand much that was said. I declined a second bowl and excused myself, stating that I had a big day ahead.

By the time I was ready, it was nine o'clock, and I had been up for three hours. I tried to pay Alain, but in his animated manner he explained that he wanted me to put the money under the pillow on my bed. He likened this situation to the tooth fairy, who places money under a child's pillow in exchange for their tooth. At first, he acted out the role of the tooth fairy in a charade, and I played along until I finally guessed. I went into the sleeping room, said goodbye to Sophia, and placed my donation under the pillow. Claire and Alain each gave me a big hug as we bid farewell. I was a little embarrassed because I wore my fleece that still hadn't been washed. I didn't dare tell them, and realize I'm probably opening myself up to ridicule by writing it here.

I had a pleasant stay at the farmhouse and was grateful for the experience. Although it was referred to as an *albergue*, I felt more like the couple's guest. Maybe if the sleeping room was full of snoring pilgrims, I would have felt different. The morning was cold, but the sun was out, and it looked to be a nice day. The farming odor was strong, even more pungent than the evening before. The walk was pleasant, through farmland, patches of forest, and hamlets – so many, I couldn't tell them apart. The Camino followed a paved country road, with one diversion around a section that was being repaired. Finally, one small stretch of the Camino in Galicia was being worked on. I could show them at least a dozen more that needed it.

A short climb took me to an alto where a light fog covered the hillside. I saw my first *hórreo*, an old crumbling wooden one, in someone's overgrown back yard. *Hórreos* are elevated, rectangular storage bins designed to hold grain and keep out rodents and small mammals. There would be many along the Way to Finisterre in various conditions, with some elaborately decorated. The Camino descended from the alto, and I only stopped at an *albergue* in the hamlet of Mercadoiro for a Coke Light. The farmland gave way to a forested area, and soon, I saw Portomarín across a bluish-green lake. After a steep descent, along a gravel road, I arrived at the highway and the ninety kilometer marker.

The lake was really a reservoir, Embalse de Belesar, created by damming the Río Miño in the 1950s. Some of the buildings, from the old town once along the Miño, were relocated up the hill, and reconstructed brick by brick. The Roman bridge and the remnants of other buildings were somewhere beneath the water's surface. As a result of the high water level, I couldn't see anything but later found out the old bridge and ruins are usually exposed in late summer. As I walked across the modern bridge on a narrow sidewalk with a railing no more than four feet high, a truck drove by and made me shake. I stopped only for a few photos and walked quickly to the other side. The surrounding area was picturesque, with hillsides of farmland, forests, and homes. On the hill, now far above the reservoir, was Portomarín.

While on the bridge, I saw a staircase leading to a portal, but when I arrived, I realized it was much more. From the side, it was an impressive stone and brick structure, with stairs leading to a walkway over a giant arch, which the road went through. Above the portal was a small, reconstructed lookout. The structure was an amazing sight, and supposedly part of the original bridge far below, although I could never figure out those logistics. The road was busy, and I waited a few minutes for a photo without vehicles. As I walked up the stairs, I wished there was someone nearby to take my photo. The closest pilgrim was on the bridge, so I continued across the walkway and through the portal.

A sidewalk climbed steeply along a road, with shops and homes on the left and a park on the right. I picked up a Coke Light, a Magnum, and some chocolate from a store and sat at a picnic table overlooking the valley. The sun was bright, and I laid out my clothes and took off my boots. I had only walked two hours, so I wasn't tired; I just needed to recharge a little. The weather was a concern, and this time, I wasn't thinking about the cold or rain. The heat, which I hadn't been accustomed to, would be a factor later, and I needed to make good time before the afternoon. Ahead, I had a long climb with over five hundred meters of elevation gain, which was going to be tough, especially if it was hot.

It was Sunday, and the plaza in the town center was busy with dozens of pilgrims, tourists, and residents who were walking and milling about. The Iglesia de San Juan resembled a castle tower, and I couldn't imagine the effort entailed by bringing it here from the valley below. Inside, the nave was large but simply decorated; however, the large, floral stained-glass window was stunning. After a quick look inside, I bought postcards at a store across the plaza and sat on a step that faced the church. As I wrote to Sarah and Adam, I watched the people in the plaza. It was easy to spot the pilgrims who started their Camino in Portomarín. Most were in groups and had small backpacks. While they looked fresh and clean, I looked like shit. Portomarín was less than one hundred kilometers from Santiago, so technically they weren't eligible for a *Compostela*. I'm sure they got one somehow, and I wondered how.

After a break that seemed to last longer than the fifteen minutes it really was, I mailed my postcard and tried to get my body moving again. Instead of being energized, I felt lazy, which was surprising because I had felt better before my two morning breaks. Along the Camino, Portomarín was clean, with many shops and cafés. One grocery store advertised bottles of wine that cost €.61 each. Amazing price, but amazing wine? Maybe I could use it later to rocket me up the hill. More likely, I would pass out under a giant chestnut tree and wake up the next day. After the town center, I had a steep drop across the highway to a pedestrian bridge over a small arm of the reservoir.

Now, I had to climb. The Camino began on a gravel and dirt road through a forest that soon opened up to farmland. I didn't know if it was from the chocolate or the Magnum, but I had energy again. I passed many people, most with their small backpacks, but one man, tall and skinny, and in his 40's, seemed to take exception. He pressed me for over two hundred meters at a pace I couldn't sustain. Finally, I stopped and let him go by. I was sweating, by far the most on the Camino. After I wiped my face, caught my breath, and had some water, I was ready to continue.

I saw the man again on the *senda* along the highway. At first, I thought he was waiting for someone else, but for some reason, he had stopped for me. Michael was from Portugal, wore jeans, and had a tiny backpack, compared to mine. He was the leader of a group that had just started in Portomarín. I asked him why, if he was leading a group, he didn't walk with them. He said many of them were out of shape and slowed him down.

We walked together, and at first, I enjoyed having someone to talk with. Michael was friendly and spoke English well, but he had a tendency to ask very personal questions, considering we had only met a few minutes earlier. He wanted to know about my job, my finances, my girlfriend, among other things. He asked for details, which I thought was inappropriate, so I managed to switch the topic of conversation to the Camino. He asked where and when I had started and how far I walked every day. I told him I averaged about forty kilometers a day which he replied was easy; he said he wouldn't have a problem. Yes, it was easy for him to say, considering it was his first day on the Camino and he was carrying a backpack about the same size as someone would find on a Labradoodle.

After a long *senda*, past industrial buildings and farm houses, we crossed the highway at a hamlet and were back on a gravel path through fields and a forest. At one point, Michael turned around and looked at me while holding his walking stick in both hands. With a huge grin, he began twirling his stick like a baton. I must interject here – for those of you who have taken that last sentence out of context, you should be ashamed of yourself. I'm trying to be serious here. Where was I? Michael glanced at an empty pop can that sat on a branch of a young pine tree, about two meters off the ground. I was behind him, but without warning, Michael swung the walking stick like a baseball bat – the pointy end sticking out – and completely missed the can. On the follow-through, I watched the pointy end as it missed my eyes by only a few inches. I was shocked and perturbed. Michael apologized, but I had had enough. I said I needed a break and told him to go ahead. He said he would wait for me, and I thought, "Don't bother." I was tired anyway from our fast pace, and I found a soft spot under a tree and sat down. I wanted Michael to get well ahead, so I took my time and rested.

In Portomarín, I had meant to do something that involved my bum on a toilet seat but never found a washroom. When I started walking again, I realized what I was holding wasn't going to hold for much longer. I looked around and saw pilgrims spread out as far as I could see, and the sparse forest had no real cover. I walked and grimaced until I found a small pile of brush that barely covered my squatting self. Why couldn't I have gone at the *albergue*? It was cozy and much more private than in the bush. I emerged back on the Camino as two guys were walking by. They stared at me, and with a grin, gave a "What were you doing in the bush? Oh, l know, you were taking a shit," kind of look. I gave them a "Fuck you! Mind your own business," kind of a look back and walked quickly past them.

Through Gonzar and Castromaior, I only stopped for a photo of a weathered *hórreo* and a tiny church. The Camino then climbed steeply through a mix of scrubby bush and farmland. I passed a group, and one of the men called out. He noticed I was from Canada, and I told him I lived in Vancouver. He wanted to talk about the 2010 Winter Games and asked questions as if I was an expert. I told him that I didn't attend any of the sporting events, but I saw a medal ceremony and a Theory of a Deadman concert. Of course, he hadn't heard of them. I asked where he was from, and he said they were a group from Portugal but didn't know where their leader was. I asked if their leader's name happened to be Michael, and they all nodded. I told them that Michael was probably waiting for them farther along the Camino. I'm sure he was playing with his stick somewhere. I said goodbye, but I wondered how they passed me. It had to be when I stopped to take care of business. Between my break and my washroom excursion, I had spent over half an hour. I walked fast, but my energy began to wane. It was early afternoon, and although it wasn't hot, it was the warmest in many days.

The long stretch ended at the eighty kilometer marker, where the path joined the highway. A large white van used for transporting pilgrims was parked, and the very impatient driver stood outside, waving for his passengers to hurry up. I followed a gravel *senda* as it climbed along the highway to Hospital. Another break was in order, and I bought an ice cream and sat inside the busy café. I was exhausted and sensed I would have a tough afternoon. It had been a long time since I sweated so much, and I was sure I smelled horrible. I had climbed about two-thirds and dreaded the last stretch. After about twenty minutes, I was back on the Camino; I went across the highway and continued to climb along a narrow road through a dry scrubby landscape.

Ventas de Narón had an *albergue* and a casa with a café. In the middle of the pleasant hamlet, sheep peacefully grazed in a pasture surrounded by an old stone fence. The casa was a treat for pilgrims, or for tourists who wanted to say they stayed on the Camino de Santiago but didn't actually walk any of it. Those who needed the amenities of the casa and wouldn't last an hour in an *albergue*. I continued to struggle along the road through a pine forest mixed with plots of farmland. It was now about 20°C, and not only was I drained, my feet were burning. Not any one spot in particular, just an overall discomfort. When I arrived at the alto, Sierra Ligonde, I was happy for a reprieve from climbing, but there would soon be more.

The road descended to Ligonde, which sprawled along the Camino, with well-kept old stone homes among the fields and trees. The hamlet was in the middle of siesta, and the only people I saw were outside the *albergue*. From Ligonde, the road headed steeply downhill, enough to warrant a switchback. Then, a short climb to Eirexe drained most of my remaining energy. In the sleepy hamlet, I stopped at the *albergue* for another ice cream. I needed something to energize and motivate me. It was two-thirty, and Palas de Rei was still over seven kilometers away. My plan was to stay in Melide, a large town with many *albergue* beds. However, it was well past Palas de Rei, with more hills in between. I took an extended break of half an hour, composed myself, encouraged myself, and moved on.

The narrow, paved road led through farmland and patches of forest. I saw my first eucalyptus tree, and soon, there would be many. I was grateful for the shade, but it never lasted long. After a descent to the hamlet of Portos, I started climbing to the Alto do Rosario. The Camino snaked through another hamlet, Lestedo, which had the first estate I had seen for a long time. It was a large, fenced property with a double gate and figures of lions guarding on either side. At the end of Lestedo stood an ancient church in the middle of a fenced cemetery, with a *cruceiro* in front.

The hamlets seemed to run into each other and were difficult to distinguish. In one, two girls about twelve years old sold handmade jewelry from a table set up in front of a house on the edge of the road. They asked if I wanted to buy anything, but nothing interested me. Other than the postcard, I hadn't even thought about souvenir shopping at that point and wasn't planning to buy anything until I got to Santiago. Later, I felt guilty and wished I had bought something to help the girls out.

After a small climb, I made it to the alto, which was a busy place, with the highway nearby. I bought another ice cream and sat on the café patio for a much-needed break. I was exhausted and was even having a tough time on the downhill stretches. It was warm on the patio, and I didn't stay long. A short descent led me to a busy *albergue* and outdoor café on the outskirts of Palas de Rei. The group from Portugal was there, but Michael was still not with them. Again, I had passed them earlier and wondered how they arrived faster than I did. Then I remembered the van. I bid the group farewell and wished them the best. The Camino followed a gravel road through a pleasant forest, where a group of horses and riders took a break. The grass was abundant, and the horses seemed happy to rest in the shade. I passed a vast park with many picnic tables, which sat completely deserted in the beautiful weather. As I entered Palas de Rei, the horses and riders galloped past me into the town.

Palas de Rei had a modern look with many businesses, but I didn't see much that looked old or remarkable. It was six o'clock, and the streets were quiet. In front of an *albergue*, a group of young pilgrims listened to a guy trying to sing and play the guitar. It was supposed to be *Hotel California* by the Eagles, but he sung in English with a thick Eastern

European accent that was difficult to understand. The group listened intently, but I suppose there wasn't much else to do. As I walked by, a pretty woman greeted me and smiled, instantly lifting my spirits.

Once I left the center of Palas de Rei, I quickly entered a rural area with small homes and large gardens. In one yard, a sheep was perched with its front feet on a fence, and it peered at me over the top. He or she looked cute, and I stopped for a photo. From the adjacent house, a man emerged to talk. He spoke a little English, and we were able to have some conversation. Similar to sheep talk with Alain, this man didn't believe that the name of this animal was "sheep" in English. I told him a few times, but I don't think he believed me. He talked about a trip he once took to New York City, and wondered if I lived close. I told him I lived far away on the other side of North America. He wanted to discuss the topic of sheep again, which was my signal to take off. I said goodbye to both the man and his sheep and continued.

The walk out of Palas de Rei was pleasant, with trees and flowers in the evening sun. I felt better on the flatter ground but knew I'd be staying somewhere before Melide. The *albergue* in the hamlet of San Julián was full, as was the one a kilometer past it, where the Camino crossed the Río Pambre. It wasn't long before I arrived in the hamlet of Casanova, and I was grateful the modern *albergue* had a bed available. It was only seven-thirty and normally early for me to check-in, but I didn't feel like walking farther. I had had a tough day, and there was no need to punish myself any more.

After the young woman signed me in, she led me to the small dorm with seven double bunks, including two in the center that were pushed together. The only two beds available were the top ones in the center. I took one and hoped the other would stay empty because I didn't want anyone sleeping beside me. I had a shower, washed my clothes, and hung them outside. It was my first day without rain for over two weeks. I enjoyed the sun, but not the heat. However, with all my earlier complaining and begging for the sun, maybe I should just shut the fuck up. I had plenty of time, so after I washed clothes, I went to the reception area, where I talked and read while charging a camera battery. I had walked about forty-two kilometers, and my goal for the next day was the town of Arca O Pino, so there wasn't much planning.

Most of the pilgrims were German or French and knew little English, so there was only small talk, which didn't last long. I was tired and went to bed just after nine o'clock. Even if I didn't fall asleep right away and just rested, that would be fine. The dorm was warm, and the windows were open to let in a breeze. It also let in so much noise. There were dogs barking, people laughing, a baby crying, and birds chirping and squawking. I usually enjoyed listening to birds, but not when I was trying to sleep. A man on the lower bunk across from me had a bad cold, swine flu, or something else contagious or life-threatening. He coughed and hacked constantly.

I finally fell asleep but was woken many times by the joyous sounds of coughing, snorting, and snoring. At one point, the entire *albergue* woke up to the sounds of a baby crying from the other dorm. Yes, someone brought a baby into the *albergue*. Later, I heard this horrible rumbling and looked at the supposedly empty bunk beside me to see some guy snoring. What a shitty night!

I CAN WRITE GOOD ENGLISH, CAN'T I?
Day 19
Casanova to Arca O Pino
40.5 Km

After I saw the guy sleeping on the bunk next to me, and after the initial shock wore off, surprisingly, I fell asleep. At least there was a railing between us to prevent accidental fondling. I woke up at four o'clock and stayed awake for an hour before falling asleep again until I heard clashing from the early risers. I lay in bed until after seven and finally grabbed my gear and went to the reception area. Outside, it was a beautiful sunny morning, not a cloud in the sky. For the first time since the third day on the Camino, I wore shorts and was glad not to feel the constraints from the rain gear. Maybe I could have worn shorts the previous day, but I still didn't trust the weather. While I taped my feet, the French couple with the baby came downstairs. The baby was closer to a year old and cried so loudly, he must have woken up anyone still asleep. Apparently, he liked the *albergues* about as much as I did.

I was out the door at 7:45 A.M. with a simple plan: to walk about forty kilometers. The morning was cool, but I had no trouble keeping warm as I quickly followed a dirt road through farmland and forest, which included some giant oak. In the hamlet of Cornixa, I crossed the border from the province of Lugo to A Coruña and a few minutes later, entered the village of Leboreiro. In its small plaza, an ancient stone *cruceiro* was well-weathered and looked in serious need of attention with a large crack halfway down.

The small church, Iglesia de Santa María, featured a unique tympanum carved out of white stone. It depicted angels, Mary, and Child, and it stood out nicely from the grayish rock of the façade. I crossed the Río Seco on a steep one-arch stone bridge and continued a slight descent on good gravel roads through forests and farmland. The Camino then followed a flat stretch through a parkway, with the highway on the right and industrial buildings on the left. Along the way, there were many monuments for pilgrims and people important to the Camino, although I didn't understand most of the dedications. I heard a rumble and a few shouts from behind, and as I stepped aside, two horses and riders galloped past. They were followed by four more that trotted by. After the parkway, I walked down the small hill through a forest and into the village of Furelos.

A beautiful, medieval bridge with four arches spanned the Río Furelos. I wasn't expecting such a large bridge or an attractive setting. Old, stone houses with red tiled roofs adorned the riverbank, with the tower of the church in the background. A German woman took my photo in front of the bridge but declined abruptly when I asked if she wanted one with her male companion. They were jabbering at each other, and I felt bad for interrupting them. I walked through an overgrown field with ruins of houses and walls and then entered Melide.

The Iglesia de San Pedro, nestled between two palm trees, had a beige and gray stone façade and a single cross on top of the bell gable. Outside, mounted on a platform, stood an ancient *cruceiro* depicting the crucifixion. Although there were many shops and cafés along the Camino, most were not yet open. A bakery looked tempting, and I bought a cherry empanada that was delicious.

Melide was more modern than I had expected, without the typical old, narrow street that the Camino usually followed in the towns. Since it was Monday, I was surprised the Iglesia de Sancti Spiritus was open. A small group of parishioners waited for the morning mass while others prayed. Careful not to disturb anyone, I took a photo of the *retablo*, which was the first I had seen in days. On the outskirts of Melide, I stopped and greeted a small white horse with a long mane as he stood in a tiny dirt lot in between houses. He looked so lonely, and because I was going a little bit loopy from all the walking, I could have sworn he asked me to take him to Santiago. I sadly declined and bid the horse farewell.

A peaceful, narrow, gravel road with walls of dirt and stone went through a forest of eucalyptus, highlighted by a symphony from the songbirds. I emerged from the forest into farmland for a while before traveling through the trees again. At a covered fountain, I watched an old woman washing clothes for a moment and wondered if it was the local laundry. Small streams required a short drop and climb, and at one, a foot bridge comprised of large slabs of rock rested on smaller ones and spanned the shallow water. I had hoped to have my photo taken with the fifty kilometer marker, but instead, I saw the 49.5. It didn't have the same prestige as the fifty, so I didn't bother. The section of five kilometers to the village of Boente had so many hamlets that I lost track.

The Camino traveled along the highway through Boente and then veered down to the Río Boente. As I climbed from the river, sometimes steeply, the valley below emerged with forest, grazing land, and scattered houses. A paved road led through Castañeda until veering off through more farmland. I reached the alto near the village of Portela and then began a steep descent on a paved road that joined a gravel one. The climb to the alto had tired me out, and I thought my break would be at the upcoming village of Ribadiso. I arrived at the forty kilometer marker at noon, and stopped for a quick photo. Hard to believe, I only had forty kilometers left.

The Río Iso looked so peaceful as I crossed on the one-arch medieval bridge. The *albergue*, an old, stone building with a red tiled roof, stood on the hill just above the river. The café was packed, and there wasn't much else in the village, so I continued on a narrow paved road past fenced hayfields and scattered farmhouses. I crossed under the highway and had a steep climb on the side of a busy road. It was warm; I felt my energy depleting and cursed myself for not stopping earlier. I expected my break would be about a kilometer ahead, in Arzúa, when I came around a curve and saw a Repsol gas station. I was so happy and picked up ice cream, chocolate, nuts, and a Coke Light.

As I ate while sitting on a bench in the shade, I reminded myself for the umpteenth time to take regular breaks. It was my nineteenth day on the Camino, and I should have learned by now. Sometimes, a person – in this case, I'm talking about myself – doesn't learn until something bad happens. Even my shoulders were sore for the first time in days. Despite it being clear and sunny with no chance of rain, some of the pilgrims were dressed in rain pants and had their backpack covers on. I wasn't the only one who still had trouble trusting the weather.

I was recharged after my break and walked up the hill into Arzúa, a town famous for its cheese; it plays host to a cheese festival every March. Initially, most of the buildings along the Camino were modern and typically five- and six-story apartments, with businesses on the lower levels. I veered onto a narrow street, but only a few of the buildings looked old. Outside an *albergue*, pilgrims eagerly lined up and waited for it to open at one o'clock. There were still eight hours of daylight left.

With not much to see along the Camino, I went up the hill and into the town center, where I looked at the church and various shops. There were a few police officers around the plaza, and I couldn't remember the last time I had seen one. I said *hola* to one officer, who didn't say a word or smile. I sat on a bench and watched people, birds, and the emerging leaves on the trees trembling with the breeze. After my break, I walked down to the Camino and gently descended a narrow street into a rural area. The horses and riders who I had seen earlier rested in a woodlot, and everyone looked tired.

This began a stretch of about eleven kilometers through hamlets and farmland, up and down shallow river valleys, and through forests of eucalyptus and pine. The afternoon temperature was at least 22°C, and although there was plenty of shade in the forests, I really felt the sun in the open. Each of the short climbs from the streams was a struggle. I didn't know if the sun was affecting me, but the hamlets looked very similar, and again, I lost track of them. I began to appreciate the *hórreos* more, no matter the condition. From the Río Languello to the Alto de Santa Irene, the elevation gain was only about one hundred meters, but it was enough to completely wear me down. The long stretches in the open zapped my energy, and a large blister on my right heel felt like it was erupting. At a pop machine in O Emplame, I pressed for a Coke Light but got a regular Coke. There was nobody around to help me, and the bottle felt so cold that I drank it anyway. It had been years since I had a regular Coke. By now, I was thirsty, dead tired, and didn't really give a crap.

Sweating profusely, I sat on a covered bench near one of the *albergues* at Santa Irene. Another man soon joined me, and it was obvious he was suffering from a terrible cold. He coughed, sneezed, and looked so stuffed up that his head could explode any second. He asked if I had any tissues, but I only had napkins and toilet tissue. I offered him the napkins, which he sneered at but took, anyway. I didn't feel like getting his bug, so I wished him a quick recovery and continued. I descended along the road, and stopped at the twenty-five kilometer marker, where I noticed the discrepancy between my map and the ground was two or three kilometers. I had thought there were about five kilometers to

Arca O Pino, which was all I had energy for. After crossing under the highway, I had one more descent through the eucalyptus to the Río Burgo, followed by one more climb where I slowed down. The stretch was much longer than I thought it would be.

When I arrived at the highway, I went straight to the first *albergue* in O Burgo, just before Arca O Pino. There was a bed available, and I thanked the *hospitalera* because I couldn't continue any farther. It was only six o'clock, and I thought if it was four o'clock, and I didn't feel like crap, I could have made it to Santiago on my nineteenth day. Never mind, it wasn't going to happen. I could relax and work on my writing for a change. I had updated my audio journal throughout each day but was always too tired or had no time to work on my written journal. I still didn't know what would result from my journals, but I hoped I could publish something. I thought about a book, but at that point, I still wasn't sure. Writing a book seemed like so much work, but how hard could it be? I can write good English, can't I? I shall interject here with a brief note to Randall staying in Arca O Pino from future Randall, about a year later: It's fucking hard! You don't know what you're in for.

The dorm was packed with at least fifteen bunks, and only two beds were left. I had my shower, washed my clothes, and hung them out in the sun. The *albergue* was many blocks away from the main business district, and I didn't feel like walking far. My feet were sore, especially after I drained another large blister. I went to the nearby gas station for chips and a drink and forced myself to relax. Between periods of writing, I met a woman from Ontario, Canada who was the first Canadian I had seen in days. Later, I met a wonderful Finnish woman, someone I could have talked with for hours. She was very interested in Canada, but except for some hockey players, I knew little about Finland. We had a long Camino talk about *albergues*, blisters, and our experience. She looked forward to finishing, too.

Before bedtime, I thought I would quickly check the internet and catch up with emails. I inserted a euro for half an hour but didn't need more than a few minutes. Soon after, a woman came by and looked over my shoulder to check how much time I had left. A few minutes later, her husband also came by and checked. He left and then she followed again. They were very rude, so I did some extra surfing and only left them with a couple of minutes of my time. I was so tired that when I went to update my Facebook page, I couldn't remember which town I was in. It was nine o'clock, and I was ready for bed. I had walked about forty kilometers during the day, and the next one didn't require any planning. The walk to Santiago should be easy.

The dorm had about thirty people in the room, and it seemed that most snored. A group of young people, including my top bunkmate, came back late after drinking, and were loud. I slept for a while and then woke up in the middle of the night to some of the loudest snoring I had heard so far. One guy, across from me, made a noise from his mouth every ten-seconds that sounded like a fart. Finally, at some point I was so tired, no noises could keep me awake. Not even some guy's mouth farts. Santiago de Compostela, I shall see you soon.

LA CATEDRAL
Day 20
Arca O Pino to Santiago de Compostela
21.5 Km

Despite my poor sleep, I woke up wide awake, with a whole lot of energy and a definite sense of excitement. It was my last day, and I was happy. Seriously, I was tired of the blisters and preparing my feet every day. I was tired of restless sleeps and my daily bouts of sluggishness. Most of all, I was tired of walking, and I looked forward to some time to relax.

I wasn't finished though; I had about 21.5 kilometers left. Many of the pilgrims were out of bed by six-thirty, which ensured I wouldn't sleep in. I lay until seven, grabbed my gear, and went to the reception area to tape my feet. The blister on the top of my left big toe looked as awful as it had a week before. Although I didn't have a full day of walking ahead, I prepared like any other. There was no point in being complacent now. I've said it before, it only takes one bad step to ruin a Camino. After coming this far, I wouldn't be happy if I hurt myself before reaching the cathedral in Santiago.

At 8:15 A.M., I left the *albergue* to another sunny day. I followed the sidewalk into the town of Arca, a pleasant, modern center with a strong connection to Santiago, given its proximity. Cafés and shops lined the main street, but few were open. In front of a hostal, a driver loaded up his van with backpacks and luggage for pilgrims who carried a day pack. I believed he was the impatient one who gave a ride to the Portuguese group before Palas de Rei.

At the O Pino town hall, I crossed the highway and gently ascended to the edge of the town. A gravel path led through a eucalyptus forest that opened up to a rural area with houses and plots of farmland. After another short climb through an open area, the Santiago airport came into view, and I watched a Ryanair plane take off. The path led to the highway, past the hamlet of San Paio, and descended into Lavacolla, which was once an important pilgrim stop but now mostly caters to airport business. I walked through the peaceful town and crossed over the Río Lavacolla, once used as a washing site for pilgrims before entering Santiago. Nobody was bathing as I went by, and I decided to wait for a shower in my hotel room.

A paved road lined with pilgrims gently climbed through a rural area with scattered stands of eucalyptus. As I passed one group, a man called out. His name was Stu from Nova Scotia, Canada, and he was with his wife and a friend. Stu told me they had just passed a woman from Toronto, Canada who had recently had hip surgery. It was too bad I had missed her, as I admired her determination, and couldn't imagine the pain she must have born at times.

I bid farewell to my fellow Canadians and went ahead, hoping to see the alto at Monte de Gozo. I understood the monument there would be impressive, but had no idea what it would look like. I went past industrial buildings, large empty fields, and stands of forest, but still there was no sign. Often, there was only a narrow shoulder and no sidewalk along the road, which surprised me since it was so close to Santiago. After I emerged from a stand of eucalyptus, I entered San Marcos, a rural area with large houses, gardens, and plots of pasture, where cattle and sheep grazed. About a kilometer away, I saw what had to be the alto at Monte de Gozo.

Some people may consider the monument magnificent, while others may call it an eyesore. Modern and towering, it certainly impressed me, although I can't say it was a highlight of the Camino. The monument was about four stories high and topped by a metal cross with a scallop shell mounted onto metal supports, shaped like the number six, and placed on a large cement block. Each of the four sides of the block had a large bronze plaque featuring a pope, the Santiago Cathedral, pilgrims, and a scallop shell at the end of an index finger of a hand. I had my photo taken on one side, and then again on another. In the distance, I saw Santiago and knew I would soon be there. The alto was busy with pilgrims, tourists, and students. The outdoor café was packed and loud.

I followed other pilgrims down a hill but soon realized it wasn't the Camino but the path to the sprawling *albergue* and the adjacent hotel complex, where many people stayed. I backtracked up the hill, past the outdoor café and the screaming teenagers, and back to the relative peacefulness of the Camino. After descending a flight of stairs, I followed a sidewalk beside the highway where a sign simply stated "Santiago." The early part of the city was dominated by office and light industrial buildings, which progressed to commercial and housing, with modern art pieces along the road. Another man joined me for a few blocks, but only said a few words. At times, I walked with other pilgrims, but often walked alone. This is where I would have enjoyed the company of someone I knew.

On every block, huge piles of garbage stunk in the midday sun. It was obvious Santiago was in the midst of a garbage strike. I felt sorry for the unlucky shop owners who had to stare at a five foot high pile of garbage outside their door. The long morning walk with no more than a few moments' break really tired me. I had planned to stop after I arrived at the cathedral, but as I walked past a bakery, the wonderful odor of their goods pulled me inside. I had my choice of many wonderful-looking pastries; I easily could have selected a dozen, but I only picked two.

I sat at the sidewalk patio next to a table occupied by two young Spanish women and a man. One woman looked at me as if to say, "Why do you bother walking? You know, there are planes, trains, and automobiles." Or maybe it was, "You're one grubby-looking pilgrim!" Anyway, I smiled and kept to myself. The delicious pastries were fresh, with cream, chocolate, and fruit. Dozens of pilgrims went by, and everyone had at least a smile, while others were jubilant. The street was busy, and I enjoyed sitting there, as long as I didn't look at the massive pile of garbage a half block behind me.

As I continued, the streets turned to cobblestone, and the buildings became older. Two church towers were in the distance, and I didn't know if they belonged to the cathedral, but they looked impressive nonetheless. After I passed through the Porta do Camiño, I entered the old city of Santiago de Compostela, with narrow streets and centuries-old stone and brick buildings. Shops sold a variety of goods, including souvenirs, clothing, jewelry, and crafts. An intricate fountain depicted St. James, and the small church nearby had beautiful hand-painted frescos and a magnificent *retablo* depicting the crucifixion.

The faint sound of bagpipes got progressively louder until I passed the man playing them in the middle of a tunnel. I knew it was almost the end of my Camino. I emerged to the vast plaza, the Prazo Obradoiro and looked to my left. There it was, *La Catedral de Santiago de Compostela*. It was beautiful – so elegant and intricate – and the surrounding buildings were great pieces of architecture in themselves. At least two hundred people were in the plaza, most of whom were pilgrims and tourists. I slowly walked to the center of the plaza, where the famous scallop shell was set in concrete with an inscription and embedded between paving stones.

At 1:10 P.M. on my twentieth day, I completed the French Way of the Camino de Santiago. I was elated, but I took a moment of silence and remembered my mom. How I wished I could have called her. If she were alive, she would have been constantly worried about me as I walked across Spain. I also knew she would have been very proud.

Now what? As I walked through the tunnel and into the plaza, I had another shot of adrenaline, but this time, my walking was over. Since it was early afternoon, I had to convince myself there was no longer the need to continue. After walking for twenty days in a row, it was difficult to stop. I had planned to go sightseeing later, and the next day. That was still walking, only different. My Camino Finisterre would start in less than two days, although I promised myself to take it slower and relax. It was easier said than done.

I had three immediate concerns once I finished the Camino – obtain my *Compostela*, find a place to stay, and have a good meal. Touring the cathedral would wait until later. Facing the cathedral, on my left was the beautiful Hostal de los Reyes Católicos, which dates back to the sixteenth century, and now part of the Parador chain. I expected it to be over my budget but wanted to look inside and inquire about the price. I looked sloppy, and was very underdressed compared to the other people in the lobby. I was a little embarrassed as I approached the desk clerk. She told me that the basic room was €111, which was over my budget, especially since I was alone. If my girlfriend were with me, it would be different. When I'm alone in an elegant hotel, all I think about is having someone with me. There's no point going through all that stress.

The Pilgrim Office was only a few minutes' walk south from the plaza. I had heard it could get busy, but when I arrived, there was only a fifteen minute wait. It was a happy place with friendly staff and smiling pilgrims. The clerk reviewed my pilgrim passport and a few minutes later, handed me my personalized *Compostela*. It was a proud and special moment.

I found a reasonably-priced hotel room about a block away from the cathedral. The clerk told me the room included Wi-Fi, but I later found out it only worked in the lobby and outside. It was just my luck.

After I showered and got ready, it was time for a special meal. The Galician steamed octopus dish, *pulpo a la gallega*, was something I really wanted to try. After glancing inside a few cafés along the old streets of Santiago, I chose one that was nicely decorated and had a friendly waitress. I ordered my *pulpo a la gallega* and a glass of Albariño, a white wine originating in Galicia. Less than half an hour later, my meal arrived on a wooden platter. The octopus was good, although I found the texture a little slimy. There was no need to complain though, this was the dinner I had been waiting for. Another pilgrim sat alone at the adjacent table, and when he looked at me, I raised my glass, and he did the same. It was a quiet celebration for the end of my journey on the Camino de Santiago.

LOOKING BACK

When I returned home, a friend asked me if I would ever walk the Camino de Santiago again. At the time, I was still exhausted and all traveled out. My feet were covered in blisters that looked awful, and they wouldn't fully heal for another two months. I said no, I didn't think I'd ever do it again. Writing this book was an endeavor that proved far more difficult than I had ever imagined. Much more difficult than walking the French Way in twenty days. I wrote, rewrote, and edited for countless hours during many months, with only a few days off. And I know I'll never win a Pulitzer or an equivalent prize for writing. However, all the work furthered my appreciation for the Camino and made me think more about my journey. I studied the 3000 photos I took and saw things that I probably wouldn't have otherwise. I learned more about the history, culture, and people along the Camino, which enhanced my overall experience. I now have a longing to return to the French Way, or possibly a different Camino. I'm not sure.

I don't expect anyone else to understand why I walked eight hundred kilometers in twenty days. It's not everyone's Camino, and I appreciate that. Sometimes, I have trouble understanding it myself. It was a difficult and stressful journey, and I was proud not only to complete it, but to surpass my original goal. I was fortunate I didn't get hurt or meet any harm. My mind and body were exhausted, and my feet had never been put through anything like it. I had inclement weather much of the time, and could count the number of good sleeps

I had on one hand.

I was so focused on the Camino that never once did I slip or fall. My old body was the strongest it had felt for a long time. Maybe as I got older, I felt like I had to prove to myself that I still had something left, both mentally and physically. Sometimes, one learns more about themselves when they push to a point well past their comfort level. That's my spirituality – it comes from within. Remember, my comfort level wasn't climbing Everest but somewhere at a lower level that didn't include staying in hostels and walking up to fourteen hours every day.

My mistakes? I made a few, but nothing drastic. It's arguable if carrying the tent was a good idea. Since I didn't use it, I wouldn't take one again. I don't think I would have felt comfortable sleeping in it anyway. I would put insoles in my boots and bring foot cream. If I walked long days again, I would take four pairs of hiking socks and five pairs of underwear. One extra T-shirt would be good, too. A SIM card for my iPhone would have been great to make planning and life on the Camino so much easier. I know it's not for everyone, but it is for me.

The Camino Finisterre, and especially the visit to Finisterre itself, were excellent experiences which I recommend for anyone who has time. There, I stayed at a wonderful private *albergue* for five nights while resting and writing what would become this book. I was surprised to see both Jerry and Claudia while they waited in front of the Finisterre bus station. Jerry had hurt his foot on the Camino and took a few days off. He congratulated me on my twenty days and seemed impressed. I arrived in Santiago five days before he did, but who's counting? I know, I know, it's the journey. Jerry was counting the days, too. Everybody I met on the Camino kept track of their days.

Claudia was just about to board a different bus when I saw her. My original plan was to travel to Barcelona because I had so many extra days. She smiled and told me she was going also, but I didn't say anything because I was with Sarah. I was sad to see her go as we hugged and bid farewell. Few other people I met had the same determination as I did. I was lucky I had been passing by at that very moment and had the good fortune to see her one last time.

The Camino gave me so much time to think about my life – where I had been, where I was at that point, and where I wanted to be. I thought about time itself, which seemed to pass so slowly while walking the Camino but so quickly otherwise. I thought about death for the first time. Not necessarily how I would die, just death itself. There is so much that I want to accomplish before my time is up.

I often thought about my mom and my relationship with her. Because we were both stubborn and had some different views, we had clashed in the past. However, before her death, I think we only had one argument in five years. We definitely became closer, and learned to appreciate our differences. We also learned to ignore certain comments the other had made. I miss her so much.

I thought about relationships I had been in and my strengths and weaknesses. When I believed I had done well and when I had fucked up. Who knows, I'm probably fucking up something right now.

Sarah and I didn't last. From our initial argument, two months before I left for Europe, our relationship was on a downhill slope, with only a few minor ups. It didn't help that she was with someone who decided to write a book, despite reading only a few in recent years and never having written anything of significance before in his life. Why couldn't I have gone just to find myself? It's so much easier. I'm sure I was frustrating to be with during the first few months of writing. Similar to how I booked my flight to London after I thought we had broken up, I would have never completed this book if we were together. For that, I thank her.

So, I find myself at a new crossroads in my life. For the first time in a couple of years, I'm alone, and this time, it feels fine. I've spent so long writing this book, but I've done something for myself – no matter how it turns out, or what others may think. For I have found a new love in my life: the Camino de Santiago.

Thomas Jefferson once wrote, "Though an old man, I am but a young gardener."
And if I may paraphrase him – or better yet, if I dare:
Though a middle-aged man, I am but a young pilgrim.

And my next Camino will be a far greater challenge.

THE END

NOW I HAVE TIME TO CLEAN UP MY MESS
(AND I DON'T MEAN JUST IN MY SPARE ROOM)

Acknowledgments

I would like to thank everyone who put up with me during the entire book publishing process.
Mirabella Mitchell, Sebastian Weber, and Anna Karin Tidlund for their work.

John Steenson and Andrea Buchanan-Smith for their additional proofreading.

Lily Wang and Shelley Hitz (www.self-publishing-coach.com) for their advice and guidance.

Family and friends who supported me while I walked the Camino and wrote this book (I won't name anyone but you know who you are).

My tired, old body for not falling apart during the Camino (although I think my brain is fried from writing this book).

My precious iPhone. I don't know how I survived without you.

Dragon Dictate for Mac, although sometimes you frustrate the hell out of me.

The cool and rainy Vancouver spring and early summer weather of 2011. It's far easier working inside without any outside distractions such as warmth and sun.

The people in Spain who greeted me and talked with me as I walked through their hamlets, villages, towns, and cities. How I wished I could speak Spanish better.

The pilgrims, hospitaleras, and hospitaleros who I met along The Way.

Sources and Suggested Reading

Gitlitz, David M., and Linda Kay Davidson. *The Pilgrimage Road To Santiago*. New York: St. Martin's Griffin, 2000.

Brierley, John. *A Pilgrim's Guide to the Camino de Santiago*. 2003. Reprint. Scotland: Findhorn Press, 2010.

Davies, Bethan, and Ben Cole. Updated by Daphne Hnatiuk. *Walking the Camino de Santiago*.
Vancouver: Pili Pala Press, 2009.

Made in the USA
Lexington, KY
07 April 2012